M000214042

TROUBLE IN CENSORVILLE

TROUBLE IN CENSORVILLE

THE FAR RIGHT'S ASSAULT ON PUBLIC EDUCATION – AND THE TEACHERS WHO ARE FIGHTING BACK

Edited by

NADINE M. KALIN and REBEKAH MODRAK

disobedience press

Copyright © 2024 by Rebekah Modrak and Nadine M. Kalin

All rights reserved. This book or any portion thereof may not be reproduced or used in any manner whatsoever without the express written permission of the publisher except for the use of brief quotations in a book review.

Printed in the United States of America
First edition 2024
1 2 3 4 5 6 7 8 9

ISBN: 978-1-964098-00-5

disobedience press

Disobedience Press
Ann Arbor, Michigan
www.disobediencepress.com

Cover by Ben Denzer
Book design by Rebekah Modrak

TROUBLE IN CENSORVILLE

"I'm an elementary school art teacher who was placed on leave after only four days in the classroom. My kids loved me, the principal told me I was doing a great job, but because I used a nontraditional gender pronoun (the nonbinary 'Mx.') and wore insufficiently 'feminine' attire – khakis and a button-up shirt – I had to go."

"I'm a high school librarian who was accused of 'supplying pornography and grooming children' because books about LGBTQ+ people are available in the library."

"I'm a high school art teacher who was censored and silenced by my school district for my efforts to increase access to learning, promote cultural awareness, and support positive social change."

FOREWORD
THE FIGHT TO SAVE PUBLIC EDUCATION

Jonathan Friedman
Director of Free Expression and Education Programs, PEN America

As I write in May 2024, across the United States teachers, librarians, and school administrators are reporting a chilled educational climate in which they are more concerned with running afoul of new censorious laws than with educating their students. This climate is the result of numerous legislative efforts to restrict what is taught in public schools, which have been scaffolding upon one another since 2021.

In my work at PEN America, I have watched a protean movement that has evolved in numerous directions. These pervasive efforts to suppress free expression are issued from state legislatures and advanced by local and state-based advocacy groups, targeting and undermining faith in public schools, public libraries, and higher education institutions – institutions that we also view as foundational to our democracy.

Again and again, the political movement to suppress information and ideas in public educational institutions relies on authoritarian tactics of fear, intimidation, and silencing. It has strained the ability of public schools to meet their goals of educating students with knowledge and critical thinking. It continues to foment mistrust and divide communities, disrupting the unification that undergirds a pluralistic society.

Our daily news cycle highlights the role of these individuals, organized groups, and legislators in driving this campaign against public education, calling to ban books like *This Is Your Time*, a letter about the struggle for racial equality by Ruby Bridges, or the graphic adaptation of *The*

Diary of Anne Frank, or *Stella Brings the Family*, a picture book about a girl, her two dads, and the meaning of family. We see calls to restrict curricula, prohibit DEI initiatives, and cancel plays, field trips, films, and more. We see educators anxious to teach about art, history, literature, and even science; too fearful to discuss current events. In September 2020, former President Trump set the tone for such an assault, alleging that "critical race theory, *The 1619 Project*, and the crusade against American history is toxic propaganda, ideological poison that, if not removed, will dissolve the civic bonds that tie us together." In January 2021, the nation's very first state-level educational gag order was then introduced in Mississippi, proposing to strip state funding from any school where *The New York Times' 1619 Project* was taught.

Since then, PEN America has tracked the introduction of over 300 educational gag order bills by 45 U.S. state legislatures. Such bills limit instruction on race, gender, and U.S. history in public schools and public colleges and universities. Initially, these bills focused on so-called "critical race theory" and "divisive concepts." However, more recently, there has been an explosion of educational gag orders restricting instruction on sexual orientation and gender identity.

These legislative efforts work in tandem with locally coordinated campaigns by groups of activists, many of which are intent on banning books in public schools and public libraries.

The demonization of teachers and librarians – treating them not as professional educators but as potential criminals – has real effects. It is no coincidence that Florida, the site of the nation's most punitive educational censorship bills, is also now leading the country in terms of teacher vacancies.[1] At the start of 2023, teacher vacancies in Florida stood at nearly 5,300, more than double the number in January 2021.[2] And in Texas, 77 percent of teachers have considered leaving the field – and 72 percent have taken steps toward that goal – citing not only low pay but a lack of respect from parents, community members, and state legislators.[3] Data shows that more than 50 percent of teachers working in states with educational gag orders have changed how they teach because of these laws.[4] Given the continuing effects of these restrictive laws and policies, this crisis will likely continue to worsen.

At the same time, across the country, teachers, professors, students, parents, and community members are pushing back.[5] The teachers who share their testimonials in this collection are part of this wave of resistance. These educators are fighting back by refusing to be silenced and telling their stories to help document the attacks on public education in the U.S. today. Their courage in the face of being dismissed and demeaned is a testament to their commitment to public education, and the need to tell these stories for the public to hear them.

Though each of these cases is different, they are united by the dynamics that have animated contentious episodes at school boards and parent-teacher association (PTA) meetings across the country, as some have tried to impose a rigid ideological interpretation of what is acceptable to discuss in public schools, and thereby trample on the freedom of all students to learn and read.

In the face of these shocking and unprecedented attacks on public education, it is vital that a large share of the public raise their voices in unison against them. The testimonials from educators in this collection kickstart that urgent effort.

I urge you to consider joining them.

AN INTRODUCTION

Nadine M. Kalin and Rebekah Modrak

A merica is in the middle of a far-right war on public education, its teachers,* the communities they serve, and the belief in universal education as a common good and cornerstone of democracy. Cloaked in the "parents' rights" and "religious liberty" movements (both intent on eroding the separation of church and state enshrined in the Constitution) and fueled by white supremacists, Christian-nationalist zealots, and white suburban Trump moms, radical forces are transforming the landscape of K-12 public education in the United States. In small towns, cities in conservative regions, and states across the nation, they're undermining the democratic vision of publicly funded education for all in favor of privatized schools controlled by for-profit corporations. The lunatic fringe behind these attacks is on the march, implacably opposed to public schoolkids' freedom to read what they want and to be taught the hard facts – and hard truths – of American history and social reality, not to mention the cornerstone civic virtue of critical thinking.

As we write these words, conservative activists are mounting a take-no-prisoners assault on public education in America. Many are funded by far-right think tanks, such as the Heritage Foundation and the American Principles Project; conservative foundations, such as the George Jenkins Foundation and the Bradley Foundation; lobbying and advocacy groups, such as the Alliance Defending Freedom, FreedomWorks, and Parents Defending Education; and political action committees, such as Moms for Liberty (M4L), Patriot Mobile Action, the American Legacy, and the 1776 Project. Backed, in many cases, by powerful outside interests, these "grassroots" activists –

---

* The editors use "teachers" to refer to classroom teachers and school librarians. The umbrella term "educators" encompasses both.

AstroTurf* activists, really – are manufacturing false accusations and issuing death threats against K-12 teachers. As well, they're targeting public school libraries, long revered as democratic spaces allowing for the free exchange of ideas, calling for the banning of young-adult (YA) novels featuring LGBTQ+ characters, sex-ed titles, and books about African American history that include inconvenient truths about slavery, institutional racism, and everyday white supremacy. In some cases, conservative pressure has even compelled schools to replace their libraries with disciplinary centers for misbehaving students.[1]

Across the country, right-wing moral panic (or ideological opposition to diversity and changing social mores *masquerading* as moral panic) has resulted in book bans and, in Republican-controlled statehouses, the passing of an unprecedented number of laws that invoke the "divisive concepts" premise to legitimate discrimination. (In essence, the logic of the "divisive concept" goes like this: America is a meritocracy where individuals' pathways to "life, liberty, and the pursuit of happiness" are not potholed or blocked by prejudices based on race, sex, gender, or religion. Thus, classroom discussions of bigotry and discrimination are, paradoxically, needlessly "divisive.") Twenty twenty-three saw the passing of at least 21 anti-trans bills prohibiting educators from referring to a student by his/her/their preferred pronouns and requiring that the teacher use the pronouns related to the sex assigned at birth.[2] Conservative politicians, pressured by Christian Nationalists and "anti-woke" activists, have passed laws prohibiting trans youth from using the bathroom suited to their gender identity. Twenty-one states, almost all of them red, and most of which went handily for Trump in the 2020 presidential election, along with 145 local governments or public school districts in those states, have passed not only discriminatory laws but penalties for educators who violate them, ranging from a letter of reprimand to suspension or revocation of their license to teach.[3]

---

* *Merriam-Webster* defines "Astroturfing" as an "organized activity that is intended to create a false impression of a widespread, spontaneously arising, grassroots movement in support of or in opposition to something (such as a political policy) but that is in reality initiated and controlled by a concealed group or organization (such as a corporation)."

Doubling down on this extremist agenda, conservatives have orchestrated the rewriting of academic standards in conformity with far-right (and, not incidentally, fact-free) visions of American history, identity, and contemporary reality. Florida's notorious social-studies guidelines, which require teachers to instruct their students that enslaved people "developed skills which, in some instances, could be applied for their personal benefit," is just one of depressingly numerous examples.[4] Since 2020, legislation spearheaded by conservative politicians, often compounded by local orders (i.e., policies created by school-district administrators), has affected over one million educators and over 22 million students throughout the States.[5]

By August 2023, groups associated with these ideologies had proposed 750 legislative measures at the federal, state, and local levels, many of them under the disingenuous rubric of opposition to Critical Race Theory (CRT).[6] Critical race theory, a term coined by law professor Kimberlé Crenshaw, began in legal studies in the 1980s as a way to examine patterns of discrimination and racism enforced and preserved by institutions (such as the legal system), housing, politics, and public policy. CRT contends that racism informs all elements of U.S. life. While there may be a distant relationship between CRT and K-12 pedagogy that attempts to consider curriculum from diverse perspectives in the context of American history and current events, most public school teachers have not studied CRT, and many do not routinely touch on the question of systemic racism.[7]

To recognize the pervasiveness of white supremacism (and the racist discrimination, violence, and official – as well as unofficial – policies that maintain it) in American history, contemporary society, and powerful institutions, ranging from the federal government to local law enforcement to corporate boardrooms, would threaten that supremacy. Thus, Christopher Rufo, described by The Southern Poverty Law Center as a "far-right propagandist,"[8] visited Fox News on September 2, 2020, to raise the alarm that CRT was "an existential threat to the United States," which, he claimed, has "infiltrated" scientific, educational, and governmental institutions in a sort of "cult indoctrination."[9] Off-camera, Rufo hasn't been coy about his weaponization of the arcane term, which few outside legal academia were familiar with until he made opposition to it a far-right rallying cry. "'Critical race theory' is the perfect villain," he told the *New Yorker* reporter Benjamin Wallace-Wells.[10] Fighting the bogeyman of CRT has proven to be an attractive tool to scare the electorate, mobilize MAGA opposition to Diversity, Equity, and Inclusion initiatives and calls for racial reckoning, and, not least, win votes.

Though these attacks have been described as a culture war, it goes far beyond the specificities of prior culture wars. In truth, they're nothing less than full-on attacks, coordinated by well-funded, well-connected political interests, to take down public education and, as red meat for the MAGA brigades, suppress the teaching of Black, Indigenous, and LGBTQ+ histories. There's a covert agenda to this Orwellian revisionism: the demolition of the civil rights and social acceptance that African Americans, Native Americans, and LGBTQ+ people have fought for, through decades of struggle. Dehumanizing precedents for today's attacks on free-and-equal public education for all children are numerous and include: the forced assimilation, and even abduction, of Native American children to federally funded Christian boarding schools; the pathologizing of "homosexuals" as "deviant," as claimed by the 1978 Briggs Initiative that sought to prohibit gay men and lesbians from teaching in public schools; and, between 1954 and 1979, the firing of over 100,000 highly credentialed Black teachers and principals as whitelash[11] in the wake of *Brown v. Board of Education*.[12] In the 2020s, we're primarily hearing about attacks on white women educators, possibly due to this legacy. According to a 2023 national survey, pre-K to 12th-grade educators are disproportionately white.[13]

In effect, the United States now has two different public education systems. One is founded on the democratic values of fact-based inquiry, critical thinking, and acceptance of a diversity of identities and opinions. The other is committed to "alternative facts" tailored to far-right ideology – a reactionary fantasy of American greatness untethered from the historical record, not to mention contemporary reality – and fiercely committed to a rearguard battle against the struggle for social and racial justice and for the restoration of a prewar America where father knew best, "people of color" knew their place, and LGBTQ+ people hid in the closet. Alarmingly, many Americans aren't even aware of this pitched battle in our communities, at our school board meetings, and in the halls of our public schools. This book aims to change that.

In this collection of frontline accounts from the far-right war on public education, 14 K-12 public school teachers from across the country describe, in their own words, the human cost of the far-right's war on free thought, critical inquiry, acceptance of difference, and the questioning of reactionary, revisionist narratives about, say, slavery, the Civil War, the genocide of Indigenous peoples, and law enforcement's role in defending white power and privilege. They speak, with raw emotion and unvarnished honesty, about being fired for creating book displays that "focused too much on LGBTQ+ students and racially diverse topics" (Elissa Malespina, a high school librarian); being trolled by parents for encouraging students to make an artwork celebrating a social-justice "changemaker" (Sally Middleton, a high school art teacher); and being placed on leave after only four days in the classroom as an elementary school teacher – for no better reason than their choice of nontraditional gender pronoun and insufficiently "feminine" attire, i.e., khakis and a button-up shirt (Monica Coles, an elementary school art teacher). They have been scapegoated, harassed, threatened, and, in some cases, hounded out of their districts or even out of their profession for embracing inclusive perspectives, teaching the painful truths of American history, and encouraging students to think critically about American society and institutions. In the pages of this book, the testimonials of educators swell into a chorus of protest.

Over and over, the teachers in this collection told us, "These horrors are happening, and my community doesn't even know." Carolyn Foote, a recently retired Texas school librarian, said, "It's a phenomenal, unprecedented moment that we're in. It's surprising how many people don't know what's going on. I talk to reporters who have no idea this is going on. And they're *reporters*."

In their testimonials, educators from Florida, Kentucky, Texas, New Jersey, Wisconsin, Tennessee, and Washington, among other states, describe having to choose not only how but, increasingly, whether to discuss topical issues and the violent side of American history and current events. Tennessee social-studies teacher Matthew D. Hawn's license is now under review simply because he prepared his students for informed discussions about racial equity and white privilege prompted by the police shooting of Jacob Blake (a Black man) and their nonviolent capture of Kyle Rittenhouse (a white man), and the January 6 insurrection. Hawn provided students with materials intended to spark conversation and provoke thought: poetic manifestos on the legacy of whiteness, an essay acknowledging the privileges of white skin, an article proposing Trump's presidency as a negation of Obama's. In a suburban public school 30 minutes away from Kenosha, Wisconsin, where Blake was shot, fourth-grade teacher Melissa Grandi Statz responded to kids' questions about the Black Lives Matter rallies they were seeing on TV by creating a lesson plan about the history of civil-rights protests. As a result, she became the target of a "Parents Against a Rogue Teacher" Facebook group and the eye of a maelstrom of hate accusing her of being "a terrorist" who was "mentally abusing children." Her family was forced to install a household alarm system and move their son from his ground-floor room to a more secure bedroom upstairs. Even her then husband was worried about his safety and took to sleeping with a baseball bat within easy reach.

In some of the incidents described in this book, ultra-conservative ideology goes hand in hand with a troubling ignorance (whether actual, feigned, or willful) of the facts of students' lives. Gavin Downing, a middle school librarian just outside Seattle, cited a Washington State Department survey in which 17 percent of students report having had sex before the age of 13. Nonetheless, Downing's principal informed him that books involving anything "beyond hand-holding and, maybe, kissing" were inappropriate for middle school students and should be purged from his shelves. "She asked me, 'How can you have a book that talks about nude selfies when you know that's a problem at this school?'" says Downing. "I thought, 'Because it's a problem at this school!' It's something these students are talking about and doing. So, let's have some discussions about it in the library." Contrary to conservative assumptions, he asserts, eliminating fact-based, responsible sources of information about sexuality won't prepare students or protect them. "If anything," he points out, enforced ignorance on such subjects "makes them more likely to be victimized."

Too often, principals, superintendents, and school-board trustees who should be a safeguard against extremist agendas cave at the first rumblings of conservative discontent. Martha Hickson, a librarian at North Hunterdon High School in New Jersey, describes the dissonance between being told by her principal that she had gone "way overboard" in supporting the LGBTQ+ students and learning, in the midst of a firestorm of conservative outrage at her refusal to purge the library of books with LGBTQ+ characters, of the suicide of a trans student who had been proudly out.

Sadly, Hickson's experience isn't uncommon. The stats don't lie, says Willie Edward Taylor Carver Jr., who taught French and English in a high school in Kentucky. "Just under 30 percent of trans youth say that they're supported at home," he notes. "Of those who don't feel they're supported at home, the likelihood that they're going to die by suicide has nearly doubled." The Trevor Project reported that when schools offered protections, such as teaching history inclusive of LGBTQ+ figures or respecting students' chosen pronouns, suicide rates fell by 26 percent.[14] If one adult in a student's life accepted his/her/their gender identity, that led to a 33 percent drop in the odds that he/she/they would attempt suicide.[15] When Kentucky passed State Bill 150, which flatly states that the gender we're assigned at birth is irrevocable and sex is inherently sinful, and State Bill 1, which requires 75 percent of books read in history to be written by white (and, implicitly, straight) men, Carver Jr. knew that LGBTQ+ kids and racial and ethnic students were going to feel erased, stigmatized, and dehumanized. He feared that, in the long term, these laws would have potentially deadly consequences.

State legislation became so hostile to LGBTQ+ people that Carver Jr., the 2022 Kentucky Teacher of the Year and himself a gay man, left the profession. In his testimonial in this book, he confides,

> there's really no way to function as a teacher, knowing there's the potential that you're going to be asked to harm students. The question is not, you know, should you be a teacher or not be a teacher? The

question is, how do you reconcile what you want to do with what you're doing? If you're a teacher in the State of Kentucky and you're following the law, you're harming people.

Pressured to be agents of miseducation, teachers in this book were threatened with the loss of their jobs and the revocation of their teaching licenses. Yet they remain committed to pedagogies that embrace inclusiveness, acceptance, and critical thought while challenging homophobic, transphobic, sexist, and white supremacist control over the classroom as an exclusively white, heteronormative, patriarchal space.[16] When educators resist censorship, they often face harassment, hostile working environments, and baseless accusations by the very communities they serve. Parents on the political or religious right, outside agitators, and conservative politicians routinely accuse teachers of "sinister agendas."[17] In some states, legislators have successfully removed the classification of "educator" from exemptions within the penal codes for obscenity, stripping away the protection that permits teachers to discuss controversial subjects in the context of, say, sex education, thereby exposing them to criminal liability. Other states are jumping on board. As Carolyn Foote, the retired Texas school librarian, explains,

> If you were teaching *The Bluest Eye* by Toni Morrison, which includes a rape scene, a parent could say, 'That's explicit! This educator gave this prurient material to my child to read in English class!' and bring [criminal] charges. And while the code still says the material has to be prurient in nature and be meant to arouse, if those protections are removed, that parent could file a lawsuit. In conservative areas, [parents are] gonna overreact. Ultimately, those parents may not win, but it's not gonna prevent them from filing charges. Sometimes, the school district is penalized – like, fines or withholding money from the district – but at least one state [as of this writing, two: Arkansas and Oklahoma] has a jail penalty for teachers – like, up to five years.*

---

* In Arkansas and Oklahoma, school employees can face from six to ten years in prison for disseminating "obscene material." In Missouri, Indiana, Montana, and Tennessee, the penalty is one to two and a half years. As of January 2024, there is pending obscenity legislation in at least nine states, including Wisconsin (SB305), South Carolina (H3826), Utah (HB0029), Nebraska (LB441), Kansas (SB188), Minnesota (HF2683), Illinois (HB4247), Georgia (SB154), and Pennsylvania (HB209).

According to EveryLibrary.org, which tracks this legislation, police fielded scores of "obscenity" reports in the past year (2023),[18] but, as of January 2024, few police or prosecutors have chosen to file or prosecute charges. It hardly matters; the damage is done. The quiet threat of reputational damage (as a result of social-media rumormongering), potential fines, job loss, and even incarceration, together with what some claim are intentionally ambiguous legislative statutes and definitions of obscenity, are intimidating educators into removing books before challenges have been formally lodged.

In their testimonies, educators describe the daily challenges they face in navigating a series of complex social dynamics and national tensions, most notably the virality of social media, which amplifies ugly mobs (but also unites book lovers and activists committed to countering bans). They share their frustrations about the COVID pandemic's effects on the classroom – specifically, transitions to virtual learning and the sometimes-inept handling of the pandemic by administrators. They decry the weaponization of parents' discontent over masking, remote learning, and other COVID-related measures by vested interests eager to weaken voters' perceptions of public education in order to shift funding and control of education to for-profit corporations, effectively privatizing public education. Deploring this strategy, Mark Johnson, a high school principal who was put on leave after standing up to a smear campaign, doesn't mince words. Far-right disruptors actually "used the pandemic and the havoc it caused" to sow the seeds of mistrust in public schools, he told us. "[W]hile we were focused on giving their kids the best possible education, *they* were focusing on spewing nonsense and whipping up people's fears." Putting this strategy in its historical context, he notes that it's part and parcel of the same right-wing and white resistance to change, integration, and inclusion that's been at war with democracy since America was created.

Private money is already corrupting the public good. We learn from Monica Coles, the art teacher navigating a wealthy suburban public school, of a PTO that opens the school year by handing educators envelopes full of money – bribes, by any other name, for their deference to parental influence. Money talks in other, less conspicuous ways, too:

Misty L.C., a middle school social studies teacher, recalls legislators walking back restrictive bills intended to quash the (nonexistent) scourge of CRT. The impetus for their about-face? The business sector, whose donations fueled political campaigns, cried foul, insisting the proposed laws would hamstring their freedom of speech and their ability to attract and develop diverse workplace cultures. To placate businesses, legislators revised the bill to target only public schools. "Coincidentally, this was happening," notes Misty, "when we had an unprecedented push for privatization and vouchers" that would divert "funds from public schools toward private and home-schooling costs."

Caught in the crosshairs of the far-right war on public education, teachers rarely tell their stories – until now. In countless cases (how many, we have no way of knowing), the fear of retaliation, the use of coercive non-disclosure agreements, intimidation by administrators, and the threat of having their teaching certifications revoked ensures their silence. In light of these pressures, some of the educators speaking up have chosen to cloak identities in pseudonyms. To guard against administrative retaliation and conservative blowback, we've created a shared locale they can call home: Censorville. They live and work in rural Censorville, or the town of Censorborough, or the city of Censoropolis, all of them municipalities in the state of Censoria.

The educators we spoke with told us about hundreds of other teachers unable to share their stories beyond trusted connections – "whisper networks" of fellow teachers and retired educators. It's crucial, we feel, to acknowledge those who, for myriad reasons, did not feel safe sharing their stories.

The educators who *were* willing to speak with us are frequently the only educators in their schools and, more often than not, the only members of their communities resisting censorship. Many have been abandoned by colleagues unwilling to risk administrative disapproval and social ostracization by the community at large. Many work in states with "at-will" employment laws and without union representation, facts of workplace life that ensure compliance and silence in the face of the ever-present threat of job loss. After Florida high school librarian Julie Miller fought back against an attempt to ban the Black queer author George M. Johnson's memoir *All Boys Aren't Blue*, she received a voicemail from another teacher in her school. "She said, 'As Christians, it's really important that we are gatekeepers,'" recalls Miller. "'I really think you should be praying about what books you're putting into the hands of our students.' And I was like, 'Wow. This is a *public* school.'"

These testimonials provide educators with a much-needed public-address system for sounding the alarm about public education in peril. As important, they're a bully pulpit, offering teachers the all-too-rare opportunity to share the powerful emotions stirred by their experiences on the cultural battlefield.

They speak movingly of their fear of losing their professional identity if the state takes away their teaching licenses, their shock at administrators' brazen disregard for their expertise, and parents', principals', politicians', and school boards' attempts to police their classroom speech, censor their libraries, even limit their gender expression or sexual identity.

Trouble in Censorville offers each teacher a platform to give readers a rare glimpse of the institutional, political, ethical, and emotional forces public school teachers are forced to contend with at a historical moment when far-right extremism is infiltrating school boards and fraying parent-teacher relations, upending teachers' lives and shredding the fabric of previously tight-knit communities.

As mentioned earlier, many Americans, disengaged from politics or simply too confident that their school boards or administrators are minding the store, are unaware of the far right's full-court press, at the local level, to roll back gains for marginalized groups of every sort (racialized persons, LGBTQ+ students) in the name of "Making America Great Again." Then, too, as Miller says of Clay County, Florida, where she lives and teaches, "most of the people who *do* know about it either don't care enough to go to a school board meeting or write a letter, or they're fearful of speaking out because we're in Trump country."

The news media, in these testimonials, don't exactly cover themselves in glory. In too many cases, media outlets act as stenographers to power, uncritically amplifying unsubstantiated claims by ideologues with an axe to grind. In researching educators' claims about media bias, we discovered that an alarming percentage of the news stories related to far-right attacks on public education repeat, without comment or context, misinformation spread by the "parents' rights" movement and groups associated with extremist ideologies and right-wing politics.

As well, mainstream coverage often omits any mention of systemic causes/effects, such as the role of race or sexual orientation and gender identity. Also rarely mentioned is the long-lasting trauma inflicted by these attacks, ranging from the loneliness and depression brought on by social isolation (whether as a result of losing their jobs or being shunned at work and in their communities) to high blood pressure and other symptoms of stress. Almost every educator in this collection describes experiencing panic attacks, debilitating depression, hives, hair loss, weight gain, insomnia, being on the verge of tears for weeks on end, or avoiding interaction at school with formerly friendly staff and fellow educators who now treat them as pariahs.

Trouble in Censorville teachers give vent to their pent-up anger over institutional betrayal – administrators' or Board of Ed trustees' refusal to stand by them in the face of public abuse at board meetings, anonymous threats, stalking, social-media mobs smearing them as "pedophiles" and "groomers," and calls for their firing. A common, dispiriting theme among the stories collected here is the invertebrate cowardice of school administrators who, in the face of COVID hardships or the outrage of even a single community member with no child enrolled in the schools, seem to forget their official policies or, as significant, the years of professional excellence held by the educator who is their employee.

The way Jill James, a language-arts teacher, tells it, parents in her district condemned her and other educators' participation in a summit supporting students' emotional needs – a summit administrators had enthusiastically supported. Hectored by conservative parents suspicious of the summit's "woke" agenda, these same administrators succumbed to what might be called sudden-onset amnesia, claiming, in their frantic attempts to distance themselves from the event, never to have known about it. James wasn't having it. Marching into the vice principal's office, she said, "You sanctioned this; you have to stand behind me." At that point, she recalls, "the vice principal stepped up. He did an about-face, agreeing that the administration had supported our initiative and that it did fall within our mission as a school to support social-emotional learning."

Many of the teachers in this collection note that it's the parents and outside political groups, not the students, who want to ban books, censor conversations about challenging topics, and curb the teaching of factual history. Most students, they repeatedly insist, *want* to have these conversations. When students are implicated in attempts to ban books or muzzle teachers, they're often prompted, it turns out, by parents – parents who cling to the social hierarchies and obsolete values of their youth (specifically, to the powers and privilege of their whiteness) in a rearguard battle against social change and calls for racial reckoning.

Ellen Barnes, a middle school social studies teacher, recounts the story of a colleague who assigned students to read about the historical roots of racism:

[O]ne of the students who was assigned this book was instructed by their [parent] to walk out of the classroom when the topic came up or if the book was even mentioned. So, this child walked out of the room and told the front office that they felt unsafe. I have no problem with students interrogating my authority – students asking me "why?" – since I should be able to answer their questions. But telling your child to do that as soon as a subject is brought up is dismissive of a reasonable conversation and an intellectually engaged relationship with your teacher. It disregards the possibility of mutual understanding. It's unhealthy problem-solving and disrespectful to the learning environment.

Barnes and other educators worry about what the future will be like for a generation of students who are told to walk out of the room in the face of discomfort; who no longer have access to books and even academic research databases that speak to their needs, their concerns, their interests; and who, in Florida, aren't even allowed to thumb through a *Webster's Dictionary for Students* because the experts who write dictionaries have chosen to acknowledge "sex" within the English language.[19]

Yet despite the opposition they face – and, too often, face alone – the everyday heroes of these stories decided, time and again, to put their jobs on the line and themselves in the line of fire between the ugliest elements in American society and the most vulnerable among their students. Despite considerable risk and stress, they refused to be complicit. They refused to act as gatekeepers for the forces of reaction and bigotry barring students' access to ideas that might lead them to question conservative doctrines meant to bolster their political power. They refused to clear the way for white-supremacist, patriarchal attempts to cling to power and impose on K-12 students ideas whose time has gone: the belief that only heterosexual relationships are normal, the demand that everyone identify with the gender of the body they're born with, and other obsolete notions that the far right has in mind when it says it wants to "make America great again."

Thrillingly, the teachers we spoke to are fighting back and fighting back fiercely. They've mobilized colleagues, parents, and community members who shared their faith in the freedom to read, the freedom to think critically, the freedom to challenge small-minded provincialism, anti-Black racism, homophobia, and the inexorable creep of white Christian nationalism and Trumpist illiberalism.

In her testimonial, Hickson, the intrepid high school librarian, describes her response to conservative book banners: a counteroffensive of imaginative, skillful, and effective tactics. First, she says, she "reactivated" a group that had fended off such challenges before, the self-styled North Hunterdon-Voorhees Intellectual Freedom Fighters (North Hunterdon-Voorhees being the name of their district).

> I said, "We gotta bring the band back together 'cause the fur is flying over here." We sprang into action. We're a two-high-school district, and each school has a GSA, a Gender and

Sexuality Alliance, so I reached out to their officers. The first time around, [with the first book challenge, I'd been] reluctant to do that. My union said, "Don't involve the kids, don't involve the kids." This time, I thought, "No, I need to involve the kids; these are their books, and the way these people are talking about their books is just a proxy for what they think about LGBTQ+ people." So, I reached out to the kids, who were immediately on fire.

Many of the testimonials in *Trouble in Censorville* offer this kind of strategic roadmap for resisting censorship and rallying support. Elissa Malespina is the only public school librarian who's also an elected member of a school board in New Jersey. Using her expertise, she revised district policy to protect their diverse curriculum and to proactively curb book challenges.

When the Christian-nationalist politician Matt Krause tried to claw his way to the top of the political pile by releasing a list of 850 so-called "pornographic" books that, in his ultra-conservative opinion, should be banned from Texas schools, Carolyn Foote and her fellow school librarians managed, despite their lack of tech savvy, to orchestrate a Twitter counterattack so effective it resulted in their Freedom to Read hashtag (#FReadom) going wildly viral. They beat back the book banners and, as of this writing, continue their work as an advocacy group, preparing parents and school librarians around the country to fight the extremist right at school board meetings.

It's our hope that this collection will provide embattled educators with a sense of solidarity and crank up the volume of resistance to these attacks. As educators, we want to ensure that each student has the opportunity to thrive in a diverse, supportive, thought-provoking educational environment that will prepare them to become part of a critical and informed citizenry. If the idea of America and the dream of democracy are to make it through the deeply un-American, anti-democratic onslaught we're witnessing, educators must be empowered and emboldened to fight back. Dedicated public school teachers and librarians can make a world of difference – in their students' lives, first and foremost, but also in the survival of the dream, too long deferred, of democracy in America.

Downing, the school librarian from the state of Washington, captures this flicker of hope and the vitally important role educators can play in fanning it into a fire. He recounts his administration's capitulation to right-wing moral panic over his decision to purchase LGBTQ+-friendly titles and create displays showcasing books about marginalized groups – a witch-hunt that inspired him to leave the middle school where he'd been a librarian for years and take a job at a more enlightened high school. During his last weeks at the middle school, he noticed a kid he'd often seen hanging around the library, "a very quiet student" who was often in the library but didn't say a lot and kept to himself for the most part." The teen seemed to have something on his mind.

> He came up to me and said, "Mr. Downing, I just wanted to thank you for always having such *great books* in the library." He put that emphasis there. He looked around to make sure no one was looking. Then he raised his fist, and he said, "Happy Pride."

IT DIDN'T BEGIN WITH TRUMP:
THE ATTACK ON PUBLIC EDUCATION –
A TIMELINE

Nadine M. Kalin and Rebekah Modrak

This timeline provides historical background and contemporary context for the current events, social and political dynamics, and organizations and individuals referred to by the teachers, librarians, and administrators profiled in this book.

The tactics used by reactionary elements fighting a rearguard battle against racial progress and social justice – efforts to muzzle free speech about American history and demonize teachers who believe in critical thinking and diversity – didn't come out of nowhere. In the words of Ta-Nehisi Coates, "Two hundred fifty years of slavery. Ninety years of Jim Crow. Sixty years of separate but equal. Thirty-five years of racist housing policy."[1] A full accounting of the toxic fallout on public education of the racism, misogyny, homophobia, and xenophobic bigotry that blight American history would require a timeline stretching from 1619 to now. We encourage readers interested in a deeper dive into these subjects to begin with *The 1619 Project* by Nikole Hannah-Jones, *Stamped from the Beginning: The Definitive History of Racist Ideas in America* by Ibram X. Kendi, *Black AF History: The Un-Whitewashed Story of America* by Michael Harriot, *A Queer History of the United States* by Michael Bronski, and *The LGBTQ+ History Book* by DK. The histories chronicled in these trailblazing titles haunt the controversies around public education described in the pages of this book.

In this timeline, we focus on relatively recent history and, in particular, on the events and trends discussed by the teachers who share their testimonials here, most notably the anti-leftist Red Scare and homophobic Lavender Scare of the McCarthy Era, *Brown v. Board of Education* (and other court cases involving racial justice, education, and the First Amendment), antigay and anti-Black legislation, the right's weaponization of the COVID pandemic for political purposes, the Black Lives Matter movement, and the presidency of Donald Trump and the rise of Trumpism (loosely defined as the white-supremacist/ Christian-nationalist backlash against the struggle for racial and social justice). Prominent in our compressed history of the attack on public education is the growing use, by far-right activists, organizations, and politicians, of book-banning, legislation that disguises anti-Black racism as principled opposition to "divisive concepts," and inflammatory, potentially dangerous rhetoric that uses baseless charges of "grooming" and "pedophilia" to pervert public perceptions of sexual health education and LGBTQ+ sexuality to undermine trust in teachers and public schools more generally.

The trends and events chronicled by our timeline reveal the tensions that, from the first, have complicated the dream of a truly democratic America. Those fissures and fractures include the opposition between solidarity (*E Pluribus Unum* – "Out of Many, One") and pathological individualism; between federalism and states' rights; between an informed citizenry participating thoughtfully in public debate and the "madness of crowds" (lynch mobs, Trump rallies, far-right disruptors at school-board meetings, the January 6 insurrectionists, etc.); between white power and the promise of universal human rights; between untrammeled capitalism and labor rights; and between the First Amendment and hate speech calling for violence.

Trouble in Censorville teachers mentioned in the timeline will be in bold, all-caps. As you read, bear in mind that this timeline, while designed to help readers understand the testimonials that follow against the backdrop of past events and current controversies, isn't just a history lesson. It's a desperately urgent call for action.

Reconstruction: 1865-1877

After the Civil War, Republican President Andrew Johnson reneges on President Lincoln's promise of granting every formerly enslaved person 40 acres of land and returns the lands to their prewar Southern owners. Freed Blacks are forced to sharecrop for white landowners with low wages and restrictive contracts.

At the same time, the Equal Rights League, founded by abolitionist Frederick Douglass, advocates for equal rights – full citizenship, the right to vote, and, crucially, access to education. One of the most significant achievements is the creation of the first public education system in the South, made possible by the actions of Black communities who raise funds, give land, and build schools, with support from the Freedman's Bureau – established in 1865 to aid formerly enslaved African Americans, and Northern aid. By 1870, all Southern states had incorporated a provision for a free public school system into their state constitutions.

Throughout this period, Southern Blacks advocate for public education and compulsory education laws in the South, which hadn't existed prior to the Civil War (a crusade for educational justice that benefits poor white families as well).[2] Between 1865 and 1869, the Thirteenth Amendment ends slavery, the Fourteenth Amendment ensures African Americans the rights of citizenship, and the Fifteenth Amendment guarantees the right to vote for Black men. Political activism by Black Southerners puts more than 2000 Black men in public office, from local seats to the U.S. Senate, which exerts pressure on white legislators to pass the Civil Rights Act of 1866, entitling all, regardless of race or color, to "full and equal benefit of all laws."

When the federal government fails to enforce the Thirteenth, Fourteenth, and Fifteenth Amendments, the Southern states seize the opportunity to enact "Black codes" that restrict the movements, rights, and advancement of Black people. African Americans are prohibited from voting, serving on juries, owning guns, and assembling in "groups of six or more after sundown, using insulting gestures or language toward whites,"[3] among other oppressive and unconstitutional restrictions. Most consequential, for our purposes, is the prohibition on attending public schools, either the all-white schools or schools developed by African Americans. White supremacist groups, mainly the Ku Klux Klan, enforce these codes through a campaign of intimidation and terror. President Andrew Johnson, a former owner of enslaved people, ignores the racist Black codes and vetoes numerous bills meant to promote civil rights.[4]

In 1877, President Rutherford B. Hayes buys Southern Democrats' votes by pulling the last federal troops out of the South, a decision that gives Southern whites carte blanche in their assault on the advances Black Southerners had gained during Reconstruction. The fallout from Hayes's decision has a devastating impact on the lives of Black Americans.

Thurgood Marshall Litigates: 1930s and 1940s

After graduating from Howard University Law School in 1933, **Thurgood Marshall, whose mother was a schoolteacher, litigates unequal-salary cases for Black teachers**, who are paid 50% of what white teachers earn. National Education Association data shows that, by the period of public school desegregation, 85 percent of Black teachers held advanced degrees (as opposed to 75 percent of white teachers). Yet, Black teachers are denied higher salaries because of their race.[5] By 1945, Marshall had won nearly all of his unequal-salary cases, resulting in more equitable pay for Black teachers. Ultimately, Marshall's efforts ended salary disparities across 10 Southern states.

Midterm Elections: November 5, 1946

For the first time in 15 years, **Republicans win control of the House and the Senate by exploiting fears about mounting Cold War tensions with the Soviet Union and by falsely accusing Democrats of being tools of the Red Menace – "pink puppets."**[6] Republicans use red-baiting to scare voters by falsely linking communism with former President Franklin Delano Roosevelt's policy successes, liberal initiatives such as the New Deal, social-welfare programs such as Social Security, and FDR's support of organized labor. Aside from calls for a rhetorical counterattack by FDR's former vice president Henry Wallace, who dismisses Republicans' anti-communist rhetoric as a "deliberately created crisis," progressive voices on the political left remain largely silent.[7]

The Hunt for "Subversives" Begins: March 21, 1947

Democrat Harry S. Truman panders to escalating anti-communist hysteria on the right by back-tracking from FDR's social welfare agenda and issuing Executive Order 9835, which requires federal workers to proclaim a loyalty oath and be subject to investigations into their political beliefs. EO 9835 inspires the Attorney General, the FBI, and the State Department to create a massively publicized blacklist of "subversive organizations" such as the National Negro Congress and the Council on African Affairs. The list is then shared with and adopted by state and local governments. When the House Committee on Un-American Activities (HUAC) gets hold of The List, young politicians eager for power and influence, like Richard Nixon and Joe McCarthy, see an opportunity to scapegoat others for political gain.[8] By conflating communism with "un-American," "subversive," and "immoral" threats, such as civil rights activism, union activism, and "homosexuality," the HUAC and its many subcommittees launch what amounts to a cultural offensive to preserve the racial, heteronormative, capitalist order.[9] McCarthyism launches an era of political paranoia, now considered a betrayal of America's democratic principles.

"The Lavender Scare": April 27, 1953

President Dwight D. Eisenhower's Executive Order 10450 tasked the FBI to hunt out and identify federal employees who posed "risks" to "national security," including any "sexual perversion." EO 10450 sets in motion the removal of gay men and lesbians from serving in the federal government on the baseless grounds that their closeted sexuality put them "at risk" of being blackmailed by Soviet agents who, the story went, would threaten them with exposure if they didn't agree to spy for the Soviet Union. Otherwise known as the Lavender Scare, this offshoot of the anti-communist Red Scare forces thousands out of their jobs.

Brown v. Board of Education: May 17, 1954

The United States Supreme Court's *Brown v. Board of Education of Topeka* decision ends school segregation. In retaliation, white school boards across the Southern states orchestrate changes so that all-Black schools close and all-white public schools with all-white administrators and faculties take in Black students.[10] As a result, between 1954 and 1979, over 100,000 highly credentialed Black teachers and principals, many of whom hold master's degrees or doctorates, are demoted or lose their jobs as white school boards and legislators stripped the resources of all-Black public schools to maintain the supremacy of white public schools.[11] The ranks of Black educators are decimated, a calculated assault whose effects are still felt today. According to a federal survey from 2020-2021, only six percent of public school teachers in the United States are Black.[12] In 1955, the Supreme Court responds to requests for aid in facilitating desegregation by ruling in *Brown II* that district courts oversee compliance with "all deliberate speed." The ambiguity in not calling for more urgent action leads to increased Southern resistance.

Introducing the Public School Voucher: 1955

In his 1955 essay "The Role of Government in Education," Milton Friedman, an economist, outlines his vision for transforming K-12 education by providing parents who opt out of public schools with government-issued vouchers that will underwrite the cost of sending their children to private schools, whether religious or secular, non-profit or for-profit. While cloaked in the language of free-market fundamentalism and parental choice, Friedman's proposal aids and abets segregationist defiance of *Brown*.

The Gray Commission: November 11, 1955

The 1955 Gray Commission, 32 white-male-legislators commissioned by Virginia Governor Thomas Stanley, issues a report calling for a state tuition grant program for parents who would prefer that their children attend private segregated academies rather than integrated public schools.

Pledge to Reverse Desegregation: February 25, 1956

In 1956, 19 Southern Senators and 82 Representatives (97 Democrats and 4 Republicans) **sign the "Southern Manifesto criticizing the U.S. Supreme Court for its ruling in *Brown v. Board of Education* and** pledging to "use all lawful means to bring about a reversal of this decision."[13]

Conservative Democrat Senator Harry F. Byrd, Sr. of Virginia advocates for a policy of "Massive Resistance" with proposals for Southern state laws blocking public school segregation. His state legislature passes a law allowing districts to withdraw funding from public schools that integrated Black and white students.[14] In a final act of defiance, in 1959, Prince Edward County, Virginia, closes its public school system without provisions for African American students, leaving them to devise their own alternatives, such as relocating children with northern relatives or going without schooling. White students attend the Prince Edward Academy, an all-white private school set up through a private fund drive. This effectively delays, by over a decade, the desegregation of public schools in Virginia.

The Johns Commission: 1956

In 1956, during the second wave of anticommunist witch-hunting, the **Florida Legislative Investigation Committee (aka the Johns Committee)** is established as the Florida version of the House Committee on Un-American Activities. In hopes of making political hay from the white Southern panic over school desegregation, the committee investigates alleged links between the National Association for the Advancement of Colored People (NAACP) and communism in Florida.

After this proves fruitless, the committee investigates and persecutes gay men and lesbians, including public school teachers, claiming, without evidence, that they're a threat to national security. By 1963, the Johns Committee has revoked 71 teacher certificates.[15] Present-day antigay rhetoric about "predatory gays" and the conflation of Marxism, LGBTQ+ people, and pedophilia are a tired refrain of the right-wing's baseless accusations of "moral perversion," often conflating "Communists and queers," during the McCarthy era.[16]

The Voucher-Based Vision Continues: 1964

Economist Milton Friedman becomes an advisor to the 1964 presidential campaign of the Republican candidate Barry Goldwater, who runs on an archconservative platform whose goals include opposition to *Brown* and the 1964 Civil Rights Act. Though Goldwater is defeated, his voucher-based vision continues to motivate the **Republican Party's support for the privatization of K-12 schooling** (and, not incidentally, the demolition of public education).

In the 2000s, vulture capitalists, such as Trump's Secretary of Education Betsy DeVos (who has donated to Christian schools and voucher programs since 1989), have redoubled their attempts to divert taxpayer dollars to voucher funding for private charter schools, private online schooling, and homeschooling. As of 2016, nearly two-thirds of the 1.7 million home-schooled kids were Christians.[17] Homeschooling became more diverse since the pandemic, with families citing school shootings, dissatisfaction with special learning instruction, children no longer have access to books and instruction in states with "divisive concepts" laws, and Black families concerned with systemic racism.

Organizations, such as the EdChoice, a "scholarship program" co-founded by Friedman in 1996, use public funds to create vouchers to, presumably, send public school students from "underperforming public schools" to private schools. However, studies show that, across states, 69 to 95 percent of those students receiving vouchers were already enrolled in private schools.[18] All of these options siphon tax dollars out of the public school system, degrading public schools and depriving their students – who are more likely to be nonwhite than those attending private schools – to the equal education guaranteed by *Brown*. This conservative strategy of slow death by defunding has the effect of making public schools less desirable, thereby bolstering support for free-market alternatives. As of February 2024, 29 states and the District of Columbia have all implemented at least one "private school choice program," in which families can use public funding toward private school.[19]

As recipients of federal funding, public schools must provide education free of discrimination. However, voucher programs created by states don't rely on federal funding.[20] Less than half of the nation's 62 voucher programs have built in the necessary statutory protections to prevent racial discrimination, and even fewer states' voucher programs offer protections based on sex, religion, sexual orientation, gender identity, and disability status. For example, a private school with a dress code banning cornrows, braids, or extensions may expel a student, leaving the student with no recourse to challenge this action.[21]

Keefe v. Geanakos: November 12, 1969

In *Keefe v. Geanakos*, the U.S. Court of Appeals for the First Circuit rules that an Ipswich, Massachusetts **public high school teacher's classroom lesson about the origins and varying cultural and social contexts of the word "motherfucker" was proper** because the word was already accessible in several books in the school library and in spoken language in common use. Chief Judge Aldrich, in writing that the teacher's speech was protected, surmises that most students are familiar with the word and, in considering the question of whether the "shock" of the language was too great for high school seniors to stand, wrote, "If the answer were that the students must be protected from such exposure, we would fear for their future."[22] Fifty-two years later, on May 5, 2021, Tennessee social studies teacher **MATTHEW D. HAWN** is dismissed because, among other things, the administration alleged that he affronted high-school students' delicate sensibilities with a recital of Kyla Jenee Lacey's poem *White Privilege*, which contains six curse words. (*see pp. 111-124*)

The Southern Stategy: 1965-1972

Exploiting opposition to school desegregation and the Civil Rights Act, the Republican Party whips up race-based fear to attract white Southern voters. Dubbed **the "Southern Strategy,"** political campaigns that capitalize on racial fears appeal to the ugliest elements in American society; Richard Nixon employs the strategy in his 1968 presidential campaign.

"Save Our Children": June 7, 1977

Anita Bryant, a pop singer of the squeaky-clean Pat Boon variety who found Jesus, learns that Miami-Dade has amended its Human Rights Ordinance to prohibit housing and employment discrimination based on sexual orientation. As well, public school teachers can no longer be fired for being gay. Bryant, inspired by her pastor saying that he would rather burn a school down than allow children to be taught by "homosexuals,"[23] launches the **"Save Our Children" campaign to overturn the Miami-Dade anti-discrimination ordinance.** Her crusade receives major media attention, providing a platform for Bryant to spread her wildly false claim that schoolchildren need to be protected from "deviant" gay "recruiters of children." As a mother and Christian, she has the right to control "the moral atmosphere in which her children grow up," she says.[24] "Save Our Children" is successful in its efforts to rally conservative voters, who repeal Miami-Dade's Human Rights Ordinance. Antigay conspiracy theories and homophobic smears similar to those used by Bryant in 1977 are still part of the far right's arsenal: Moms for Liberty and other ultra-conservative groups calling for the removal of LGBTQ+-themed books from school libraries often employ them.

Targeting Gay and Lesbian Teachers: March 15, 1978

On March 15, 1978, the **Oklahoma Senate unanimously passes H.B. 1629.** Conceived by lawmakers John Monks (Democrat) and Mary Helm (Republican), the law allows "school boards to fire teachers who engage in public homosexual conduct." Following Oklahoma's lead, John Briggs, a Republican senator from California ardently support-ed by Anita Bryant, sponsors Proposition 6, aka the Briggs Initiative, which seeks to ban gay people from working in California's public schools despite evidence showing that "the overwhelming majority" of crimes involving child molestation "are committed by heterosexuals."[25] Opposed by San Francisco Councilman Harvey Milk, President Jimmy Carter, and, despite his rock-ribbed conservatism, former California Governor Ronald Reagan (who had been warned that any student with a failing grade might accuse the teacher of being gay, causing chaos in classrooms), the ballot initiative is defeated on November 7, 1978. Oklahoma H.B. 1629 is ruled unconstitutional by the Oklahoma Supreme Court on March 26, 1985.

Island Trees School District v. Pico: June 25, 1982

The **U.S. Supreme Court ruling for** *Island Trees School District v. Pico* upholds the idea that a student's right to a plurality of viewpoints trumps a school board's right to determine the curriculum. In 1975, three members of the Island Trees School District Board of Education went outside their community to meet with a conservative group called Parents of New York United (PONYU), who gave them a list of 33 "objectionable" books, which they described as "anti-American, anti-Christian, anti-Semitic, and just plain filthy."[26] Most of the books on the list were by or about racialized people. Without reading the books in their entirety, the Island Trees School Board members went into one of the public schools in the middle of the night and removed all of the "objectionable" books listed in the catalog.[27] Justice Brennan, writing on behalf of the majority, argues that "local school boards may not remove books from school libraries simply because they dislike the ideas contained in those books and seek by their removal to 'prescribe what shall be orthodox in politics, nationalism, religion, or other matters of opinion.'"[28]

There are many parallels between the Island Trees episode and present-day attacks on public school libraries: agitators from outside the community attempting to influence local policy, conservative book banners who can't be bothered to fully read the books they want banned, the flouting of official policy by covertly removing books rather than petitioning for their removal through official channels, and the racist characterization of writing by racialized authors as "obscene."

The Federal Marriage Amendment: July 18, 2006

After the Massachusetts Supreme Court ruled that it was unconstitutional to ban gay couples from marriage, and San Francisco begins issuing marriage licenses, President Bush fears that "activist courts" may strike the Defense of Marriage Act as unconstitutional. He **attempts to write homophobia into law** by resurrecting the Alliance for Marriage Act as a constitutional amendment, the Federal Marriage Amendment, defining marriage as "between one man and one woman." Senator John F. Kerry of Massachusetts, the leading Democrat in the presidential campaign, calls Mr. Bush's endorsement a campaign ploy seeking "a wedge issue to divide the American people."[29] On July 18, the motion fails in the House of Representatives. It will be reintroduced by Republican legislatures in 2008, 2013, and 2015.

The Weaponization of Facebook: September 26, 2006

The first social media platform, initially intended to assess the attractiveness of women, launches. During the COVID pandemic, many right-wing parents and activists will use the platform to spread misinformation about curriculums, stoke moral-panic fears about nonexistent perils to students in public education, and to harass, troll, and dox teachers to intimidate them into resigning or to chill their speech and restrict their freedom to teach diverse perspectives. Conservative parents form groups with names like "Concerned Parents" or "Parents Against a Rogue Teacher." (*see pp. 225-238*) Meanwhile, teachers' freedom to express themselves on social media is often limited by their district.

Marriage Equality: June 26, 2015

In *Obergefell v. Hodges*, the court rules 5-4 **in favor of marriage equality**, writing that "same-sex couples may exercise the fundamental right to marry in all States," and that "there is no lawful basis for a State to refuse to recognize a lawful same-sex marriage performed in another State."[30]

The Election of Donald J. Trump: January 20, 2017

Donald Trump is inaugurated as the 45th president of the U.S. A real-estate mogul and reality-TV star with no prior public or military service, Trump campaigns on the slogan "Make America Great Again," a promise to return to a time when racism, misogyny, and homophobia were facts of everyday life in America, and white supremacy and the patriarchy reigned supreme. Trump, who during Barack Obama's presidency had promoted the "birther" conspiracy theory that Obama was born in Kenya (rather than Hawaii, as documented on his birth certificate) and was therefore not eligible for the presidency, kicked off his 2016 presidential campaign with yet another racist lie: the vile falsehood that Mexican "rapists" were swarming over the southern border. During the campaign, Trump regularly traded in Islamophobia, racism, homophobia, and misogyny. His campaign rhetoric and, after his election, tweets, rallies, and policies normalize unabashed bigotry and intolerance, inspiring a wave of hate speech and hate crimes across the country.[31] During his four years in office, Trump "fueled already smoldering racist animosities,"[32] exploiting the right-wing "whitelash"[33] of racist hostility to mounting demands for social justice and racial equity.

MARK JOHNSON, a non-white high-school principal interviewed in this collection (*see pp. 263-274*), believes Trump's "racist fearmongering" gave far-right extremists "permission to speak what they've felt for so long." **WILLIE EDWARD TAYLOR CARVER JR.**, a former English and French teacher from Tennessee (*see pp. 147-171*), observes that "after Trump's election, the dial on bigotry of all kinds got turned up. Suddenly, hatred became protected political speech." During his presidency, Trump deploys tactics familiar from autocratic regimes: he demonizes asylum-seekers and undocumented immigrants, claiming that America is being "unfairly victimized by foreigners,"[34] threatens military force against BLM protesters, referred to veterans of American war as "losers," and attacks the media as "fake news" and the "enemy of the people."[35]

The 1619 Project: August 2019

Journalist Nikole Hannah-Jones' *The 1619 Project* reimagines 1619 – the date marking the arrival of the first enslaved people in the United States – as the year of the nation's birth. By doing so, Hannah-Jones re-centers America's historical narrative around the impact of slavery and, in telling that story from an anti-racist perspective, highlights the previously neglected or downplayed contributions of Black Americans.[36]

The Weaponization of the COVID-19 Pandemic: 2020

On January 21, 2020, the Centers for Disease Control and Prevention confirms the first case of COVID-19 in the U.S. By March, many cities go into lockdown, requiring or encouraging people to stay at home to reduce the spread of the virus, and many businesses require patrons to wear masks. **Public schools shift online during the early days of the COVID pandemic**, giving parents a front-row seat to their children's classes. Some conservative parents are outraged by discussion topics and reading materials that question "essential facts," such as the myth that America, in the 21st century, is a "race-blind" meritocracy. As well, they're dismayed by the recognition of non-binary gender identities or the teaching of perspectives on U.S. history that challenge the white-washed versions they were taught. Far-right parents use school board meetings as political platforms to decry these trends, in effect resisting a changing world. **MARK JOHNSON**, a high-school principal (*see pp. 263-274*), tells us that "far-right disruptors really used the pandemic and the havoc it caused us to their advantage because, while we were focused on giving their kids the best possible education, *they* were focusing on spewing nonsense and whipping up people's fears." **MISTY L.C.**, a middle school social studies teacher (*see pp. 173-184*), adds, "Those trying to privatize education saw this parental dissatisfaction over how COVID was handled – the school closures, the mask mandates, the online learning – as their moment to mobilize parents against public schools and toward private education. They moved as swiftly as possible to whip up as much fear as possible about what was happening in the schools."

"The Racial Reckoning": February 23, 2020

Ahmaud Arbery, a 25-year-old Black man who recently enrolled in college to become an electrician, is chased, then shot to death by two white men while jogging in a suburb of Brunswick, Georgia. As with many hate crimes and racially motivated murders, the white men falsely claim that Arbery was a suspect in a recent burglary. On March 13, 2020, **Breonna Taylor**, a 26-year-old Black woman and an award-winning EMT is fatally shot by police in her home in Louisville, Kentucky. Based on flawed intelligence, the police raid Taylor's home late at night, spraying it and two neighboring apartments, with occupants, with 32 rounds. On May 25, 2020, **George Floyd**, a 46-year-old Black man, beloved by his family and Minneapolis community for his gentleness and generosity, is murdered by a white police officer who kneels on his neck for more than nine minutes while arresting him on suspicion of using a counterfeit $20 bill. The murder is recorded and widely broadcast; international audiences watch Floyd struggle to breathe and then die while witnesses plead for the officers to release him.

May 27, 2020, is the date cited as the first protest leading to a worldwide uproar about systemic violence against Black people. Black-led organizing and mass protests for racial justice continue through the summer of 2020. **The Black Lives Matter (BLM) protests, also known as the racial reckoning**, advocate for more counselors and fewer cops within police departments, increase turnout of voters of color, and call for public school curriculums that tell the full story of Black history, teaching the origins of racism so that students can analyze, contest, and ultimately overturn white supremacy.[37] Many public school educators trying to teach American history, engage with current events, and be responsive to communities grappling with racialized violence develop lesson plans that allow for research and discussion about the murder of these and other African Americans by white cops and white vigilantes.

"Saving American History": June 2020

In June 2020, **Tom Cotton, Republican Senator for Arizona, introduces the "Saving American History Act" in the Senate**. The proposed bill prohibits the use of federal funds to teach *The 1619 Project* in elementary and secondary public schools. State governments can withhold funds proportional to the expense and time a teacher spends teaching *The 1619 Project*. This act is not voted on and therefore is never enacted.

Jacob Blake: August 23, 2020

Jacob Blake Jr., a 29-year-old Black man and father of six who was training to become a mechanic, is shot in the back by a white police officer responding to a domestic incident between two women in Kenosha,

Wisconsin. Blake survives but is paralyzed and endures excruciating pain. The Kenosha prosecutor chooses not to bring charges against the police officer, Rusten Sheskey, who returned to work in April 2021.

Kyle Rittenhouse: August 25, 2020

Kyle Rittenhouse, a white Trump fan and self-appointed security for local businesses, shoots three protestors, two fatally, during the Kenosha uprising in response to the shooting of Jacob Blake. He is taken into police custody peacefully and later acquitted of all charges, including two counts of homicide.

The Weaponization of "CRT": September 2020

In what Kimberlé Crenshaw describes as "a post-George Floyd backlash,"[38] the "far-right propagandist"[39] **Christopher F. Rufo weaponizes the term "Critical Race Theory"** (CRT), which he encounters in the footnotes of books on anti-racism. CRT is a form of academic analysis, developed by legal scholars, which studies how racial inequality is perpetuated through housing, banking, the legal systems, and, of particular relevance to the issues discussed in this book, education.[40] Rufo recognizes the obscure term's ideological potential when used as "political kindling" to play on right-wing fears of "radical" and "Marxist" indoctrination.[41] During the summer of 2020, he spins the concerns raised by BLM protests – specifically, the role of slavery in American history, the continuing legacy of racism, and calls for historical literacy and racial justice – as "leftist indoctrination" being taught in K-12 public schools and workplaces. Publicized by right-wing media, Rufo's disinformation campaign incites outraged opposition on the right.

Christopher Rufo catches President Trump's interest when he appears on Fox News's *Tucker Carlson Tonight* on September 1, 2020. Imploring Trump to abolish critical race theory-based workplace training from all branches of the federal government, he denounces "Black Lives Matter and neo-Marxist rhetoric." Rufo's manufactured threat of "**CRT indoctrination**" – an "un-American" plot to "brainwash" schoolchildren with leftist ideologies – proves effective at revving up Republican Party energy and mobilizing conservative white, suburban voters.

Trump Enters the Anti-CRT Fray: September 4, 2020

President Trump wades into the anti-CRT fray by sending a memorandum to federal agencies claiming that "according to press reports" government workers are being trained "to believe anti-American propaganda."[42] The Trump memo prohibits spending on training programs used in federal workplaces and the armed services if the programs in question incorporate CRT, critique "white privilege," or suggest that institutional racism is a fact of American life or that any race or ethnicity is inherently racist (a claim that CRT does not, in fact, endorse).[43] Later in the month, Trump's executive order will identify phrases used in four federal training sessions in which discussants acknowledged their privileges, considered how racism is "interwoven" into American systems, and questioned the relevance of concepts, such as "the nuclear family." Critics of the Trump memo contend that such topics provoke useful questions for government and military employees considering American society critically. CRT, it bears noting, was not mentioned in any of these sessions.[44]

Parents Against a Rogue Teacher: September 2020

Burlington, Wisconsin parents start a "Parents Against a Rogue Teacher" Facebook group to harass fourth-grade teacher **MELISSA GRANDI STATZ** (*see pp. 225-238*), condemning her as a "Marxist," a "terrorist," and an indoctrinator and calling for her firing because she led a class discussion about protests in nearby Kenosha, Wisconsin, sparked by the shooting of Jacob Blake. She and her students discussed the Black Lives Matter movement and systemic racism in American society. Members of the Facebook group post pictures of their guns and encourage others to arm themselves, presumably to intimidate Ms. Grandi Statz into resigning.

1776 Commission: September 17, 2020

Seeing an opportunity to manufacture further moral outrage for political gain, President Trump announces a new **committee to promote "patriotic education," the "1776 Commission."**[45] Warning of innocent white children being corrupted by leftist ideologues "portraying

American as racist" in public schools, he calls upon parents to revolt, predicting that "patriotic moms and dads are going to demand that their children are no longer fed hateful lies about this country."[46]

Trump Executive Order 13950: September 22, 2020

The Trump White House issues EO 13950, "Combating Race and Sex Stereotyping," to prohibit U.S. Armed Forces and federal agencies from so-called "divisive concepts" training. The EO defines "divisive concepts" as the idea that the U.S. is fundamentally racist or sexist, that an individual may be racist or sexist, "whether consciously or unconsciously," and that "an individual should feel discomfort [or] guilt ... on account of his or her race or sex." Assuring Americans that "racialized views of America" were "soundly defeated on the blood-stained battlefields of the Civil War" and that "in the 57 years since Dr. [Martin Luther King Jr.] shared his dream with the country," America has attained a state of racial harmony and equality, the order warns patriots to beware racist indoctrination that "some people, simply on account of their race or sex, are oppressors" who bear responsibility for past actions committed by members of the same race or sex.[47] The EO purports, in the name of a principled opposition to such "divisive concepts," to unify the nation. In reality, Trump's executive order is designed to suppress speech about the historical origins and present-day effects of race-, gender-, and sexuality-based inequities and to retain white, patriarchal power.

"Divisive Concepts" Legislation: January 2021

Republican state legislators begin drafting bills banning "divisive concepts" in K-12 public school curriculums, with language borrowed – in 78 out of 99 national bills – from model legislation crafted by staffers at the Heritage Foundation, a conservative think tank.[48] In turn, public schools begin to self-censor, avoiding any reading materials or discussion topics related to race or gender that conservatives might deem "divisive." The barely concealed intent of "divisive concept" laws is the marginalization or erasure altogether of the historical narratives and contemporary perspectives of non-white and/or non-heterosexual/non-cisgendered students and teachers. As the authors of "Educational Gag Orders" note, the chilling effect of "divisive concepts" legislation disproportionately affects the First Amendment rights of "students, educators, and trainers who are women, people of color, and LGBTQ+."[49] In fact, the whitelash in the decades following *Brown v. Board* had, in large part, already accomplished these racist goals. The whiteness of public education has played a key role in aiding and abetting this reactionary agenda. The firing of 100,000 Black teachers in the 1950s through 1960s [*see the entry,* Brown v. Board of Education: *May 17, 1954*] had a chilling effect on generations. As of 2018, 79 percent of all teachers in public education were white.[50] U.S. public schools are run mainly by white educators whose approach to curriculums and pedagogy view American history and current events, more often than not, from a white perspective, reaffirming the white-dominated social order, consigning non-white voices to the margins, and depriving all students of a diversity of viewpoints and critical challenges to received truth.

Teacher Accused of Being "Marxist": January 2021

MISTY L.C. (*see pp. 173-184*), a middle school social studies teacher in Censorville, is accused by two conservative school board candidates, in their campaign fliers, of teaching "critical race theory, a Marxist ideology." As their smears spread, conservative parents join the uproar on social media.

Moms for Liberty: January 1, 2021

Tina Descovich, Tiffany Justice, and Bridget Ziegler, wife of Florida Republican Party Chairman Christian Ziegler, found **Moms for Liberty (M4L)**, a right-wing group whose "anti-woke" activism the Southern Poverty Law Center later characterizes "as "extremist."[51] Well-organized and well-funded, the group leads the charge to discredit, defund, and dismantle public education. M4L is especially effective in influencing school board policy and races. With the assistance of political PACs such as the 1776 Project, M4L funds school board candidates running on a "pro-parents' rights" platform.[52] The group uses the term "parental rights" to argue that they're providing parents with more control over school library books and classroom instructional content. In reality, they're not only attempting to limit classroom discussions and students' access to informational materials about race, gender identity, and sexual orientation; they're infringing on the rights of parents who want their children to be taught critical, factually accurate history and sociology that takes into account the experiences, perspectives, and dissenting views of marginalized peoples.

The Insurrection: January 6, 2021

A violent **insurrection at the U.S. Capitol** marks an end to a presidency organized around the politics of white grievance. In the run-up to the election, Trump questions the legitimacy of the voting process. After losing the election to Joe Biden, he continues to circulate baseless lies about election fraud and attempts to use his position to pressure officials to alter voting results. On January 6, Trump directs hundreds of his supporters to storm the Capitol Building to prevent Congress from counting votes certifying Joe Biden as the next president. About 150 officers are injured in the attack and five who defended the Capitol die, one from injuries sustained during the confrontation and four from suicide in the days and months that follow. On August 1, 2023, a grand jury votes to charge Trump and six co-conspirators with four charges, including conspiracy to defraud the U.S.

Biden Rescinds EO 13950: January 20, 2021

In one of his first official acts, on the day of his inauguration, **President Joe Biden rescinds Trump EO 13950.** Nonetheless, the whitelash it has already inspired will have ripple effects for years to come.[53] In May 2023, a parent at a Miami-Dade school will complain about the "hate messages" in a book of poems by the African American poet Amanda Gorman, who spoke at Biden's inauguration. At Biden's swearing-in as President, Gorman read "The Hill We Climb," her poem about the insurrection, the "harsh truths" of the United States, and the potential for unity, even in a nation wracked by racism and political polarization: "We've seen a force that would shatter our nation, rather than share it," she declares. "Would destroy our country if it meant delaying democracy."[54] In response to the Miami-Dade parent's objections, the elementary school removes Gorman's book from its library.[55]

Targeting History Teachers: April 2021

High school art history teacher **SALLY MIDDLETON** (*see pp. 101-109*) is accused, by a Facebook group of "concerned parents," of advancing an ideological "agenda" because she assigned a video exploring how an activist or cultural changemaker made a difference in his, her, or their community. In a related project, students are asked to make an award for an agent of positive change in their community. This, too, enflames conservatives.

Tennessee State Bill 623: May 5, 2021

Tennessee legislators give final approval to SB 623, which gives lawmakers the power to deny state funding to public schools whose curriculums incorporate, and/or teachers whose courses discuss, "divisive concepts" such as systemic racism, white privilege, and unconscious bias. During the debate, Democratic Senator Brenda Gilmore argues against SB 623, pointing out that the law "robs teachers of the ability to teach true history. And, contrary to what some people may think, being an African American, I do not cast blame, but I think we do have to admit that slavery did occur. It was a dark period in our history. We have to acknowledge the wrongs of our society, even when it's a difficult conversation to have. And as a result of slavery, that today, in 2021, racism still does exist."[56]

On May 5, 2021, **MATTHEW D. HAWN** (*see pp. 111-124*), a social studies teacher and a baseball coach in Northeast Tennessee, is dismissed for discussing white privilege and racial equity in a high school class on contemporary issues.

The Zinn Pledge: May 17, 2021

The Howard Zinn Education Project, dedicated to providing students with instruction on U.S. histories that includes the role of racialized peoples, working people, women, and social movements, invites teachers to sign its pledge as a way of publicly declaring their refusal to be intimidated from teaching factual U.S. history and examining current events from a critical perspective. The pledge commits teachers to "develop critical thinking that supports students to better understand problems in our society, and to develop collective solutions to those problems." As well, signatories to the pledge affirm, "We are for truth-telling and uplifting the power of organizing and solidarity that move us toward a more just society."[57]

Doxxing Teachers Who Sign Pledge: June 25, 2021

ELLEN BARNES (*see pp. 201-213*), a middle school history teacher, learns that some of her colleagues have been doxed by a website called "Granite Grok," which describes itself as a "gun-toting conservative political forum." Rated a "Questionable Source" with "extreme bias and "consistent promotion of propaganda" by MediaBiasFactCheck.com, *The Granite Grok* publishes a list of names and locations of teachers who signed the Zinn Pledge.

McAuliffe Decries Book Bans: September 28, 2021

In his last **campaign debate against Glenn Youngkin (R), Virginia gubernatorial candidate Terry McAuliffe (D)** affirms, "I'm not going to let parents come into schools and actually take books out and make their own decision. I don't think parents should be telling schools what they should teach." He is referring to a 2017 bill that proposed labeling books as sexually explicit in ways that ignored literary merit and context; McAuliffe, then governor, vetoed the bill.[58] He goes on to note that Youngkin only resurrected the topic to stoke parental fears, a campaign tactic that uses children and public schools "as political pawns" to win an election. McAuliffe calls the silencing of Black authors "a racist dog whistle designed to gin up support from the most extreme elements of his [Youngkin's] party – mainly his top endorser and surrogate, Donald Trump."[59]

Far-Right Challenges to LGBTQ+ Books: October 2021

Far-right parents challenge five books, all with LGBTQ+ themes, in the library at North Hunterdon High School, New Jersey, where **MARTHA HICKSON** is the librarian. (*see pp. 79-98*) Armed with district policy, Hickson rallies the community and authors to fight the ban challenges.

Principal is Put on Leave: October 2021

MARK JOHNSON (*see pp. 263-274*), an educator and the first non-white principal of Censor City High School, is put on leave after talking with the media about not being publicly supported by an all-white administration after a white, far-right parent railed against him at a school board meeting for "destroying schools" and promoting "critical race theory." In fact, the initiative Johnson was promoting had "nothing to do with CRT," he notes. In the aftermath of George Floyd's murder, at a high school where half the student body is non-white, he had called for the community to come together to dismantle systemic racism.

Matt Krause's Hit List: October 25, 2021

Texas State Representative **Matt Krause sends a list of 850 books** to the Texas Education Agency and to superintendents of school districts around the state, asking them to confirm whether any of the books are in their libraries or classrooms. The list provides no descriptions, qualifications, or assessments of the books listed, just their titles. In his cover letter, Krause directs the agencies to identify other books that "contain the following topics: human sexuality, sexually transmitted diseases, or human immunodeficiency virus (HIV) or acquired immune deficiency syndrome (AIDS), sexually explicit images, graphic presentations of sexual behavior that is in violation of the law, or contain material that might make students feel discomfort, guilt, anguish, or any other form of psychological distress because of their race or sex or convey that a student, by virtue of their race or sex, is inherently racist, sexist, or oppressive, whether consciously or unconsciously."[60]

CAROLYN FOOTE, a retired Texas librarian (*see pp. 241-250*), notes that, "Krause had aspirations to run for Attorney General of Texas, and the release of the letter seemed to be ... a play for attention." Infuriated by right-wing book-banners, Foote and her public-school library colleagues organize a Twitter counterattack using their Freedom to Read hashtag (#FReadom) paired with the Texas legislative hashtag. On November 4, their Twitter campaign goes viral, drawing national media attention to the right-wing assault on the First Amendment in public education.

Greg Abbott's Moral Panic: November 10, 2021

Texas Governor Greg Abbott sends a letter to the Texas Education Agency directing them to scour public schools to "prevent the presence of pornography and other obscene content in Texas public schools."[61]

Far-Right Bounty Hunters: November 12, 2021

In New Hamphire, **Moms for Liberty offers a $500 bounty** for "the person that first successfully catches a public school teacher breaking this [anti-divisive subject matter] law."[62]

OK and TN Strip Protections from Educators: 2022

Section 251.4 of the American Model Penal Code outlines the prohibition of the distribution of obscene materials but allows an "affirmative defense" if disseminated by "institutions or persons having scientific, educational, governmental or other similar justification for possessing obscene material."[63] "Affirmative defense" means that, for example, a librarian loaning a book of literary and educational merit with anatomy, sex ed, or sexual themes would not be criminally liable. In 2022, Oklahoma and Tennessee pass laws **removing "educational purposes," "education," and "libraries" from the list of workplaces or professions exempted from these obscenity laws**. School employees can face prison time or fines for violating these laws. In 2023, Arkansas, Florida, Indiana, and Missouri follow suit.

"Pushing" the "Gay Agenda": January 2022

At a town meeting in Censorville, Republican committee members and parents claim that **JILL JAMES**, a middle school language arts teacher (*see pp. 253-260*), is "pushing books" that feature LGBTQ+ protagonists and "encouraging students to become trans, to come out as gay." On January 10, 2022, Iowa's Republican Senate President **Jake Chapman accuses educators of a "sinister agenda occurring right before our eyes"** in "disguising sexually obscene material as desired subject matter and profess[ing] it has artistic and literary value."[64] In penal codes related to obscenity, Republican legislators begin challenging the assumption of "positive intent" on the part of educators. On January 19, 2022, Washington state middle school librarian **GAVIN DOWNING** (*see pp. 187-198*) is notified by his principal, in flagrant violation of the district's book-challenge process, of three books she wants removed from the library. All three books address the perspectives of LGBTQ+ kids and LGBTQ+-related issues.

"Don't Say Gay": March 28, 2022

Florida Governor Ron DeSantis signs the so-called "Don't Say Gay" bill, which prohibits teachers at the pre-K to Grade 3 level from acknowledging sexual orientation or gender identity in their classes. This prohibition is later expanded to include Grades 4 through 12.

Fired for Book Displays: April 2022

ELISSA MALESPINA, New Jersey high school librarian (*see pp. 215-223*), is notified by her principal that she will not be rehired based on the unfounded perception that her book displays focus too much on LGBTQ+ students and racially diverse topics, which, according to the principal, "has created the perception that the library is about only two things."

"Stop W.O.K.E. Act": April 22, 2022

Florida Governor Ron DeSantis signs HB 7 (Stop Wrongs to Our Kids and Employees Act or "Stop W.O.K.E. Act") into law, banning teachers from discussing race or criticizing the U.S. "meritocracy" as racist. According to DeSantis, the law "gives businesses, employees, children, and families tools to stand up against discrimination and woke indoctrination."[65] In November 2022, in response to a lawsuit filed by eight Florida professors, a federal judge rules that the parts of the law that restrict conversations about race in public universities violate the First Amendment. U.S. District Judge Mark Walker refers to HB 7 as "dystopian," noting, "the First Amendment does not permit the State of Florida to muzzle its university professors, impose its own orthodoxy of viewpoints, and cast us all into the dark."[66]

Teacher of the Year Resigns: May 21, 2022

2022 Kentucky Teacher of the Year **WILLIE EDWARD TAYLOR CARVER JR.** (*see pp. 147-171*) resigns from the high school where he'd taught for 15 years because recent state laws (SB 150 and SB 151) require teachers to misgender students and to prohibit them from using appropriate bathroom facilities, among other harmful directives.

Fired for "Looking Different": August 22, 2022

Elementary school art teacher **MONICA COLES** (*see pp. 67-76*) is placed on paid administrative leave without cause, after only four days in the classroom. Parents alarmed by Coles' insufficiently "feminine" attire spread rumors that Coles was "lecturing" elementary kids on "gender and pronouns" and that drawings from an art course she'd taken in college, posted to her private Instagram, were nude drawings of minors. These charges were baseless as the drawings were created for assignments in a university figure drawing course that used adult models.

Book Bans Up by 33 Percent: September 21, 2023

PEN America, a center for the protection of free expression, releases a report about national public school book bans, reporting an increase in bans by 33 percent from the 2021-2022 school year. According to their report, Florida banned 1,406 books, accounting for 40 percent of nationwide book bans.[67] PEN America describes the bans and legislative efforts to restrict teaching subjects the right disapproves of as an "Ed Scare" intended to suppress free expression and critical thought in public education.

Christian-nationalist Book Challenges: January 8, 2024

Clay County's district reconsideration list, a list of books that parents, administrators, or community members have challenged between November 2021 and January 8, 2024, expands to over 745 titles. As a result, nearly 306 titles are permanently removed from school library shelves. According to the district, 94 percent of the challenges have come from one man: Bruce Friedman, founder and president of the

Florida chapter of a far-right group called No Left Turn in Education, identified by the Southern Poverty Law Center as a white, antigovernment, Christian-nationalist group. Of the 439 titles that the committee chose *not* to remove from school libraries, Friedman has appealed every decision. This includes a challenge to Marc Brown's beloved children's book *Arthur's Birthday* because the monkey Francine suggests a game of spin-the-bottle at a birthday party.

In June 2023, **JULIE MILLER** (*see pp. 127-144*), the lone Clay County school librarian who spoke out against Friedman's book challenges, is unceremoniously reassigned to a teaching role in a subject she had never taught. The principal alleges that Miller violated the "parameters of allowed reading materials" defined by "Florida Statute" while working as a librarian. However, Miller believes that the reassignment is actually an act of retaliation for her resistance to the district's book bans.

Ban Books, Then Burn Books: February 6, 2024

Valentina Gomez, a candidate for Missouri Secretary of State affiliated with Trump's MAGA movement, tries to advance her political career by posting a video of herself on X, Facebook, and Instagram **setting fire to** *Queer: The Ultimate LGBTQ Guide for Teens* and *Naked: Not Your Average Sex Encyclopedia*, books meant to educate teens about their bodies.

Nationally, Teachers Self-Censor: February 15, 2024

Since January 2021, legislators in 44 states have passed or attempted to pass bills restricting the teaching of topics related to race and gender.[68] On February 15, 2024, the 2023 State of the American Teacher Survey, published by the nonpartisan think tank RAND Corporation, reports that 51 percent of K-12 teachers across the nation are subjected to local and/or state restrictions prohibiting the discussion of racism and sexism in the classroom.[69] Most startlingly, **55 percent of respondents who** ***aren't*** **subject to state or local restrictions are** ***choosing*** **to self-censor** when it comes to social and political issues, reflecting the chilling effect that threats of public harassment and administrative pushback are having on the teaching of sociopolitical topics, even in ostensibly liberal school districts.[70] One of the findings of the testimonials in *Trouble in Censorville* is that most educators who push back are alone in their fights. Being liberal or able to acknowledge bias and bigotry doesn't necessarily mean that a teacher will have the support, courage, stamina, or protections to push back when the administration may not have their back, their colleagues may ostracize them, and when many live in states with weakened teachers' unions.

A NOTE TO THE READER

This project began when a public school teacher reached out to us to ask how they might bring to the public's attention their story of being placed on leave. This appeal led us to reach out to other K-12 teachers, who generously responded to our e-mails. Our collective decision to publish these testimonials sprang from the belief that someone needed to alert readers to the far right's campaign to discredit and defund public schools and, as important, its human cost. Educators targeted by far-right activists deserve a platform unconstrained by the soundbite limitations and biases of the news media and the algorithm-driven corporate commons of Facebook and X.

The educators (teachers, teacher-librarians, and at least one administrator, a principal) whose testimonies appear in this book tell their stories in the urgent hope that their firsthand experiences will drive home the collateral damage inflicted by the far-right assault on our public schools. More immediately, they hope to rouse readers to action. "This is what happened," educators are saying. "This is how I resisted, and this is why it matters." Their testimony is a call to action and a form of self-healing; many of our interviewees told us they found the acts of sharing their stories cathartic and empowering.

Interviewees reviewed their oral histories at every step of the editorial process to ensure that the published results were scrupulously factual, true to their unique voices, and reflected their intent.

Readers should be aware, too, that some contributors chose to use pseudonyms and remove identifying details to protect themselves from workplace retaliation, job loss, and the like. If colleagues or friends are mentioned in testimonials, we requested that every contributor confirm that individual's willingness to be included and, if willing, whether to be identified by name. Bad actors are provided with pseudonyms when necessary to protect the educator. Otherwise, political and religious extremists, legislators, administrators, and school board members who violated district protocols or professional ethics, social-media trolls, and others whose treatment of educators reflects poorly on them are named and should answer for their actions in the court of public opinion.

Interviewees received honorariums and, when the book went to press, an additional sum. One hundred percent of the profits from this book will go to the teachers whose testimonies made *Trouble in Censorville* possible – a small contribution to the welfare of those whose courage cost them their jobs or impacted their well-being and an investment, we hope, in the activism many of them continue to pursue.

MONICA COLES
THEY DECIDED THEY DIDN'T LIKE THE WAY I LOOKED.

"I'm an elementary school art teacher who was placed on leave after only four days in the classroom. My kids loved me, the principal told me I was doing a great job, but because I used a nontraditional gender pronoun (the nonbinary 'Mx.') and wore insufficiently 'feminine' attire – khakis and a button-up shirt – I had to go."

It began in August 2022, before school had even started. The kids weren't back yet. We were still in training and had barely started setting up our classrooms.

I had just graduated from art school with my BFA and a teaching certificate that May. I got an amazing job opportunity: teaching pre-kindergarten through fourth-grade art in an elementary school in a small, extremely wealthy district. They're the one percent of Censoropolis, if you will. I was super, super excited and just up and left everything in Censorborough and moved to downtown Censoropolis.

I had previously provided the principal with a short profile and photo for the "new hires" section of the school newsletter. In my bio, I called myself Mx. Coles. Mx. is a non-gender-disclosing prefix; I'd used it throughout my student-teaching and substitute-teaching career. I'd never had an issue with it. But the next day, when the principal asked me to come into the main office to get my school identity badge, she and a woman from Human Resources advised me very, very respectfully that "this neighborhood is something out of the 1950s – extremely conservative – and it probably wouldn't be a good idea to use a different prefix right off the bat," in my first year at the school.

This hurt my feelings. I felt stuck in an odd situation. I was put on this pedestal, under this spotlight, with everyone looking at me. Even though it was just my principal and a woman from Human Resources, I felt as if I was on display. As I said, they were super sweet, but it felt like an attack on my gender expression and identity. It was just so personal and dehumanizing to even ask me to change my identity like that. I don't know if either of them was aware of this, but homophobic conservatives don't like the nonbinary prefix Mx. because, in their eyes, it blurs the firm line between male and female, making gender more fluid, defying firm gender binaries, which they believe should be assigned at birth – and stay that way.

When the principal and the HR woman were talking to me, I was thinking, 'Well, I don't want the parents to think I'm some radical' and 'I don't want to put myself or my job in any sort of danger.' I explained my nonbinary identity and how it had never been a problem for me before, but eventually, I just compromised and said, "I understand. Okay, I'll go by Ms. Coles." It was my first year, so I wasn't going to fight for it.

School started with students arriving for their first art classes on Wednesday, August 17, and it was fantastic. I had a dream team with our specials teachers (physical education, music, and art). Multiple people came into my classroom on my first three days of school; my principal visited, and HR people came in. It felt like I was being checked out informally, but I felt really good. I was in my zone. I was teaching, and I had my classroom management all set up. I mean, for a first-year teacher, I felt like I was in a pretty good spot, and people were noticing that. My principal and HR people were telling me, "You're probably going to be the next Teacher of the Year." Things were going really, really, really well – which is what made the next rapid turn in events so shocking.

That Friday, two days after the start of classes, my principal came into my art room during my lunch period and said, "I'm 100 percent sure this didn't happen, but I have to address this with you." She tells me there's a rumor going around, specifically that a fourth-grade boy in one of my classes raised his hand and asked about the way I dress. I have a short haircut and usually wear what some might say is a men's button-up shirt and khaki pants. The other teachers in the school have long, curled blonde hair and wear dresses and heels all day, every day, so my appearance is different from the rest of my staff, admittedly, but it's nothing crazy. According to the rumor, when the student asked about the way I dress, I went into a philosophical harangue about gender and pronouns and all of these ideas that trigger the far right. Supposedly, this happened on the first day of my art class.

None of this happened. None of these kids – elementary school kids, mind you – ever asked about the way I dress. The allegation was completely false. I told my principal that, and she said, "Yeah, of course, of course." She told me, "I like the way you dress; I think it's great," although she was probably just trying to make me feel better.

That Friday, I went out with a colleague who's a floater teaching at different schools in the district. Like me, she was – I'll use the term "visibly queer" – so we hit it off immediately and found solidarity with each other. We became instant friends. In the wake of my being blindsided, she and I went out for dinner to talk about the rumor and my conversation with my principal.

I believe this is where the momentous event happened. My colleague asked about my art, and I told her about my art account on Instagram. Now, this art Instagram dates back to when I started college; I was just tracking my art journey. It was under an alias, completely disconnected from my legal name and my teaching career. But it *was* public, and I let her follow it.

By Sunday night of that same weekend, I was getting tons of follows by what were obviously moms from my district. I could tell it was them because I could see their profile pictures, and they were all young, white, wealthy-looking women with their sweet little babies in their pictures. These are exactly the types of moms I'd seen at school.

My belief is that they were stalking this other queer person, and the second that she had an additional follower – because I'd followed her back – they found me. You had to do some searching to find a photo of me, four pictures into a post from well over a year ago, with an image of me next to a piece of art, which makes me think they were stalking me to find whatever they could to smear me.

Shortly after getting those followers, I got an e-mail from HR. It said, "You need to come in first thing Monday morning before school." I did, and they handed me administrative leave paperwork that said, "You are now placed on paid administrative leave." The woman from HR who had previously praised me just that week was now requiring that I leave the school before my fourth day of teaching. This about-face, without warning, was purely for self-preservation. She was joined by a second person, a man from HR, at this meeting. They didn't want the school to draw any attention to itself over this matter. They were willing to throw me under the bus to stop any anticipated bad publicity for the school and the district.

I was at my lowest. I'm not a big crier, but I did sob during this meeting. I sat there and cried, and they got me tissues, and I couldn't breathe. I left like that, I think. It was a short meeting, maybe 15 minutes.

I talked to my mother every day, but I couldn't bring myself to call her and tell her what had happened. I called my stepdad, and I said, "This is the situation. I can't talk about it right now, but this is what's going on." And he was like, "Okay, I'll try to tell your mother for you." I was so upset.

The two people from HR had some of my Instagram posts – all art projects from college – printed out. The most notable one was a charcoal drawing from a figure-drawing class two years ago, where, of course, we were drawing nude figures. This wasn't the first photo in the post; it was the fourth photo in, which means you had to click through the first three in the series to find it. The parents were saying that my drawing studies from college were actually drawings of minors – that I was drawing minors, and I later learned that the parents had actually called 911 that Monday morning, saying that their children would be in danger in my classroom.

I never got any information on who the parents were, and I didn't ask either. I just knew it was several of them and that they were parents of my students because, as an art teacher, even just for those three days, I had already seen the whole school through my art room in my classes.

They also took other projects of mine from other art classes completely out of context. They said that I was promoting suicide because, in a photo of a performance piece, I had a plastic bag near my face. It was intended as a metaphor for the feeling of being suffocated by certain things I was dealing with, not promoting suicide by suffocation.

One of the HR people told me, "Obviously, these allegations aren't true. You're an art teacher. You went to art school to get an art degree, to be an art teacher, and had to complete art assignments that you placed on your Instagram page." The two people from HR were upset over the situation. I had a lot of meetings with these two people from HR, and the woman would always tell me how much she's cried over this, and the man would always confirm that: "I've seen her cry." Then, they'd say, "This whole situation is obviously wrong, but we need to put you on leave because it has created a distraction." They asked me to make a file describing what each artwork represented.

For example, they'd printed out one of my charcoal nudes, so I described it as a charcoal study completed at my art school, and I gave the course title, Figure Drawing, and included the professor's name. This was intended to drill home that this was a required assignment at a university and that the model had to be over 18 years of age, not a minor.

Throughout the next few weeks of HR meetings, they told me that I could not go back to my elementary school for fear that moms would be picketing out in front and that there would be a ton of heated meetings between them and the superintendent.

I haven't been back to my classroom ever since that Friday, the first week of classes. I'm not banned from the building. I could go with my principal to collect my personal items if I wanted to, but I just haven't wanted to. It's too hard.

I'd heard of educators being found and harassed online, but my Instagram art site was completely unconnected from my legal name, which is the name they knew me by. Now, I don't think educators are protected in any way. Our teacher training should be blunter. They should say, "You can lose your job because someone makes up a story about a particular post, even if it was years ago, involving the fifth photo into a series of images. Your life can be changed."

Nude drawings were made as far back as the 15th century. Figure studies aren't new. Posting them isn't against the platform's rules. You can have a nude drawing because it's a drawing. But people who likely know nothing about art history and have an ideological agenda can still misinterpret it, maybe intentionally. As HR told me, "They can interpret it however they want."

During the Friday evening before the first week of school, we had Meet the Teacher Night, where the parents came into our classroom. I remember I wore a navy pinstriped suit with pants and a matching blazer because my Censoria Education Association representative, who was trying to help me through this situation, later told me, "The principal and HR said you wore a suit," and I was like, "Okay?" However, I didn't get the sense that my suit alarmed anyone. Everyone that I met during that parents' night was super, super kind, and excited that I was there. The only questions I had were about my curriculum, which I was excited to talk about. I didn't spot any red flags, such as a parent wearing a MAGA hat. Everyone was shaking my hand and being really, really friendly and excited. I met a lot of the kids, and it was awesome.

Also, parents could have spotted what I was wearing that first week of school when I had after-school carpool duty. I recall wearing khaki pants and a button-up shirt tucked into the top of my pants. My theory is that the parents who saw me at Meet the Teacher Night, who couldn't have been nicer to me in my classroom, started talking about my suit and the way I looked, and then other parents recognized me at carpool and joined them in talking about how I looked different from the other teachers in the building. I figure they would get together regularly for brunches or whatever and gossip. Whatever form of dialogue they had, things escalated really quickly over that weekend, I believe. Meet the

Teacher happened the Monday evening before school started, which was on Wednesday; by Sunday night, my career at that school was over.

They decided they didn't like the way I looked and, perhaps out of gossip-fueled hatred, concocted these stories from whatever they could dig up on me, such as the stuff in my artwork. They said I was drawing minors and promoting suicide and promiscuity. Before that, they started a rumor that I had an intense liberal gospel I was promoting about gender and pronouns.

Some of my older family members told me that being a teacher in Censoropolis requires swallowing your identity. It's not like anything you've ever seen before. Some of the things that I saw going through my training would make your jaw drop. These moms are a very, very tight group of people. They're housewives. They have brunches every morning in each other's mansions. They're beautiful and perfect, and they don't do anything. It's wild. It's a trip. It made me sick. When I first started getting ready to teach there, I was already coping with the wealth. That was a challenge for me to get through since I had never seen anything like it. It makes them feel indestructible.

Because of the wealth in Censoropolis, our school was almost completely funded by our PTO.* So, let's call a spade a spade: it's bribery. Before the kids even came back, we had a PTO-teacher luncheon. When we all finished eating and talking and meeting, the president of the PTO stood up and handed everyone an envelope. When we got back to our classrooms, we opened up our envelopes. Inside was a check. Let's just say

---

* It's worth noting the difference between Parent Teacher Association (PTA) and Parent Teacher Organization (PTO). The National PTA is a national organization established in 1897 that advocates for public education policy and provides resources for local, affiliated school groups. PTA secured universal kindergarten and the National School Lunch Program. School groups that join PTA pay dues in exchange for a voice in the organization and benefits, such as by-laws that outline roles and elections, insurance, and assistance with non-profit status. PTO usually indicates a single-school group that operates under their own bylaws or without bylaws and focuses only on issues at their school, rather than impacting public schools at a national level. Coles' account raises the question of whether PTOs are more susceptible to dubious practices, as opposed to PTA, which states that "PTAs advocate for the adequate funding of schools from governmental sources. They do not replace funds not supplied by governments. Therefore, supplies purchased using PTA funds should be given directly to children, not to teachers." (pta.org > Family Resources)

it was *enough*. It was $1,000 each. This was not for classroom expenses; they told us it was a gift.

I wasn't paid by the district while going through my school training or my teaching. Our first paychecks aren't until September 20, and we'd been working since June. The PTO gave us these supplemental funds to set up a classroom. There was a suggested percentage that should go toward our classroom and a suggested percentage to go towards us as a gift, but you didn't have to show receipts. It was implied that the $1,000 could be used to help tide us over until our first paycheck. In my case, all the money I got in that check from the parents, I spent on my classroom.

The district itself has money to spend on its schools and its teachers, but the parents want to fund it, and they have been. They have heavy, heavy, heavy, heavy, *heavy* donors. Yet, during my crisis, the school never offered me any mental health support. HR told me to "go get a massage." My first paycheck wasn't until September 20 – four weeks after they'd fired me – and they told me to go get a massage.

As part of my separation agreement, all I can say is that I resigned from that district. That's about all I can say. During my last couple of HR meetings, where I signed my release paperwork, they said they wanted to meet again and get some statements to the parents from me. Even though I'd just been with the students as their teacher for three days, they wanted me to write something from me to the parents. They wrote some words for me, and I agreed to their suggested statements. I don't recall what they stated, but their intention was to share these statements with the school parents to kind of put a bow on the situation in a newsletter or an e-mail. It was a flag of my defeat for them to frame on their fridge.

They also wanted to give me a script I could use in job interviews or some kind of letter I could give to my next school district to explain my very short job tenure in Censoropolis. We had a conversation about how to answer questions in a job interview, such as, "Why did you leave your previous job?"

The painful irony is that they then gave me really good reference letters. But you know what? It just gave me a sense of fire, an angry, passionate fire that really motivated me to get another job. Like, "Okay, with these references, I might actually come out of this alive."

During some of my initial HR meetings, I had said, "You know this is slander, right? Why aren't you telling these parents, 'Monica graduated from art school, she did her artwork, we hired her as an educator, and that's all that matters'?" When I said the word "slander," they immediately said, "As the human resources team, we can't recommend you take legal action, but you clearly have a case." My lawyer and I would have to subpoena them to give us the records of what those people said about me because I never actually saw any of the e-mails or any of the screenshots from their phones. I never heard the 911 call or anything like that. The fact is, I don't want to see some of the things they said if I don't absolutely have to.

I did consult with an attorney. I met with one who was very highbrow. He wanted me to get a Netflix special and get on the news and all this stuff, probably to advance his profile. I told him, "That's not what I need. I just want to know my legal rights." Eventually, I was able to resign from my position without legal counsel. I wanted to get on with my life and not bring added attention to my situation. I didn't feel like the lawyer or the legal system had my back.

Having me in that school was supposed to be an education in itself, just by virtue of my being someone who looks different. I never opened up about my queer identity. I just looked a certain way. If people like me were to go public with their stories and call out these districts that have their own unwritten laws, made by the parents who took me down the way they wanted to, if they were held to any sort of accountability and educated, and the rest of the public was educated, on the injustice of what's happening, at the very least, teacher training would be different. But I didn't fight back by pursuing a lawsuit or telling my story to the media, mainly because I didn't want to add further attention to myself. I wanted to keep my life. I was afraid of becoming a poster child of a disgraced teacher or discriminated queer person.

I haven't slept a night since. I'm stewing in my own anxieties about the people out there with my name and information who have ill intent against me. They had the power to remove me from this amazing opportunity that I moved to a new city for. I'm being paid for being on leave, so I'm not struggling financially, but at what cost? I felt targeted and disgusted at the thought of people looking through everything about me, so I no longer have any social media whatsoever. I'm completely isolated. I live in a city where I don't know anyone, and I'm disconnected from everything. I can pay my rent, sit at home, not have to do anything, and lose my mind, but my sense of purpose is gone.

Teacher staff and the HR people told me, "We wanted you to be Teacher of the Year. You were a rock star. You were doing such a great thing," and all of that. And my team members, when this first happened, said, "Do not give up on being an educator." That's the hardest thing. A big part of me is super discouraged.

From the beginning of this, I almost felt guilty for not feeling guilty because I truly never felt like I did anything wrong. The parents took one look at me and had an immediate hatred response, I think. I'm having the worst punishment, yet I did nothing but good.

This could literally happen to anyone.

MARTHA HICKSON
"DEBAUCHING THE MORALS OF MINORS."

"I'm a high school librarian who was accused of 'supplying pornography and grooming children' because books about LGBTQ+ people are available in the library."

I've been a librarian in this school since I started my career in 2005. The idea of challenges and objections to books is part of our training as librarians. Throughout the last 19 years, there have been objections to books from time to time. Those objections always come from parents, never kids.

In the old days – and when I say old, I mean before 2019 – a parent would raise a concern through a classroom teacher or an administrator, saying, "My kid is reading this book, I don't like this, that, or the other. Can you get that book out of the library?" Then, I would be notified, and that would launch a process. It's called *having a conversation*.

The conversation would involve me listening, making every effort to understand the nature of the parent's concern. Most often, it has to do with language or sexual content: the kind of language their kids use in the cafeteria or on the school bus every day; the kind of sex teenagers have under the bleachers or in the backseat of their parents' car every day. Okay, maybe not every day, but regularly.

Often, I'll raise points like, "Why is the book in the library? What is its literary merit?" Generally – in fact, *always*, prior to 2019 – we were able to come to an agreement, something along the lines of, "You know what? If that book's not a good fit for your child, I totally get it. There's a lot of books I don't care to read either. For example, I'm not a sci-fi or fantasy fan. The same thing holds true for your child: If it's not a good fit, put the book back on the shelf. I have 20,000 other choices for you, and if you give me a little direction, I can find a better fit." That worked great – until 2019. I keep referencing 2019 because that's the year I had what I'm gonna call my first "serious challenge," to the graphic novel *Fun Home* by the author Alison Bechdel.

She's an award-winning writer and artist, a MacArthur "genius" grant winner. *Fun Home* is her memoir of growing up in her family's funeral home and her growing awareness as a tween, teen, and young adult of her sexuality and her realization that her father was a closeted gay man. It was made into a Tony Award-winning Broadway musical starring an 11-year-old actor as the young Bechdel.

In 2019, an administrator told me that there was a parent complaint about the book, and it needed to be removed from the library. I said, "Okay, there's a parent complaint, but we don't remove books solely on the basis of a parent complaint. There's a process for that, and we need to follow the challenge process." Long story short, it became evident that there was no parent complaint. It was the superintendent who wanted the book removed – on his say-so alone. The last four years have demonstrated to me that superintendents or administrators often feel entitled to remove books from libraries because of their own particular sensitivities, usually with matters of sex but sometimes with issues around race, religion, politics, whatever. And, in most cases, the only thing standing between *them* and the removal of that book is somebody like me – a librarian – who reminds them that, "No, we have policies around this."

As it happens, my husband, who is now retired, was still working as a drama teacher at that time, at a high school about a half an hour away from the school I work at, called Watchung Hills Regional High School. They were in the midst of their own *Fun Home* uproar; parents in *that* community were trying to have it removed from the books students could choose to read as part of their senior English language arts curriculum. *Fun Home* was included in response to previous student requests for more representation of diverse identities in their English curriculum.

Anyway, parents were up in arms about it, and the furor was getting coverage in the local press because it was so unusual, and the complaints were so vociferous.

My speculation is, my superintendent heard about what was happening at Watchung and called my principal to say, "Do you have this book in your library?" and when he learned that, yes, we did have this book, he demanded that it be removed because he believed it was pornographic or, as he said in response to me on Valentine's Day, 2019, that it "risked debauching the morals of minors." He actually used the word "debauching"! Whenever I picture him typing that e-mail, he's typing with one hand and clutching his pearls with the other.

So, in response to the superintendent's request to remove *Fun Home*, I tried to explain that this isn't the way things work, because to give him, or anyone, that power and privilege would enable parents or administrators or whoever to walk through this school and remove things at their whim just because they don't like them. Moreover, sitting quietly by, or even enabling that sort of censorship, isn't what I get paid to do. I get paid to make sure there's a wide range of compelling, accurate, high-quality reading material for students to choose from. And part of making sure that compelling, accurate, high-quality reading material is available to students is ensuring it isn't removed on a partisan, political, or ideological whim.

My refusal launched a protracted battle that led to the Board of Education changing the selection policy for library materials, giving the superintendent sole control of all library acquisitions and removals. *That*, in turn, led to a big kerfuffle, which is when I became an activist, taking a stand and getting the community involved. In the end, we won that battle. *Fun Home* is still here. The original selection policy – which had been viewed as the gold standard in the state of New Jersey – was restored.

The most recent episode – and please God let it be my last, but something tells me it won't be – began on September 28, 2021. I was eating my lunch and reading *The New York Times Book Review* when my principal entered my office, which he very rarely did. So, I knew this couldn't be good. He told me that he had heard a rumor that there was going to be a complaint about a book at that evening's school board meeting. (Afterward, I wondered if there really *was* a rumor or if someone had complained directly to him.) I said, "Oh, really? What book?" and he said, "*Gender Queer* by Maia Kobabe." I immediately pulled up the overwhelmingly positive reviews of the book and printed them out for him. I also gave him our selection criteria, our challenge policy, and the form community members are supposed to use to challenge a book.

Finally, I reminded him that having a fit at a board meeting is not the way to challenge a book – which he knew because he was involved in the 2019 situation – and I sent him on his merry way.

Ironically, this happened during the American Library Association's "Banned Books Week," the week in September when, since 1982, libraries, schools, museums, and bookstores around the country celebrate the right to read by acknowledging the fact that, over the years, certain titles have been repeatedly challenged. So, I had a display up for "Banned Books Week," as I had every year for the last 17 years.

I went home that night, said to my husband, "Something weird happened at work today," and we fired up the board meeting, live, on YouTube.[1]

When the public comments started, I immediately knew I was gonna have a problem. A woman gets up and complains about two books: *Gender Queer*, which we'd had on the shelf since 2019 (it had zero circulations), and *Lawn Boy* by Jonathan Evison, which I had checked out the day before. And which student did I check it out to? This woman's son.

The woman then started on a tirade about the books. She described both books as pornographic and obscene, claimed that they were being used to groom children, and she created the impression that I had foisted these books upon her child, which couldn't be further from the truth. *Lawn Boy* is a charming and lovely book about overcoming adversity. There's a scene in which the main character talks about a time when he was in the fourth grade and he and another fourth-grade boy experimented with each other sexually. I hate to tell people, but boys of every age touch each other's penises. It happens. I should point out that the book isn't *about* boys playing with their penises. As I recall, the woman read that passage out loud, taking one paragraph, at the most one page, totally out of context (as book banners always do) and making it appear that the whole book is nothing but 250 pages of fourth-grade boys touching each other's penises.

I refuse to believe she had read the book in the 24 hours since I checked it out to her kid. Regardless, she complained about the book, and then she complained about me. How dare I check this book out to her 16-year-old, et cetera, et cetera. Then, she referred to me as a "pornographer, pedophile, and groomer of children." She also referred to the board in the same language, after which several other community members got up to speak.

There was kind of a tag-team strategy: comments building upon comments, building upon comments. The man who came after her started complaining about particular books in our Banned Books Week display. The fact that this man had never even *entered* the library revealed that he'd enlisted his children in this effort. He was calling out books like *Two Boys Kissing* by David Levithan, *Beyond Magenta* by Susan Kuklin, and *Being Jazz* by Jazz Jennings. All of these books have to do with LGBTQ+ themes.

He was also incensed that I had a "Banned Book Week" contest, where I asked the kids to use the library catalog to figure out which of the top 10 banned books of that year we owned in our library (which was my way of getting them to practice using the library catalog). I had a prize drawing; the winner got a $10 Dunkin' Donuts gift card. He went ballistic, demanding to know, "Where does the money for the $10 gift card come from?" Things continued in that vein.

One of the phrases that he used during his comments was, "brought to you by North's very own librarian, Martha Hickson," thereby continuing the demonization of the library and the librarian. His concern was, "Why are they forcing these sexualized materials on our kids?"

A few speakers later, a woman who would eventually be elected to our Board of Education stood at the podium. She didn't have much of an argument other than to just vent and say, "What is this? It's not appropriate. It's not appropriate. It's inappropriate." She rambled,

> Education is education. Basics. When I grew up, I didn't have any of these issues brought to my attention.... I have a job to raise my children the way I feel fit. My children would not speak about religion, politics, social issues, in front of family or friends.... We don't discuss those things. We're not hiding it from our children. It's not hiding. It's respecting.

At home, my heart is *ba-boom, ba-boom, ba-boom,* damn near leaping out of my chest. I started experiencing all sorts of crazy panic-attack symptoms. Fortunately, I'm a member of a teacher's union. So, the very night this happened, as the meeting was going on, I was contacting the president of my union saying, "I'm gonna need help."

The union was my life support (along with my family, of course, and the broader library community). I reached out to all of my librarian peeps immediately, and they were incredibly supportive. I have a wonderful, wonderful library clerk I work with every day, Pat Stark. I couldn't have made it without Pat; she held me up.

I came into school the next day, expecting that the man who had stood in my office and said, "Oh, I heard a rumor," would be trotting right down to see me and talk about what happened the night before. No sign of him. Because I was a meeker, milder person back then, I thought, "Oh, well, the principal is a busy man. The library's not at the top of his priority list." Now, I'm like, "What was I thinking?" I should have demanded a meeting with the principal and an immediate investigation of the false charges made against me.

The day after that, the assistant superintendent showed up in the library and, in front of my coworkers and students, said, "You sure stirred up trouble. How did you pay for that Dunkin' Donuts gift card?" I told him, "I paid for it out of a $500 honorarium I received when I won the New Jersey Association of School Librarians' Intellectual Freedom

Award." He muttered, "Okay," and left. That's the last time I ever spoke to that man. He hasn't spoken to me since that day.

So, I didn't hear from anybody – administrators, decision-makers, anybody above my pay grade – for several days. Finally, when I expressed frustration that I was getting no information about the situation, my direct supervisor said to me, "We have no obligation to communicate with you." Then, he demanded to know how it is that books with language like that could be in a school like ours. I had to explain to him, "Well, that's the language kids speak; students deserve to read books written in their own vernacular."

Finally, at about two that same Friday afternoon, I happened to encounter the principal in the hallway. I asked him if there was any update from Tuesday's meeting and if any book challenges had been filed. He said, "Nothing yet." I replied, "Will there be any action against me?" He said, "There's nothing planned." Finally, I asked him, "Well, will the district make a statement of support for me?" He said, "Why would we do that?" I said, "Because I've been an employee in good standing for 17 years, and it would be nice if there were a statement asserting my integrity, performance, and professionalism." He said, "No, we won't do that." He did not offer an explanation, and I didn't ask for one. At that point, I was livid – and I was concerned that if I stood there for five seconds longer, it was going to escalate into something that would not reflect well upon me.

Ultimately, there were challenges to five books, all with LGBTQ+ themes. In addition to *Gender Queer* and *Lawn Boy*, challenges were filed to *All Boys Aren't Blue* by George M. Johnson, *This Book is Gay* by Juno Dawson, and, for old time's sake, *Fun Home* by Alison Bechdel.

The thing I find so interesting about the five books as a group is that four of the five are nonfiction. So, not only do we want to *remove* books from the library, we want to remove facts, too. *All Boys Aren't Blue* is a memoir by George M. Johnson, who happens to be a New Jersey native; they grew up a half an hour away from our school in Plainfield, New Jersey. The book is about growing up Black and gay. Part of it talks about sexual molestation at the hands of a family member. It's an important book, and it talks about sensitive things that happened in real lives.

This Book is Gay by Juno Dawson is kind of a handbook for young gay kids who are exploring their identity as an LGBTQ+ person, wondering, "What does gay, queer, trans, or whatever, mean for me in the world?" It covers every aspect of life – your family life, your school life, your dating life, your religious life, and, oh yes, P.S., your intimate life.

There's one chapter about sex in the book, which comes with a preamble that says, "This chapter is about sex. If you're not ready to read about sex, go to the next chapter." Dawson worked as a sex-ed teacher in Britain, and the book is based on her interviews with, I believe, more than 300 LGBTQ+ people around the world. So, it has an international perspective, too. It talks about the experiences of LGBTQ+ people in multiple cultures.

The book has a very conversational tone. It's written in the teen vernacular, the way kids really speak. It's as if you had an older gay friend in your life and you were asking them questions; it's like having that conversation in book form. Of the five books, it's the one that was the most heavily circulated in our library. The reason I became so attached to *This Book is Gay* is that, when it hit the book ban list, I could already see, in my mind's eye, the faces of the students to whom I've checked that book out over the years.

Unlike 2019 when the superintendent tried to remove the books by fiat, the district at least *attempted* to follow its own process in this case. A "Reconsideration Committee" was formed, with members chosen by my principal. It consisted of the principal, the department head – the same assistant principal who demanded to know how books with language like this could be in a school like ours – a school board member, an English teacher who's no longer in the classroom, and a librarian. Since I was part of the complaint, my union said, "You should not serve on the Reconsideration Committee. It would just call any decision into question." So, a public librarian from our county library sat on the committee.

The committee was also supposed to have a community member with expertise in the subject area of the books being challenged. All five books had LGBTQ+ themes, so I recommended to that same supervisor – the "how could this happen to a school like ours" guy – that he consult our guidance counselors or a staff member from our school's child study team, all of whom have specialized degrees and experience working one-on-one with kids who have particular social-emotional needs. Perhaps they could recommend a practitioner in the community who works with LGBTQ+ kids or families who are dealing with the coming-out process. Instead, the principal chose for their Reconsideration Committee the president of the school's Booster Club, a mom who possessed no expertise in issues related to the LGBTQ+ community. The administration thought they'd stacked the deck, but it didn't work that way.

In the meantime, while the committee was meeting over the next three or four months, I was working behind the scenes to prepare for the worst. Back in 2019, when *Fun Home* was first challenged, I knew I was gonna need community help with what I naively thought was an isolated incident. I have some library groupies, parents who just love the library, so I reached out to those folks. My brother and sister-in-law, business owners who are very active in Democratic politics, are residents of this district, so I tapped into their network, too.

Through that networking, I'd assembled a group that we named the North Hunterdon-Voorhees – that's the name of our district – Intellectual Freedom Fighters. They helped me get people to the board meetings back in 2019 during the initial *Fun Home* situation. I reactivated that group. I said, "We gotta bring the band back together 'cause the fur is flying over here." We sprang into action. We're a two-high-school district and each school has a GSA, a Gender and Sexuality Alliance, so I reached out to their officers. The first time around, with *Fun Home*, I was reluctant to do that. My union said, "Don't involve the kids, don't involve the kids."

This time I thought, "No, I need to involve the kids; these are their books, and the way these people are talking about their books is just a proxy for what they think about LGBTQ+ people." So, I reached out to the kids, who were immediately on fire.

The Reconsideration Committee meeting is a closed meeting, but the monthly Board of Education meeting is open to the public. By the time of the October board meeting, they had to move the location from the board office, which holds about 40 people, to the auditorium here at the high school. There were roughly 400 people in that auditorium. The vast, vast, vast majority of them were there to stand up for intellectual freedom. "Under no circumstances are you gonna ban books in this district," is what most of the people wanted to say. There were about 40 people there who were in support of book banning, who were there to say really horrible things – all in the name of their Lord and Savior, Jesus Christ, of course, whose name was displayed on the placards they were waving around.

But the most compelling speakers by far were our students. At least 10 of them spoke. They were unbelievable, so prepared, so professional. They spoke from the heart about their lived experience – what the books meant to them, what the loss of the books would mean to them. It makes me cry even thinking about them. Plus, the people holding their Jesus signs were making fun of them – jeering, booing, hissing, gasping (if the kids talked about themselves being bisexual or gay), that kind of stuff. A couple of the kids left the microphone in tears, but it was a very, very compelling evening. I think the board was quite moved by what they saw and heard.

From then on, it was just one shitstorm after another. Every day I walked into the building, I had no idea what I was gonna face. This environment became so hostile – and there was no relief. The antagonism from the administration – the accusatory tone – was constant. Frankly, that relationship is pretty much broken. I mean, we play nice now, but I have no trust in these people. There were some teachers who shunned me. A few of those have come back into the fold, but there are some who continue to believe I'm peddling pornography in the library. Those relationships are forever broken.

Students were involved in the attempted ban, as well. Obviously, the student who was sent to the library by his parent to check out that book on September 27 was part of it. Before the September 27 checkout, that kid had been coming to the library every day during his lunch period for about two weeks and just roaming the stacks. Any time I saw him out there, I would say, "Do you need any help or are you just browsing?" And he would say, "I'm just browsing." I always leave kids alone in that situation; I don't want to be breathing down their necks. For some kids, just walking around is their coping mechanism. So, when I saw him on September 27, he had *books* in his hands.

I said, "Ah, you found something!"

Other students aligned with the book banners kept coming to the library, behaving strangely, lingering in the stacks or in front of displays. After they left every day, we would find books on the floor. As we were reshelving books, we started finding books that were mis-shelved way out of their Dewey range or shelved backwards so you couldn't see the spine. In every case, they were books about gender identity or LGBTQ+ issues. One of these students spoke at the initial meeting on September 28 to tee up the accusations.

I reported this mischief to the administration on a daily basis, asking for help in controlling this behavior. There are cameras all over the place. I asked the administration to review the security footage to see who was doing this – I knew full well who was doing it, but I wanted it documented – and they said, "Oh, we're too busy. We don't have time."

I'm not privy to everything the administrators are dealing with, but I suspect that the parents of these kids had been making trouble for the administration for quite some time. In light of all of the situations that administrators have to deal with, the mis-shelving of library books isn't at the top of their list, and rightly so. But when you look at it as an overall pattern of censorship, it's a matter of concern.

If that wasn't bad enough, parents and members of the community who didn't even have kids in our school were sending me hate mail and trolling me on social media, saying I was "sick and disturbed," "guilty of distribution of pornography," and a "domestic terrorist." One of them said, "She should be fired; such a pig." Between the hateful e-mails, the online trolls, the antagonism from the administration, vandalism from students, and being shunned by some of the teachers, I was getting it from all sides. It was a perfect storm of bullshit, and there came a day in late October when I had what I now understand was a stress-induced breakdown – physical, mental, emotional.

I had to be removed from the building. My union reps called my husband to pick me up. I was in tears in the school nurse's office. I could not stop crying. I could barely speak. I couldn't catch my breath. My blood pressure was through the roof. My husband took me to my doctor, the same doctor I've been seeing for 25 years, and she did not recognize the creature sitting before her.

Her first instinct was, "We need to get you away from this." She took me out of work for several weeks. She put me on anti-anxiety medication, which I take to this day, Lexapro. She connected me with a therapist who gave me tremendous coping skills to help me get through this.

I didn't come back to school until December 1. What was I gonna do while I was at home? I had nothing else to do except figure out ways to fight censorship. For those few weeks, I could turn the advocacy and networking piece of it into my full-time job. So that's what I did.

In November, there was another board meeting. Still no word from the Reconsideration Committee, by the way. There was another big turn-out, not as big as October, but the ratio was the same. People who opposed book banning dominated the book banners. December, no board meeting. They were taking a Christmas break, I guess. So, the Intellectual Freedom Fighters sent "Seasons Readings" cards to every board member, asking them to give students the gift of intellectual freedom. I sent my own greeting card to every board member, saying, "All I want for Christmas is my reputation," because they hadn't uttered a word in my defense regarding the false charges against me; those lies were still hanging over my head.

As we turned the calendar page into 2022, there was *still* no word from the Reconsideration Committee – until the very last week of January. On a Friday afternoon, the board published its agenda, as it normally does before the next Tuesday's meeting, and on that agenda was a link to the committee's report. No one gave me a heads-up about the announcement. I just found it there, buried in the agenda.

I fired that thing up and discovered that the committee, to my amazement, recommended *keeping* four of the books. To my chagrin, though, they wanted to ban *This Book Is Gay* by Juno Dawson. They dispatched it in 132 words. It's hard to explain their rationale, but the committee – which was not unanimous on this point – wanted the book banned because they said it was missing citations. Also, they had questions about whether it was appropriate; they didn't like the slang that described sex beyond what would be taught in school. By the way, their job was to evaluate the book against the selection criteria for library books as stated in board policy. None of those elements was on the selection criteria.

There was a resolution on the Tuesday agenda for the board to vote on banning the book. I'm sitting there on Friday afternoon, reading this, and I'm like, "No way in hell are they banning this book." It's been in the library since 2015, and I've checked it out so many times and, every time I do, I'm stunned, maybe because I'm an old lady, and I can't imagine having this much courage when I was a teen. Some 14- or 15-year-old goes to the shelf and gets this rainbow-colored book with the title in huge block letters – you can read it across the room – *This Book Is Gay*. There's no problem with being gay, but when you're 14, and you feel like the eyes of the world are on you, and you're taking this book up to this old bag to check it out, well, I consider the relationship of trust implied by that transaction to be such a blessing. The student feels safe enough to take this rainbow-colored book off the shelf, walk through the library with it, and hand it to me, someone that they might not know all that well. I consider it a gift and a blessing because it tells me I've created a space in the school where kids can feel safe enough to be themselves and to expose that part of themselves to me.

I don't have kids of my own. For those six, seven hours a day, these kids are my kids, and I want the very best for them. It means so much to me that they can find something helpful and useful on those shelves. I build this collection for them.

So, there was no way I was gonna let the board take books like this away from kids who need them.

That Friday night, I was looking at the book and I noticed, right there on the cover, next to the word Gay in the title, in teeny tiny mouse letters, it says, "Introduction by David Levithan." He's the acclaimed author of loads of young-adult books, including *Two Boys Kissing*. And I'm like, "Martha, why didn't you notice this before?"

David Levithan, I knew, is a native of New Jersey who works in New York City for Scholastic. I was convinced *somebody* in my library network must know how to get in touch with him. So, first thing Saturday morning, I'm sending out the Bat Signal to my librarian peeps through our New Jersey Association of School Librarians listserv, asking, "Does anybody have a way to get in touch with David Levithan?"

One of my friends, Michelle McGrievey, lives in Hoboken, where David lives, and goes to the same independent bookstore where he shops. She got in touch with the owner of the bookstore, who said they could put me in touch with him. Two hours later, I'm e-mailing back and forth with David, asking him if he can send some sort of message to the board. "I'll write you a message," he wrote. "Please have a student deliver it for me."

In the meantime, I'm reaching out to other folks, asking them to participate in the meeting, which was held virtually, "thanks" to COVID. So, geography was not an obstacle. I was able to reach out to out-of-state alumni. When Tuesday night rolled around, there were about 50 people in the queue to speak in defense of the book.

David Levithan sent a beautiful message. As he'd requested, a student read it to the board. It told the board about all the feedback he'd received from readers, telling him that books like his helped them understand who they are, and that their lives had worth. Some even said books like his had encouraged them to stay alive. Juno Dawson wrote *This Book is Gay* to be clear and honest with kids about their lives, David said. He mentioned that he would have wanted Juno Dawson's book when he was a teenager and that there are tons of kids who need it now. He urged the board to listen to the students who were talking to them because those are the people board members are supposed to be serving.

I think David's message really affected the board, not so much because it was from David Levithan (they have no idea what a rock star he is in young-adult literature), but because, in a really powerful and elegant way, it called attention to all the student comments the board had heard since October.

That was also the night when I finally got to speak. Basically, I refuted the Reconsideration Committee's recommendation to ban by telling the board about the numerous times the book had been checked out, quoting some of its rave reviews, and noting that one of the top library collection guides listed it as "essential," meaning that every high school should have it. All of that information could have been available to the committee, but they'd never even bothered to check with the library.[2]

When it came time for the board to vote, I was biting my fingernails at home. In the end, the board did not accept the recommendation of its own Reconsideration Committee; it voted to keep all five books. At that point, I just lost it. I mean, it's trite to say, but it was a ton of bricks falling off me in that moment.

After the decision, the Intellectual Freedom Fighters submitted a 17-page report to the board about our observations of the process: what worked well, what could have gone better. To date, they've taken no action on any of our recommendations. In May, I had a conversation with my principal in which he reflected on the events of that school year and told me that I had gone "way overboard" in supporting the LGBTQ+ students. When I asked him what "way overboard" meant, he talked about the fact that there were too many LGBTQ+ books in the Banned Books display. I tried to help him understand how these books ended up there and why certain books are challenged. The very nature of the fact that books on this subject are targeted is how they end up in the display, I explained. That's beyond my control. And my principal, this machine-like individual, responded like a wall. There was no agreement or disagreement or even understanding expressed. I felt like I was saying words and they were going out into a void.

In November of 2021, I was contacted by *School Library Journal*; they asked if I would tell my story. I was on the fence about this for several days. I remember saying to my husband, "I do *not* wanna become the poster child for banned books." But as I thought about how many of us were going through this and how lonely I felt when I was going through it, I decided, "Well, if I can be helpful to some other librarian, then I'm willing to do it." I was so naive; I thought, "Oh, well, just librarians are gonna read it." So, I wrote my story and, of course, it ended up everywhere.

Since it was published in February 2022, I don't think a week has gone by when I haven't talked to somebody about this, whether it's a fellow librarian, a teacher, or a member of the news media. Although I didn't want to be the poster child for this, that's exactly what I've become. But I feel like: if not me, who? One of the reasons I can speak out is, I have tenure. Plus, I'm at the tail end of my career. So, I feel like I have the ammo to do it.

In June 2022, a really great thing happened. Remember I told you how critical the kids were to our success and how the Gender and Sexuality Alliances were involved? Well, the New Jersey Library Association gave our district's Gender and Sexuality Alliances their Intellectual Freedom Award. One of the proudest nights of my life, let alone my career, was going down to Atlantic City to cheer on three of the student officers, who were there with their parents. When the kids took the stage, the entire ballroom full of librarians leapt to their feet and cheered. It can bring me to tears just thinking about it. It was so beautiful. The rest of that night and the next morning, 'cause the kids stayed over, they were treated like honest-to-god rock stars when they walked around that conference. People were mobbing them. I was so, so proud.

The sad thing is – and I'm looking at that picture right now – only three out of the four officers who planned to go were there. One of the kids – an out, proud trans student – texted me to say, "I can't make it to Atlantic City. There's a family emergency." I was sad that they missed it. I was even sadder – devastated – come October when they died by their own hand. I've often wondered if the affirmation from that crowd could have kept them going. Their death has been a huge loss for the school community and especially for the GSA kids. But, you know, according to the principal, I had "gone way overboard."

Unfortunately, it didn't stop there. Around the same time our student died, three of the people who'd been active in trying to ban the books were running for the Board of Education. Our Freedom Fighters organization was very active in trying to get the word out about who to vote for, who not to vote for, and why. But despite our best efforts, one of those people, a Moms for Liberty T-shirt-wearing community member who denies being a member of Moms for Liberty, now sits on the board.

A year later, in November 2023, there were elections again for four more board of education seats. Unfortunately, things did not go the way we wanted. Of the four contested seats, two were taken by extremist book banners. One of these newly elected board members ran unsuccessfully last year, tried again, and now has a seat on the Board of Education. Her husband has been very active on social media, is associated with an ultra-MAGA extremist group here in New Jersey called New Jersey Fresh Faced Schools, and he posts regularly about banning books. He created a video in which he goes after me and our library. And now his wife sits on our school board.

I'm trying to keep all this in perspective. Looking at the national picture, Moms for Liberty endorsed 134 candidates for boards of education in 2023, and more than two-thirds of them lost.[3] In New Jersey, of the 20 candidates that Moms for Liberty endorsed, 15 lost. So, I think the tide might be turning – slightly.

Unfortunately, in my little corner of the world, they're slow to catch on. Hunterdon County, New Jersey, where I work, is a very red area. These extremist candidates are closely tied to a Republican machine that offers them all kinds of support in terms of marketing and election strategies, things like robocalls, robotexting, and mailers. In the closing days of the board campaign, we learned, extremist candidates specifically targeted senior citizens in our community, making the false claim that drag queens were coming into the schools to do book readings. You know, drag-queen story hours. Completely untrue. (Even if it *were* true, I still don't understand what's the big deal; drag queens are delightful and wear fabulous costumes.) Essentially, they sold snake oil to senior citizens to get them out to the polls and vote their way. I guess it worked.

My advice for other educators is: know your institution's policies and processes. When that principal showed up and said, "I heard a rumor," I knew what the policy was, so I could talk him through it. I keep multiple copies of the policy right here in my drawer to hand out to whoever needs it. Odds are, if you know the policies and processes forwards and backwards, you may well be the only one in your institution who does. I've dealt with a lot of administrators – it's a revolving door – and every time this has come up over the last 19 years, their first instinct is always to get rid of the book. Every time, I tell them, "You can't do that, and here's why. You have a policy." And every one of them has said, "There's a *policy* about that?" Administrators around here are more afraid of the parents than they are concerned about the safety of the students or staff. It's easier to placate the parents than it is to do the hard thing and stand up for students' rights to read.[4]

I'm fearful about what lies ahead. Not long ago, one of the book-banning parents created a video that included footage from my school library and posted it on Facebook. In it, he is yet again accusing me of imposing a left-wing agenda on students. That's the man whose wife has since been elected to the board of education. So, he's going after me. It's not going away. The seeds that were sown in 2019 are still bearing poisonous fruit.

I feel unsafe here every day, especially after things escalated again as a result of this video. The video showed footage shot in the library in September 2021. At that time, I had a display up about the history of protest movements. Among others, I had the 1960s anti-war movement, the civil rights movement, a book about the climate-crisis activist Greta Thunberg (because she's a teenager who is taking action on an issue that's important to her and to the world). When you're building a library collection for teenagers, it's important to show kids that they're not just consumers of information; that they can be producers of information, movers and shakers in the world who make things happen. I had the Farm Workers' strike, all different kinds of protest movements.

Why did I have that display up? Because the previous summer – we were still in the depths of COVID at that time – every Saturday for about a year and a half, across from the Dunkin' Donuts in the town where I live, not far from our high school, a gang of people would stand there for about six hours at a time, protesting vaccines and mask mandates. At our board meetings, there were families coming to protest having to mask their kids to go to school. And who was protesting with those parents? Their own children. I thought, "Well, this is interesting." The previous spring, some of our students had marched in protest of George Floyd's murder. Clearly, our kids are interested in this idea. So, I thought, "Let me put up a display about protest movements to harness what's going on in the world, as an attempt to get kids to read about it." This is what set these people off. They are – it boggles my mind – protesting a display about protesting. You can't make this stuff up.

As a result of the video that this man posted, I was getting e-mail and social media posts by the dozens, crazy people calling me a groomer. I alerted my union and my principal; I let my administration know that I don't feel safe.

We're a suburban high school. We have five armed police officers in this building every day. For what? They stand around and talk sports. It's very performative. I asked if I could have the presence of a security officer in the library. The administration refused my request. I said, "All right, can you patrol the building, at least? Make a show of acting like a police officer instead of standing around? And when you patrol the building, can the library be part of your beat?" So, I got the administration to agree that one of our uniformed police officers would enter the library at least once a day to create the illusion of some security. That kinda fell by the wayside this year. They did a good job of it last spring, then they let it slide.

The people who are after me are avid gun owners. In fact, the husband of the Moms for Liberty book banner who won a seat on the Board of Education in 2022 wore a T-shirt to her swearing-in – classy guy – that says, over a picture of an AR-15 rifle, "I am 1776 percent sure no one will be taking my guns."

In terms of its direct impact on our library books, 2019 is the start date of all of this, but if I was gonna be totally honest, I'd have to say this has been building steadily since 2016, the year Trump was elected. I got a huge wake-up call on the first Tuesday of November of 2016. Let me say that again to be clear: The first Tuesday of November of 2016. I'm walking around the library, and I discover swastikas drawn on the library chairs in chalk. I called my administrators. At that time, the man who's now my principal, the guy who told me I'd gone way overboard in supporting LGBTQ+ kids, was vice principal. The man who is now the assistant superintendent, who told me I had stirred up trouble and wanted to know how I paid for the Dunkin' Donuts gift card, was the principal at that time. These two came down to the library, looked at the chairs, and said, "Oh, just wipe it off." And left.

I was like, "Yeah, I'm not doing that." I took pictures of the swastikas, and I sent them to the Southern Poverty Law Center, which at that time was collecting examples of hate speech that were cropping up around the election. The other sad fact about this is that LGBTQ+ students have told the board that, since the attempted book bans, they are experiencing more harassment, more bullying, more intimidation, more homophobic slurs in the hallway.

One of the students, Mitchell – who is a sweetheart, just the loveliest, most eloquent, intelligent young man – received death threats because of his support for these books. Our building, by the way, labels itself as "no place for hate," but that's just a glossy veneer that the school puts on and never looks below the surface of. What is the day-to-day life of these kids? So far, no violence has erupted in a severe way, but the GSA kids are feeling the hate. And as we know, one of them is no longer here to tell the tale.

SALLY MIDDLETON
TRUMP GOT ELECTED AND ALLOWED EVERYBODY TO BE HATEFUL.

"I'm a high school art teacher who was censored and silenced by my school district for my efforts to increase access to learning, promote cultural awareness, and support positive change."

I moved to Censoropolis eight years ago, and I've been teaching there ever since. When I started at Censorville High School, everything was awesome. I had a great team. I really liked my job. I really liked my kids. And then, you know, Trump got elected and allowed everybody to be hateful, and that's when the madness started.

I've taught AP art history, and I always felt like I was allowed to say to my students, "The majority of our art history textbooks are all white, and they have a Eurocentric viewpoint." I was very open with my kids, but I never had any issues with anyone despite telling it like it was. Then COVID occurred, and I had my first online class with 60 students in Art 1. That's when the first incident happened.

I'd always gotten students to do socially engaged art projects benefiting a cause. One year, it was "save the ocean"; you had to make ocean animals out of recycled materials. The whole goal was to show them how art can have an impact and do some good.

In my first year of online teaching during COVID, one of our Art 1 activities was to make an award for someone in your community who's a changemaker. I found this video that said, "You might think you're just one measly little voice, that you're just a high school student, but let's look at some examples of other movements where it was just one person who made a difference." It gave examples from a variety of perspectives, which, in my state, I'm required to do – offer contending takes on issues without showing a preference for any one side. The point was, "You, too, can take a stand." Whatever stand they took was of their choosing.

Apparently, a mother was listening in on her kid's class, and instead of asking me about the video, instead of asking the principal, she went straight to social media. She could have talked to me, and I would have gladly e-mailed her my lesson. Instead, she complained in a Facebook post that I showed the video in class and that it urged students, "Even you can start a movement; your voice matters."

I believe she was upset that the video encouraged protesting and joining forces with like-minded people. The video shared strategies from across history, such as sit-ins, that activists had used to call for change. I guess she thought it encouraged rioting.

This was around the time when conservatives were obsessed with the Black Lives Matter protests: "Look at all these people making such a mess and vandalizing property and yada-yada-yada." I gather she thought I was promoting violent protests or whatever because it said in the video, "You can band with like-minded people and fight for something you believe in." When she posted her comment, "Look at what my son's art teacher is doing," somebody commented, "Clearly, another teacher pushing their communist agenda."

The Facebook group is called Concerned Parents for Censorville School District. It stemmed from a Facebook group for anyone in the community. Then, after Trump was first elected, you started seeing more and more polarizing posts about school stuff. Separate groups were formed along political lines to discuss school topics. Concerned Parents for Censorville School District leaned strongly to the right and, based on my scrolling through their posts, are mostly Christian, white, stay-at-home moms with too much time on their hands. The group became a forum for gossiping and complaining about teachers and schools. I remember hearing Trump at rallies on the news questioning what teachers were teaching "our kids in schools." Many from this group would show up at school board meetings to air their complaints and begin by quoting bible verses and praying for our schools.

A teacher who worked with me and was part of that Facebook group to surveil their activity reached out and said, "Hey, I don't know which one of you five art teachers did this, but they're talkin' about you online." I was like, "Oh my god, it's me." When I looked up who her kid was, he had made an award for Dr. Martin Luther King, Jr. for the art project inspired by the video. I thought, "I don't know what the problem is here, but okay."

I went to school the next day, pretty freaked out, and spoke with the school counselor about the incident. The counselor wasn't fazed. The school had dealt with this parent before, she said; I wasn't the first one to set her off. She suggested that the counselor sit in on my next few online classes. I introduced her to the class each day, in case the parent was listening in.

You might think that having a counselor hovering over me as I am trying to teach was less than ideal, but it was quite the opposite. Anytime a teacher has one of these instances, the administration or the district just leaves us hanging without any follow-up, resolution, or support. But she was a wonderful counselor; she made me feel *more* comfortable. I had somebody on my side, seeing what I was teaching and watching the video and going, "There's no problem here; you're showing both sides." It was a relief.

Of course, that didn't satisfy this mom. She e-mailed the superintendent and said that I was "pushing my agenda onto her child." To be clear, I never said that this student had to do an artwork on Dr. King; that was her son's choice. It was ridiculous. At any rate, the superintendent called the principal, who advised me not to talk to the parent directly. I had to go in and show the principal my video, which I'd previewed before showing it to my students, as I'm required to do. I had to give my lesson plan to the Arts Director for the district.

At that point, I asked my husband to join this Facebook group because I was fearful of a parent on the group going over my head without asking me anything about my curriculum choices or about why I assigned such-and-such a project.

I'd heard horror stories from other teachers who went through this kind of crap. I've had friends who are English teachers be questioned about their book choices, History teachers fearful to talk about racism, and many teachers had to take down their "Safe Space" stickers (signaling to students who were part of the LGBTQ+ community that this teacher was a safe adult to talk to) at their classroom doors.

I was friends with another teacher at Censorville High School, Joe, who hung a Black Lives Matter sign in his classroom. A student took a photo of the sign and shared it with his parent, who then posted it to Facebook, after which parents complained to the school. The district told him, "Hey, don't come to work until we figure this out." He was like, "Screw that." He went to the news and said, "Here's what they're doing to me because I'm trying to show my students that they're welcome here, that my classroom is a safe space."

They don't fire teachers. They just ask them – very politely – to resign 'cause they can't fire you per se for some of these things. What they'll do is say that because you're in the media, you're creating an environment that interferes with students' ability to learn. That's their loophole because they can't fire you for having a sign in your room. So, they say, "Oh, you're no longer a successful teacher because you're distracting."

Of course, you know, teachers have had crosses up in their classrooms without any issues ever since I started teaching here. Our principal did tell us, "If you wanna have a cross or your favorite Bible sayings or a Black Lives Matter sign or whatever, you can have it in your classroom as long as it's on your desk *facing you*. It can't be on display." That said, there's an "In God We Trust" sign prominently displayed in the front office. It was gifted to us by a conservative, Christian cell phone company, Patriot Mobile.* This same company also supports conservative school district candidates. The state passed a law requiring such signs

---

* For a sense of how extreme this company is, see: Erum Salam, "Conservative Texas phone company fueling extremist takeover of schools," *The Guardian*, September 5, 2022.

to be displayed in a "conspicuous place" in schools if they're donated or purchased by private donations.

So, back to my teacher friend Joe, who had the BLM sign up in his classroom: Since he was in that far-right Facebook group, my husband saw the start of the uproar. He was like, "Hey, something's happening at Censorville High again. These parents are mad that this teacher has a Black Lives Matter sign on his wall."

These parents were calling him a pedophile on Facebook and referencing something called Pizzagate. Apparently, these QAnon conspiracy theorists believe that if you're eating a piece of pizza in your profile picture on Facebook, it's a secret code that you're a pedophile. Well, my teacher friend had a picture of him eatin' pizza on his Facebook page, so these parents started calling him a pedophile. And *that* got some of them to start trying to dig up stuff on *other* teachers. To be clear, he is not a pedophile; it's simply something that QAnon-ers *believe*.

So, I took a screenshot of that and sent it to my friend who worked at Joe's school, and I said, "Hey, they're callin' Joe a pedophile. Is he aware? Is he okay? This is just a heads-up." Well, that person shared my photo, and sure enough, it had my husband's little Facebook profile picture bubble in it. That got shared around, and my husband's profile picture has me in it. Somebody took that screenshot of all these parents being hateful towards the teacher and put on X (formerly Twitter), "We need to blast these parents." They made a list of the parents who were being awful and put it on X. The conservative moms saw it, went directly to HR, and said, "Sally has a fake X account and is making a hit list of moms, and, oh, gosh, we're fearful for our lives."

Long story short, I had a big meeting with HR over this insanity. I had to prove to them that I was in a graduate course the night that a fake X account was made. I was sitting in class when all of this happened. I never determined who *did* create the fake X account, but they used my picture without my consent to gain access to the parents' names and call out the "mean moms," as they called them. No one I know would have used me to create a fake X account. It isn't beyond the realm of possibility that the fake account was a "false flag" operation created *by* the moms to legitimate any retaliatory strategies they might pursue with HR.

I gave them screenshots from my and my husband's phones that showed that neither of us was on X. I showed them our screen time. Luckily, one of the ladies in the administration building was in the same class as me and said, "She was in class with me, so she couldn't have done this."

HR sat with me for a while and said, "Aren't you upset at your husband for taking the screenshot and sneakily being in this group?" I said, "Absolutely not, because look what they're doing to us. Clearly, you work for *them*. This is customer service at its finest. Whatever the parents say goes." They said they'd get back to me because this was an incredibly serious matter. They didn't get me to sign a non-disclosure agreement, even though they said they were gonna send it. I never heard from them again. This happened last year, and HR hasn't contacted me since.

But that wasn't the end of the ugliness. Since we were in a teacher shortage, the district put out a call for volunteers to substitute-teach without any training and a mom from Concerned Parents for Censorville School District got certified to substitute teach. This parent was assigned to teach my friend's English class, and she looked through all the books in that teacher's personal library, which was behind her desk. This parent/sub found a book, *Milk and Honey*, that she didn't like. It's a collection of poems and prose by the Indian-Canadian poet Rupi Kaur that refers to sexual assault. The parent/sub considered these topics inappropriate for high school, so she brought it to a school board meeting. My friend, the English teacher, almost didn't get the position of being the new librarian at Censorville High because this parent complained to the board about a book that was in her personal library.

It isn't beyond the realm of possibility that this parent became a sub with the intention of checking on district schools and their books. On the Concerned Parents for Censorville School District Facebook page, parents had been expressing great interest in what was on the shelves in schools. They might have used the opportunity to become a substitute teacher as a means of getting into classrooms to check on the appropriateness of resources on shelves.

I'm in a progressive Facebook group that has sneaky mole people in the conservative group. They try to warn us, "Hey, does anybody know this teacher? We wanna alert them before –" that sort of thing. They're trying to protect us.

The other day, a teacher had hand cream on his desk. Its brand name is Gender Bender, and it's geared toward men. It has a manly, woodsy scent. The name is a witty attempt to get around the stigma skin care products hold for some men, who perceive them as too feminine. An unknown student took a photo of it and sent it to their parent. Someone in the conservative parents' Facebook group Concerned Parents for Censorville School District said, "Should teachers be allowed to push this agenda?" I'm like, "It's the teacher's *hand cream*. On *his* desk. I can't *even*."

The other thing that's happened since then involved my being in charge of creating the AP art history curriculum for the Censorville School District. The District Arts Curriculum Coordinator said, "Could we change your unit on Islamic Art to Art from the Middle East? We really shouldn't be teaching religion; we should be teaching art." This struck me as incredibly hypocritical since this is coming from the same district whose policy allows teachers to hang crosses in their classrooms in a state that *requires public schools* to display "In God We Trust" signs, if they're given to us. I came back at them with, "You didn't have a problem with my unit on early Christian artwork." So, they let me keep Islamic Art, although not until I'd proven that a bunch of textbooks also had sections on Islamic art and that it wouldn't make sense to say Middle East when I'm teaching about the Alhambra in Spain, which is unavoidable in any discussion of Islamic art and architecture.

There have been book challenges, too. During a school board meeting, conservative parents voiced anger at the librarian at my school, who was the head librarian for the whole district, for letting the district librarians go to their state and national librarian conferences. The conference speakers were into critical race theory, they claimed. These parents were upset that their taxpayer dollars were going toward sending teachers and librarians to conferences to learn about the "woke" agenda. These parents went so far as to park outside of her house and stalk her, so she had to quit for the safety and security of herself and her kids. She left the district altogether.

In the aftermath of all this insanity, I watch what I say more than I used to, even in art history. That's hard, especially because the AP-level curriculum, which I have to follow, says that I have to teach social responsibility. The learning outcomes/goals for my course define social responsibility learning as demonstrating "the ability to place selected works in historical context by intercultural competency, civic knowledge, and the ability to engage effectively in regional, national, and global communities by a) demonstrating an understanding of the impact of visual arts on culture by analyzing art in terms of its role in culture; b) examining artists' lives and philosophies in terms of their impact on art and culture." As a teacher, I interpret this as explaining why certain works of art were created due to the historical/social contexts of the time. For example, Greek marbles were originally painted, but now, when we see them, the paint has deteriorated, and so they're the white of the marble. However, there's little effort to restore them or even educate people on their original bright coloring – reinforcing the idea that whiteness is pure, historical, and revered.

So, I'm trying to have discussions like, "Why are all of the ancient Greek marbles whitewashed? We know that they were all painted in their day." I wanna teach the activism of the feminist group Guerilla Girls, asking the questions that they asked like, "Why are most of the women in the Met the nudes in paintings and not women artists?" I wanna teach that stuff, but I'm not gonna lie, I'm scared.

Students are super aware of all of these issues, and I'm really proud of a lot of them. There's no rule where I have to censor students' artworks. It's just *my* content as an educator that's being censored. The students get to choose which artwork they wanna make to satisfy their high school art credit. I showed them examples of Emperor Justinian in the Byzantine era using his position to promote Christianity and gave them an assignment: "Make a mosaic that promotes something you believe in." I'm trying to give them space to do their thing, but I have to watch how I word it so they can make whatever they want. They feel like they can speak their truth in their artworks. One student is making a mosaic of the Black Lives Matter fist.

MATTHEW D. HAWN
I WAS THE FIRST TENURED TEACHER IN THE STATE OF TENNESSEE TO BE DISMISSED WHEN THE RIGHT WING WEAPONIZED CRT.

"I'm a tenured high school social studies teacher in Northeast Tennessee who was dismissed for discussing white privilege and racial justice in my upper-level contemporary issues class."

I'm a social studies teacher and a baseball coach in Northeast Tennessee who was dismissed on May 5, 2021, for discussing white privilege and racial justice in a high school social studies class entitled Contemporary Issues.

Sullivan County, where I taught, is in the Appalachian Mountains. I've lived here my entire life. Growing up, I was interested in politics. I would get up in the morning and watch Rush Limbaugh before school. I was very conservative. I was also homophobic, racist, and misogynist. I believed it was the man's job to go out and work and provide for the family, and the woman should stay at home and raise the kids and keep the house in order.

But then I went to Tennessee Tech, about an hour east of Nashville, in Cookeville. That gave me the opportunity to meet people whose backgrounds were different from mine. My first friend at Tennessee Tech was Black. The people I hung out with in the dorms were a very diverse group – public- and private-school kids from Nashville, kids from places I'd never heard of, people from all walks of life.

It is around this time I'm starting to realize that maybe we're not all that different, but I'm still struggling with how I look at the world. Then, I started taking history classes. Tennessee Tech did a very good job of introducing me to other viewpoints. I was taking a class called something like "The History of History," and I remember my professor saying, "Whenever we read history, we are reading it from the perspective of whoever's writing it."

He mentioned the Black Panthers and said, "If you think about the Black Panthers, they were classified as the militant wing of the civil rights movement." Then, he asked us, "Do you think the people they were giving healthcare, education, and clothing to would classify them as militant?" I'll never forget that. Something just went off in my head like, "Oh, my goodness, there's a lot I need to be educated on."

Part of why I became so passionate about teaching racial equity in my Contemporary Issues class is because, on some level, I think I'm teaching that 17-year-old kid Matt Hawn. Those kids in Sullivan County are just like I was, for the most part. They still have the perspective that comes from living in an all-white culture.

In college, I'd always thought about teaching, but it wasn't until after I graduated with a degree in finance that I decided to go back and get my degrees in education and history. It's very hard to get a job teaching social studies and coaching in Sullivan County because people tend to stay in those jobs for a while, but I was lucky: shortly after I graduated from Tennessee Tech in 2004, in the fall of 2005, I got a job at Sullivan Central High School. I ended up teaching there for 16 years. For the first few years, I taught Economics. Later on, I was given other classes, like Personal Finance and World History. Then, around 2010, the administration assigned a contemporary issues class to me. It had state standards I had to follow, but it didn't have a set curriculum. I developed the curriculum and chose the assignments students worked on.

It was a challenge to facilitate conversations with students on hot-button issues when I first started teaching that class because we don't often ask students what they think about real-world issues. Teachers must adhere to a set curriculum that wouldn't ordinarily include that sort of thing. I told my students, "Unfortunately, you're teenagers, so people won't typically ask your thoughts and opinions about pressing social issues, but congratulations, you're in a Contemporary Issues class where this is what you get to do!"

We talked about everything from nuclear proliferation, terrorism abroad and at home, and North Korea, to the #MeToo movement, racial equity, racial justice, and the COVID pandemic and related issues – how initial cases started, how the virus spread, cultural and ethical questions of individualism versus collectivism. For example, does an immunocompromised person have a right to be safe when they go out in the world? It was a really, really good class for students to engage with current events and controversial issues and to learn how to talk and listen to each other.

By the 2020-2021 school year, I'd been teaching at Sullivan Central High for 15 years. I'd never had any disciplinary issues regarding my lesson plans – or anything else, for that matter. But, like teachers nationwide, I had to adjust how I taught during COVID. I had to learn to talk to students through a computer, staring at 25 avatars – not knowing whether or not they were paying attention, not even knowing who I was speaking with. I don't know the basis for the district policy that prevented educators from asking or requiring students to turn on their cameras, but I assume it came from equity and privacy concerns. Some students may not want to reveal the conditions of their homes, or they may not have control over their environments. They could be sitting in a room where other family members are also working or fighting or getting dressed.

That school year, Sullivan County started off completely virtual. Then, we came back to the classroom on alternating days, called "hybrid learning": on A days, some of our students were in the classroom, and some of our students were at home, and vice-versa on B days. The trouble was that some of the conversations in Contemporary Issues need to happen in person, where students can ask questions openly and not be afraid to delve into the material. They need to really feel free to state how or what they think about a particular issue.

In September 2020, during a period of hybrid learning, I was listening to the radio on my way to school, and they were broadcasting the Jacob Blake family press conference. Jacob Blake is a Black man who was shot seven times, in the back and the side, by Kenosha, Wisconsin police officers allegedly answering a domestic disturbance call between two women. During the ensuing protests over the police brutality, Kyle Rittenhouse, a white 17-year-old, shot three of the protestors, killing two of them, then turned himself in to the police, who took him into custody peacefully. I thought, "Well, I have to talk about this today."

At the time, we were recording our classes, so if a student had issues while they were at home, they could watch that day's class later on my Google Classroom site. We started that class by watching the Blake family press conference, and then we talked about what Kyle Rittenhouse did. I said that white privilege is a fact, adding that Rittenhouse's non-violent reception by the cops is a prime example of it. A Black man is shot in the back seven times by the police, then a white teenager kills two people and walks up to the police with a weapon, yet is not met with a lethal response. This was a significant national story where you could compare two very different responses to different people based on the color of their skin.

When I'm in the classroom, teaching, I don't usually say, "This is a fact"; I want the students to make up their own minds. My job is to provide them with information from reliable sources and show them how to do the research to figure out what they think about the issue. In this case, the issue was whether white privilege exists and whether it explained why the police responded differently to Rittenhouse. As for me saying "white privilege is a fact," I hadn't planned on saying that, it just came out. But just because I said it, it didn't mean that we would accept that assertion as received truth and not do any research. The students would still do the research to determine whether or not white privilege was a fact, looking at economic data and other social markers, such as high school graduation rates, college acceptance and graduation rates, unemployment rates, family income, median income, homeownership rates, incarceration rates, and so on (which do prove, incidentally, that white privilege is a fact).

So, at the end of that school day, I posted that recording of my Contemporary Issues class to my Personal Finance class by accident. A parent saw it and complained, "Why is Coach Hawn talking about this in Personal Finance?" Which is a great question because that's not part of my Personal Finance curriculum. But what they really had a problem with was my statement that white privilege is a fact. That's what led to them calling the central office. These were people I know and who know me because, as I said, it's a small community. Instead of coming to me about it, though, they went to my administrator, the school board, and the central office. That led to our Director of Curriculum and Instructions sending me a letter saying something like, "Statements like 'this is a fact,' don't lead to discussion between students and don't improve their research capabilities." He informed me of the Tennessee Teacher Code of Ethics, which requires that teachers shall not reasonably deny students access to varying viewpoints. I said, "I understand. I'll make a change in my teaching." But even then, I wasn't aware there would be any consequences for saying that white privilege is a fact. I took the e-mail as a suggestion, not a directive or a reprimand. The district even confirmed my understanding much later, in the appeal hearing, when it said this wasn't a verbal warning, and wasn't a disciplinary measure.

Shortly thereafter, when COVID cases arose in Sullivan County, the school board made the decision to go back to being completely virtual. I stopped talking about racial equity and justice because Contemporary Issues was a year-long class, and I hoped we would resume in-person instruction soon, at which point we'd discuss those and other lightning-rod issues. As it turned out, we stayed virtual the rest of the fall semester in 2020, and we were still online when classes started up again in the spring of 2021. And you know what? On January 6, a group of people tried to overthrow the United States government.

I wasn't really sure how to discuss that with my students. I didn't have a lesson plan for that, and I live in a county where 75 percent of the population voted for Donald Trump. At the time, there were claims in the news media that he led the insurrection. I wanted to be very sure of the facts before I proceeded because we were still trying to figure out everything that happened. I wanted to wait until we got more news stories before I even began to create some kind of lesson that would allow the students to research and discuss what happened that day.

One of my approaches, as outlined in the state standards for this class, is to look at how historical events affect the present. I thought, "We'll look at the 2016 election as a historical event," because, after all, it *was* historic: Trump was the first presidential candidate to use social media as his primary platform, and it was the first time a candidate without any prior public service won an election. I thought we could look at what happened in 2016 and see whether the election led to the insurrection on January 6.

I asked my students, "Why was Donald Trump elected?" and they gave a lot of great answers. Some said, "Russian interference." Some said, "He's not a politician; he says what he means." "He's a good business-man." "The Clinton campaign failed to schedule stops in Pennsylvania, Michigan, and Ohio." They said all these things. So, I said, "Yes, we'll research all of those."

They had great answers, but I wanted to expose them to perspectives you don't typically hear in north-east Tennessee. My county is 95 percent white. My school system is 98 percent white. Every student I attended school with, from kindergarten to my senior year in high school, was white, and every teacher, too. So, to me, a different perspective for my students would be the Black cultural critic Ta-Nehisi Coates. In his es-say "The First White President," Coates makes the argument that, after eight years of Obama as president, the Trump campaign used whiteness as a tool to mobilize voters and win the election because they recog-nized that a lot of white voters, no matter their economic status, had felt threatened by having a Black man lead the country.

I assigned the article before Martin Luther King Jr. Day. The following Tuesday, students would return to school physically, and I believed this would be a good starting point for the unit surrounding the January 6 insurrection.

Unfortunately, I never got to teach from the article because a parent complained that it was inappropriate for high school students and that I wasn't giving them access to varying points of view. The county would eventually make the charge that this was the only material I was planning to give my students, which couldn't be further from the truth. My students would never have the opportunity to analyze other causes for the election of Donald Trump, such as "Trump Confounds the Pros, Connects With Just the Right Voters," an *NPR* article about Trump's appeal and his political acumen, or "Trump Won Thanks to Social Media," an article from *The Hill.* I talked with my principal about the entire lesson plan a few days after the parental complaint to explain the full scope of the unit and precisely what the class would do. However, my principal told me to discontinue the lesson and move on to another topic, which I did.

Two weeks later, on February third, I was given an official reprimand by my central office, which was completely unexpected. It stated that, moving forward, they wanted "balance" to everything we discussed in class. So, if I gave a liberal perspective, like Ta-Nehisi Coates's, I had to follow that up with a conservative perspective. The problem was that I didn't see Coates's perspective as liberal. I just saw it as the perspective of Ta-Nehisi Coates – the way he looks at race in the United States and its relation to the 2016 election, because he talks about Bernie Sanders and Hillary Clinton and he doles it out on both sides, no matter the person's political affiliation. I didn't look at it as liberal or conservative.

I told my Tennessee Education Association (TEA) union UniServ representative – a former social studies teacher, not a lawyer – that I was going to contest the reprimand. My argument was that the central office never provided me with due process as outlined in the employee handbook: they didn't bring me in to speak with them to decide if an investigation was warranted and didn't conduct an investigation if deemed necessary. So, I contested the reprimand.

At a March 2021 meeting of the Sullivan County Board of Education, I ended up losing six to zero. They voted in favor of the superintendent of schools, stating that he had the right to reprimand me without an investigation. Their statement directly contradicts our employee handbook, which clearly states, "Prior to disciplinary action, the administrator or supervisor involved will complete an investigation of the incident(s)." I wasn't happy about the ruling, but I knew that I was coming back to the classroom in a couple weeks and would be able to get back to a normal school year, so I said, "That's fine."

Fast forward to mid-April of 2021: the trial of Derek Chauvin, the police officer who murdered George Floyd by kneeling on his back and neck for over nine minutes, is underway. At that same time, we were doing a lesson plan about racial equity and justice. We talked about implicit bias, defunding the police, mass incarceration, and the perception of Black people as a monolithic culture. We were watching the trial live in my classroom, and, during a discussion about the trial, a student brought up white privilege. Now, before that, I'd decided not to talk about white privilege. Out of respect to my principal, I was trying to stay away from hot-button issues. I wasn't going to bring white privilege into the conversation about racial equity. This was going to be my last semester at Sullivan Central because the district was consolidating it with two other high schools, and the principal asked that we go out peacefully. He'd been my principal for 10 years, and we had a really good relationship. I had been his son's favorite teacher four or five years prior to this uproar. So, I said, "Sure, absolutely," though, again, I took it more as a suggestion from him than an official directive from the central office.

But, when a student mentioned white privilege, teacher mode kicked in. I said, "Well, what is that? What is white privilege?" In that moment, I realized that students signed up for this class to learn about things like this, and no matter what the outside pressures are, they deserve the full experience of this class. I wouldn't have hesitated to ask that question or bring up white privilege a year ago, I thought, so why am I hesitating now? Not doing so would amount to cheating the students out of an education. So, we started talking about white privilege. We read Peggy McIntosh's essay "White Privilege: Unpacking the Invisible Knapsack," then discussed it. McIntosh lists 26 advantages that she gets from her skin color, like: "I can choose blemish cover or bandages in 'flesh' color and have them more or less match my skin," and "I can arrange to be in the company of people of my race most of the time." I've used that article with students for a long time, at least seven years.

Back in 2020, I'd come upon this video of Kyla Jenee Lacey reciting her poem *White Privilege*. I was just mesmerized by this smart, strong, yet vulnerable woman performing this powerful piece of art. I thought, "Oh, my god, I have to show this to my Contemporary Issues class." So, in that mid-April 2021 class, I showed Kyla's poem after we'd read and discussed Peggy McIntosh.

There are some curse words in the poem – six, to be exact, which means that less than one-half of one percent of the words are expletives. However, someone complained about the video, and, a week later, on April 27, I was called into our central office for a meeting with the director of schools and other members of the central office staff. They wanted to know why I showed this poem to an upper-level social studies class after previously being reprimanded for inappropriate materials and for denying students access to a range of viewpoints. Then, a week later, on May 5, I was called back to our central office, and the director handed me my dismissal papers. I was fired from my job.

As it happened, May 5, 2021, was also the day the Tennessee General Assembly passed its so-called 'anti-critical race theory' or 'divisive concepts' bill (officially, Tenn. Code Ann. § 49-6-1019).[1] Later that summer, the governor would sign it into law. To be dismissed from my job for teaching racial justice on the same day the state legislature passed that bill, well, it's hard to ignore the message that sends about this political firestorm I inadvertently walked into.

* * * * *

At a school board meeting on June 8, the Director of Schools brought my dismissal charges to the Board of Education, and they voted in an up-and-down vote (yes or no) right then and there. There were six votes for dismissal and one vote against dismissal.

I never thought I'd be in this situation. Sometimes, I wake up and wonder, "How did I get here?" My identity has changed. I used to be "Matt Hawn, the teacher or the coach at Sullivan Central High School." Now, when people ask, "What do you do?" I say, "I used to be a teacher, but I was dismissed for..." So, I guess that's my identity now. That's tough to accept.

I wasn't even *aware* of this right-wing culture war against critical race theory; I still live in this East Tennessee bubble, too. My classroom was a place where I felt like I had the freedom to discuss any issue, any time I wanted to, because, for the last 10 years, I'd had complete autonomy. So, the idea that I would be dismissed for assigning a Ta-Nehisi Coates article or using Kyla Jenee Lacy's poem *White Privilege* as material for my students to engage with never crossed my mind.

I believe there are a few reasons for the pushback and culture war we see today. First of all, this isn't from our students. Our students *want* to have these conversations. However, there is a small, vocal, well-funded group of parents and community members who are leading this culture war we're seeing in schools and libraries.

After the racial reckoning of 2020, we started to see things like *The 1619 Project* introduced in academic settings. We started to include in our curriculum voices that have been left out of American history for 400 years – voices like Ta-Nehisi Coates, Nikole Hannah-Jones, and Kyla Jenee Lacey. The system has worked very well for white males like me, but now it's perceived to be under attack.

I don't know if this is ignorance or willful ignorance, but, growing up here, we didn't learn about these things. In middle school, I was taught the Lost Cause fallacy. The Lost Cause fallacy is a myth started by Southern historians, ex-Confederates, and their children after the war to redefine the narrative of the Civil War as an act of Northern aggression. We were taught that slavery was a net positive, and that it was hypocritical of northern states to condemn slavery when working conditions in northern factories were so egregious. We were taught that the North won the war because of superior numbers and resources but that Southern military officers were superior in every way; they just couldn't overcome those northern advantages. We were also taught that the Civil Rights Act and the Voting Rights Act of '64 and '65 ended racism.

I think COVID played a part, too. Parents were saying, "For the first time, we are getting to look into the classrooms." So, they hear a teacher saying that white privilege is a fact, but they don't really understand how learning happens or how lesson plans work. We educate students much differently than we did in years past. How we learn is still a relatively new science. For the longest time, we thought students were blank slates that we filled with information. Now, we're starting to move away from that model and give them the opportunity to research things, to make up their own minds based on the facts. It's a more student-centered approach.

I think this conservative culture war on educators is a combination of all these things; it's a perfect storm.

Part of me wants to be slightly optimistic and say, "They're pushing back because we're introducing a more diverse group of voices into the classroom." But current legislation like the Divisive Concepts (or "anti-CRT") bill deprives kids of a real education, a more research-focused education. These bills keep students sheltered in a racial and cultural bubble, which keeps them from empathizing with marginalized groups.

In the 2021-2022 school year, our district cut Contemporary Issues from their class offerings. You can't even take that class in Sullivan County high schools right now. I don't know how you could teach a Contemporary Issues class under Divisive Concepts, anyway. The law would say it's impossible.

Having students understand varying viewpoints is the founding principle of education: it's about challenging what they previously thought; getting them to think about what they believe and why they believe it.

* * * * *

We're coming up on two years since my dismissal. We're in the third step of the appeals process. I appealed the May 5 dismissal, and we had an appellate hearing in August of 2021 that lasted for three days. I received the hearing officer's decision that October; he said the superintendent was justified in dismissing me. So, I appealed that decision back to the school board in December of 2021 and they upheld the hearing officer's ruling, agreeing that, yes, I should have been dismissed. Now, a year and a half later, I'm waiting for the chance to plead my case in Sullivan County Chancery Court.

My colleagues have been very supportive but, um, silent. They're afraid. Teachers and librarians across the state are afraid for their jobs. When I made my appeal to the school board in December, more than three hundred people showed up to support me. But even though I'm very close friends with a number of teachers from my district and the surrounding districts, the *only teacher* who showed up from Sullivan County was our union president. Whenever I asked my friends if they were coming, they'd say, "No, we're sorry, we can't. We don't wanna be punished for supporting you."

As frustrating as that was to hear, I understood where they were coming from. I don't want any teacher to have to experience what I've gone through, fighting for my job for the last two and a half years and facing an uncertain future. So, it's hard for me to be upset with them. They've sent words of encouragement; they just haven't been very public about it.

But I've received support from many people living in many different places. I also had 16 years' worth of former students speak out on my behalf on social media. They showed up at my appeal in huge numbers, and anytime that a journalist calls and wants to speak to any of my students, I have a Rolodex full of names I can call, and they're like, "Yes, absolutely; I'm there for you."

My sister started a GoFundMe two years ago,* and people have been very generous in their donations; that's what I'm living on. It pays all of my living expenses and 100 percent of my health insurance premiums. I do have a summer job. I coach T-Ball and baseball for five or six weeks weeks in the summer. Other than that, you know, I've done some small speaking engagements, which pay honorariums. But I'm living without a paycheck.

---

* "Stand with Coach Hawn," GoFundMe, https://www.gofundme.com/f/stand-with-coach-hawn.

I could try to teach in another system in Tennessee, but you can look up the license for any public school teacher in the database on our state website, and if you look up Matt Hawn, it says "license under review." When this is all over, I'll be called in front of a licensure review board; they can decide to strip me of my license for another six months, a year, or even indefinitely.

We need some kind of safety net in place for teachers so they can fight these disciplinary measures resulting from the culture war. Not only financially. We're talking emotionally and spiritually. Also, teachers need to be taught how to talk to the media.

In Tennessee, the appeals process for dismissed tenured teachers favors the school system. (If you're untenured, you're not afforded the opportunity to appeal.) The school system appoints and pays for an "impartial hearing officer" to oversee the first step in the appeals process. The next step is an appeal of the hearing officer's decision, which sends the teacher back to the school board. School boards are elected officials, and they have one employee, the Director of Schools – in other words, the very person who dismissed the teacher. It would be hard to justify to voters why you hired a director, then voted to overturn a decision they made. The third step is the local chancery court. The teacher's lawyers are going to go to court and argue that the dismissed teacher didn't violate the tenure law. To do that, it needs to be an obnoxious violation – indisputable unprofessionalism or brazen insubordination.

When all of *that* concludes, I'll go in front of the licensure review board; my lawyer, Jenny McCoy from the TEA, will represent me. I thought this entire process would last 18 months. But here we are, two years later, with no end in sight.

Being in that first hearing was very difficult. To have them throw back at me every mistake I'd made, in a very public setting – and, you know, I've delivered some doozies of lesson failures – it's hard on you. It was tough to sit there and have them ask me, during my testimony at my August hearing, "Well, why did you do this? Did you not think about this?" It started to make me question, "*Should* I have been fired?" Their whole case is, "You did all of these things wrong, so we don't trust you to teach our kids anymore." I walked out of there feeling really beat up and defeated.

I probably did make some mistakes. But that's why we reflect and change. I don't think I've ever delivered a perfect lesson yet. But to not even be given the opportunity to change or given a chance for some professional development, like, "Listen, if you're gonna teach about racial equity and racial justice, we're gonna send you to this professional development workshop so you can become better." I would have loved to do something like that because I was doing this all on my own.

Lawmakers who pass legislation like the "Divisive Concepts" bill use words like "indoctrination": "Teachers are indoctrinating students with *The 1619 Project* or the writings of Ta-Nehisi Coates." But isn't the *absence* of those perspectives also indoctrination? The classroom may be the only place where students like mine, who live in an all-white, evangelical, conservative environment, have an opportunity to hear these perspectives. People misunderstand the purpose of a class like my course on contemporary issues. I'm not trying to convince my students to believe one way or another; I want them to be able to understand that there are differing viewpoints and that those perspectives deserve consideration, too. We have to live with one another, so let's do our best to try to understand each other.

As difficult as all of this has been, had I not been fired, I wouldn't be friends with Kyla, the poet whose poem I showed. She's like my sister now. We talk or text almost every day. I still wish I had my job, but having her as a friend ... You know, it would be hard for me, simply because of my friendship with Kyla, to look back on this as a total loss. I tell her all the time, "I can't imagine a life where I didn't know you."

JULIE MILLER
I FEEL LIKE I LIVE
ON THE VERGE OF TEARS.

"I was removed from my position as a high school librarian for fighting back against all the book banning in my school district in Florida."

live in Crazy Town – Florida. In March 2022, the state legislature passed three bills. One, House Bill 7, the Individual Freedom Act, dubbed the "Stop W.O.K.E. Act" by Governor Ron DeSantis, pertained to how students are taught about racial issues – in other words, don't teach anything that can make a white kid feel bad about being white. Another, House Bill 1557, determined that we're not supposed to discuss gender and sexuality with K-through-third-grade kids. Later, that was expanded to K-through-eighth grade and, then for high school. It's incredibly limited what can now be discussed when it comes to gender and sexuality.

And finally, there's House Bill 1467. This one has to do with making it easy for people to demand the removal of library books and instructional materials, while simultaneously making it harder for school personnel to purchase and use these materials. Now, what a lot of people don't realize is that library books and instructional materials are two separate things: instructional materials are used in the classroom; library materials are on a shelf in a library. With instructional materials, you have a captive audience. If I'm a teacher in a classroom and I say we're going to read this novel, then that's a captive audience. But a book in a library is self-selected, a free choice for the reader. But they're not distinguishing between the two in the bill because they don't know what they're talking about because they're legislators, not educators.

The law states that a district's school board is responsible for all instructional materials used in a classroom, made available in a school library, or included on a reading list. It mandates that every district must have a policy regarding objections by parents or residents of the county, and that every item in our library catalog must be publicly accessible on our school website.

Florida's obscenity law, Statute 847.012, prohibits the distribution of "any book, pamphlet, magazine, printed matter, however reproduced, or sound recording" that contains "actual or simulated sexual intercourse, ... masturbation, or sadomasochistic abuse; actual lewd exhibition of the genitals; actual physical contact with a person's clothed or unclothed genitals, pubic area, buttocks, or, if such person is a female, breast with the intent to arouse or gratify the sexual desire of either party," as defined in Statute 847.001.[1] It goes on to prohibit "explicit and detailed verbal descriptions or narrative accounts of sexual excitement, or sexual conduct and that is harmful to minors."[2] Lastly, it mandates that all library materials must be suited to student needs and appropriate for the grade level. The law also requires school librarians, media specialists, and other personnel involved in the selection of library materials to complete a training program on developing our collections before they're permitted to review and select age-appropriate materials and library resources.

The Florida legislators passed the law, and then they were like, "Okay, now make a training program." So, the Florida Department of Education (FLDOE) put together a workgroup, but the way they did the whole thing was very weird. In May, they put out a call to superintendents to recommend media specialists for the workgroup, and then they selected six from around the state, most of whom were district media specialists (who basically oversee all the school media specialists in that county). A few months later, they put out a *second call* to superintendents, asking them to recommend *parents* to serve in this workgroup because [*sarcastically*] it's very common for professionals to be trained by parents. What's *awesome* is that two of the four parents who were selected to serve in this workgroup are leaders of Moms for Liberty chapters. I learned from a trusted source that they self-nominated; they just e-mailed the chancellor or commissioner of education or whoever and they were approved. Meanwhile, a child psychologist and a retired principal were *turned down*. People who are actually knowledgeable about what is being discussed were turned down.

The two Moms for Liberty women have essentially held the workgroup hostage. All of the workgroup meetings have been crazy, with the media specialist members outlining proper selection and weeding processes while the Moms for Liberty members are hellbent on focusing the entire training on so-called "porn." Over and over, these two moms have tried to get ridiculous stuff included in the training, like photos of illustrations or text from books that they consider to be pornography, in order to demonstrate that school libraries are *filled* with porn. They want *their* definition of pornography to determine what is allowed and what's not. Basically, they believe that *anything* sexual *at all* should not be in any school libraries. Thanks to this rhetoric, school districts fear putting anything beyond "taking off clothes" in high school libraries and "a kiss on the cheek" in middle school libraries.

You can watch the meetings on YouTube if you want to see the tomfoolery, thanks to the Florida Freedom to Read Project. The group is a godsend of a nonprofit started by moms in Central Florida who were not okay with libraries removing books, the closure of classroom libraries, and books with BIPOC or LGBTQ+ characters being targeted. So, they started tracking censorship activity in the state, submitting public record requests to find out who is calling for book bans across counties and what's being removed, and teaching people how to talk and write letters to school boards. They requested the video recordings from the Florida Department of Education Library Workgroup and posted them on YouTube.[3] In the most illuminating video segment, the FLDOE's general counsel explains the Miller test for obscenity to the workgroup, making it clear that an illustration in a graphic novel or the existence of sexual activity in a young-adult book does not automatically classify the work as obscene or pornographic; the work must be considered as a whole.[4] Context is important.

I should note that I believe completely in a parent's right to determine what their child is allowed to read. There's no librarian who's going to say, "Oh, no, I don't believe in parents' rights." But what's not okay is for one parent to determine what *my* child can read or what *all* children in the community can read. That's a bridge too far.

* * * * *

I've been a media specialist/librarian at a public high school of 1800 kids in Clay County, Florida, near Jacksonville, for nine years. Our county has seven high schools, six junior highs, and 30-plus elementary schools. Each school's demographic is a little different. My school is 50 percent white, 25 percent Black, and the rest is made up of Hispanic, biracial, and Asian students.

It's the best job I've ever had. I love teaching, collection development, and working with students. I've got a great book club. Thirty to forty kids show up every month after school on Fridays to talk books. We've got a thriving program going on here. But things changed for me in November 2021 when my principal called me in to say that a complaint had been made about a book in our collection called *All Boys Aren't Blue*.

Groups from outside our community, including No Left Turn in Education and Moms for Liberty, complained to the district about the book. *All Boys Aren't Blue* is a memoir by George M. Johnson, who is Black, queer, and nonbinary. In the book, they describe their first sexual experiences. Their description is explicit, as in – it's detailed; but it's not titillating, which, to me, is the difference between what's acceptable and what's not.

When the principal called me in to let me know about the complaint, she asked if I had read the book. I said, "Not yet, but give me a few days and I will. In the meantime, I'll provide you with the resources you'll need because I know that our policy manual states what to do in case of a book challenge." At that point, it wasn't a challenge, just a complaint. I provided her with the district policy, and we both agreed to read the book.

After I finished it, I came back and said, "I think it's fine. The author gives context for why they're going into detail, which is because many areas of the country have so little sex education happening, and when there *is* sex education, it's always heteronormative. What safer way to learn about what you might expect from sexual encounters than reading about them in a book?" Because who knows what our students are going to learn from their phones, you know? Also, keep in mind that this whole situation preceded HB 1467. It preceded the viral school board meetings and newspaper headlines. I had no clue that we were at the beginning of what would later become a nationwide censorship movement.

The principal said, "Well, I feel it violates the Florida obscenity statute, S. 847, so I'm going to challenge the book formally." I don't know what conversations had been had, but my Spidey senses were telling me that she was receiving pressure from the district to get rid of this book. So, she filled out the form and e-mailed the curriculum council, which comprises the administrators and department heads in the building, and, per our policy, asked for a meeting.

The school curriculum council came together the next afternoon, after school. The principal started by providing everyone with an orange folder that held the Florida state statutes with the highlighted parts about obscenity. Then, she had the *five pages* from the book that describe the sexual stuff, which she read *out loud* to the group.

Then, I spoke. I went through the numerous starred reviews the book had received in professional journals, the awards it had won, a statement from the author to *Time* magazine about why their book is not pornographic, pointing out that it's not written for eight-year-olds but for readers 14 and up, and that it's marketed that way.

I also shared with them the sheriff's office report about recent events in Flagler County, nearby, where a school board member had called the sheriff about the *very same* book and filed a criminal complaint against the other school board members, the superintendent, and the school librarians who had the book in their collections. The detective and the lawyer for the sheriff's office dismissed the complaint because it wasn't a crime. They said, in so many words, "This is ridiculous; stop wasting our time," because, according to the Miller obscenity test, it wasn't obscene.[5]

Finally, I told them, "I disagree with this process because, as of right now, the only people in this group" – of 16, by the way – "who have read this book are the principal and me. You've seen *five pages* of a 300-page book; context is important."

The whole thing was a violation of district policy. At the time, our policy stated that "the school leadership team reviews each request and examines the materials for reconsideration." The word "examine" implies a thorough inspection of a material, which, in the case of a book, implies *reading it* rather than being shown two percent of its contents.

So, this group checked all the boxes, technically, but the review was not conducted in an above-board manner, really. At that point, we voted – it was a blind vote – and it was 14 to two to remove the book. I was devastated by the outcome and angered by the whole process. I felt like I had failed so many people: students who would relate to the book, other libraries and librarians, and the author.

The curriculum council meeting was very difficult for me. I felt like it called my professional judgment into question in front of my colleagues, and it definitely put a strain on my relationship with my principal, which, prior to that, had been very positive, fully supportive.

It wasn't until many months after that, in mid-June 2022, that my principal and I had an informal talk. I told her how awful the meeting was for me and how it made me feel. She said she was receiving a lot of pressure from the district because the district was receiving pressure from these outside groups. She felt she didn't really have a choice in the matter, but that, in general, she's not for censorship.

I let the principal know I'd received a voice memo from another teacher in my school who had heard about what happened at the curriculum council meeting. In her voice memo, she said, "As Christians, it's really important that we are gatekeepers. I really think you should be praying about what books you're putting into the hands of our students. I'm praying for you about that because I know this is a difficult thing." And I was like, "Wow." At the end of the day, this is a public school. This is not a church school. But, also, I'm a minister's wife. My husband is a teacher, but he's also a part-time music minister who plans and leads the music for services at our church. I'm a worship leader on Sundays – essentially a lead singer for the songs played by our band during services. To have my faith called into question and to be reprimanded by another teacher over my defense of *books* was very hurtful.

During our discussion, my principal told me that, earlier that week, someone local had posted a video of herself on Facebook, reading passages from "one of those Court-of-something books." She meant *The Court of Mist and Fury*, the second novel in Sarah J. Maas's fantasy series *A Court of Thorns and Roses*. My principal said, "She read some pretty graphic passages from it and tagged the Facebook pages of every high school in the county that has it in their collection. It's been crazy." I imagine there were comments posted on the video, parents contacting the principals, and that the district had been alarmed as a result.

I knew the series she was talking about. I'd read the first book. It gets a little spicy, but it wasn't beyond the pale. It was within the bounds of what's acceptable for a high-school collection. Not middle school, to be sure, but high school, definitely. However, a few months prior, in the spring of 2022, a public librarian brought to my attention the fact that the series *starts* at a young-adult level but, by the third book, it's full-on *adult* romance. The third book is *very* explicit when it comes to the sexual scenes. And I'm like, [*sarcastically*] "Oh, that's fantastic. Thanks so much, publisher and author, for shifting in the middle of a series from young adult to adult without warning."

The following Monday, based on that librarian's input, I went back – because I had all five books in the series in my collection – and took a closer look at the last three books and decided, "Yeah, these last three books in the series can't stay. These are beyond what we should have in our library (based on our community standards)." So, as a professional decision, I deselected them.

That's one of those things some people get concerned about. "Is that soft censorship?" "Soft censorship" is a term that's used when there's a quiet removal of things. But you have to know your community. A high school in New York or even in Miami may be totally fine with all of the

Sarah J. Maas books whereas, in a very red county like mine, I knew I could not justify having them on our shelves. So, I deselected the third through the fifth books, but not the second one because it hadn't been mentioned. Naturally, the second book is the one they go after.

After the meeting in which my principal told me about the video, I went back to the library to get some things done. I was looking through the shelves to retrieve a book when I noticed an empty space. Sure enough, my three copies of *A Court of Mist and Fury* were gone. So, I went back to my computer and ran a report to see what had been weeded out of my system. Four days prior, those three copies of the book had been deleted by an unnamed person with administrative rights.

I alerted my school administrators. They said they knew nothing about it. I alerted the union; they knew nothing about it. I contacted the district media specialist, the library supervisor for the county, and she *acted* like she didn't know anything about it, though it is likely that she's the one who took the books from my shelves, following an order from our chief academic officer, Roger Dailey, the number two guy in the district.

When the Moms for Liberty or No Left Turn in Education go to the district to complain or threaten lawsuits, they go to Roger Dailey. He isn't in an enviable position. So, after the Facebook video came out, Roger had instructed other district personnel to go to the schools, get the books off the shelf, and delete them from the catalog.

A couple days later, toward the end of June, Mr. Dailey and I had a meeting. He admitted he hadn't followed district policy or procedure. He was just trying to deal with the problem before the upcoming school board meeting, he said. He apologized for how he handled things and assured me he wouldn't do that again. I let him know, "If you had simply reached out to me or any of us, we probably would have made the decision to deselect it based on the material in the book."

At that point, Mr. Dailey got very interested in deselection, a term he had not heard of before. I explained that deselection is when you're taking a book out of the collection because you discover that its contents don't fit your library selection criteria or the collection development policy. It's like, "This was a mistake, and I'm correcting an error." I quoted Maya Angelou: "Do the best you can until you know better. Then when you know better, do better." I told him, "We recognize that some books that may not belong in the collection have slipped through and we're doing our best to deal with them, but it's really not okay for you to come in and take them off our shelves." He said, "Well, I really didn't think anyone would notice until August."

When I left that meeting, my husband told me, "The school board has just put up their agenda for tomorrow night's meeting, and they've got the library policy manual update on the agenda." They were voting on it the next night, June 30, without advertising it first because it was an "emergency measure," they said, to ensure compliance with the new law, which was going into effect on July 1, 2022. I took a look at the updates and saw that they'd taken the reconsideration process and poured weak sauce all over it. It was awful.

The new policy took the challenge from being at the school level, on a school-by-school basis, to the district level. Under the existing policy at the time, if more than one school in the county had a book that's being challenged, it had to be challenged at each school. Under the new policy, whatever the decision is for one school goes for the whole district.

Also, the proposed policy would change the make-up of the reconsideration committee. In the revised language, if you only appointed the required three people on the committee, you could completely leave out a school-based media specialist. You could have the chief academic officer, the supervisor of instructional resources, and a principal, and there you go. That's your three people right there.

Another change in the new policy was that, when a person challenges a book, they don't even have to have read it. Even the reconsideration committee that would vote on whether the book should stay or go won't have to read it! Any citizen who lives in the county can fill out a challenge form online and attach a summary of "objectionable content" found at booklooks.org, a website tied to Moms for Liberty that offers a registry of books with page numbers and lines or paragraphs of "offensive content" in the guise of "book reviews." Someone can use that to say, "I don't like this book!" and the district will say, "Okay, we accept your challenge. We're going to assign this group to vote on the book, we're not going to require you to submit anything saying that you read the book, and we're not planning to read it either."

All these school board policy updates were finalized. They're our policy now. The board made only one change to the new policy based on my feedback: they made it mandatory for one of the people on the committee to be a school-based media specialist.

Within six months of the school board updating its library policy, 102 books had been put on the district reconsideration list.[6] The list is publicly available, even though we media specialists weren't informed early on about the public nature of the list. Many of the books are contemporary titles. There's a lot of Ellen Hopkins books. She writes novels in verse. They're like poetry but they tell stories about social issues like drug abuse (*Crank*), teens impacted by gun violence (*People Kill People*), and human trafficking (*Traffick*). Hard topics. But there's also classic YA novels on our reconsideration list, like Lois Lowry's *The Giver*. *Flowers for Algernon* by Daniel Keyes. Kurt Vonnegut's *Slaughterhouse-Five* is on it. So are *The Bluest Eye* and *Beloved* by Toni Morrison. *The Bluest Eye* addresses the rape of a child; *Beloved*, which won the 1988 Pulitzer Prize for fiction, takes inspiration from the true story of an enslaved woman who killed her daughter in 1856 to spare her from the terror of slavery and sexual assault. There's Marjane Satrapi's *Persepolis*, a stalwart in the graphic novel genre, about growing up in Iran during and after the Islamic Revolution. It's been criticized for portrayals of torture and other acts of violence.

Most of the books that have been targeted for sexual content aren't anything beyond what you'd expect to find in a high school library. But it's not just books dealing with sexual content. If a book talks about race and racism, like *Dear Martin* by Nic Stone; *The Hate U Give*, one of my faves, by Angie Thomas; *Anti-Racist Baby*, a picture book by Ibram X. Kendi; and *Stamped: Racism, Anti-Racism, and You* by Kendi and Jason Reynolds, the conservative activists claim they're about "CRT." Most people who have actually looked into this claim have learned that CRT, or "critical race theory," is only taught at the law school level. There is *no* CRT being taught in K-12. The book banners are just using a catch phrase they learned from social media or Fox News pundits. Look up *Christopher Rufo* and *CRT*, and you'll see exactly how the whole ruse started.

In addition to targeting books touching on race and sexuality, they're attempting to ban books about LGBTQ+ characters. They even object to just the *presence* of LGBTQ+ characters. If we're learning about the queer experience or the Black experience at all, those are the books that are being targeted.

There's absolutely nothing wrong with these books. They just happen to address racial issues. They happen to have a gay kid in them. We're talking books like *Drama* by Raina Telgemeier, which is a graphic novel about eighth graders putting on a play. The big deal? One of the young teens is gay, and there is a same-sex stage kiss, a scripted kiss that's part of the school play.

These folks are using the charge of sexual content to get their foot in the door. Start with the most shocking passages they can find to trigger a response from school districts. Then, once they've opened Pandora's box of challenging books, they slip in all these other books centering non-white or non-straight characters. There are a lot of these groups out there, and they are very organized. In Florida, the big three are Moms for Liberty, No Left Turn in Education, and Florida Citizens Alliance. They're working together, crowdsourcing "book reports" on spreadsheets and websites like booklooks.org. Again, by book reports, I don't mean they give a summary of the plot or anything like that; it's just any sentences or paragraphs they find offensive, sometimes including a profanity count at the end. You can just print these things out as PDFs, go up to the podium at your school board meeting, and say, "I'm here to challenge this book, and here's why."

They try to use the "shock-and-awe" tactic by reading passages to get attention. At the June 30 school board meeting, Bruce Friedman, a new citizen of the community, got lots of attention when he went up to the podium and read a rape scene from *Lucky*, Alice Sebold's memoir. Friedman is the founder and president of the Florida chapter of a far-right group called No Left Turn in Education and, he claims, the parent of a student at my school. When Friedman started to read, the school district's lawyer very foolishly said, "Stop – you can't read that! This is being broadcast and children may be watching; you can't read pornography." I felt like slapping my forehead when he said that. It's like, "That's not pornography! Aren't you a lawyer?" A school board member called for Friedman's mic to be cut off because he wouldn't stop reading. It became news: "Parent's mic is cut off while trying to read porn from library book at school board meeting."

I spoke at that meeting, too. It was the first time I'd spoken at a school board meeting about any of this. I said, "I'm a high school librarian in this county. I'm a mom. I'm a minister's wife. I'm a minister's daughter. I lead worship at church. We're your neighbors. We sit next to you at church. We're not these words that are being thrown around – groomers, indoctrinators, et cetera. There is no insidious agenda at play here. A lot of us have inherited our library collections. Some of these books have been on the shelves for years. I've only been here for nine years, so there are books that precede me, and I buy hundreds of books every year. We can't possibly read every book on the shelves. But when we do see a problem, or when a member of the community identifies what they believe is a problem, then we're going to do our due diligence."

I gave them the example of the third through fifth books in the *A Court of Thorns and Roses* series, telling them how and why I deselected those titles. The school board didn't even stop me at the three-minute mark; I spoke for seven minutes. I felt like it was received really well. Everyone applauded after I spoke, even the Moms for Liberty group and Friedman.

After the meeting ended, I went over and started a conversation with Friedman and our local Moms for Liberty chapter leader. I was trying to build a bridge. I said, "Try to work with us. Be patient with us. This doesn't have to be a splashy go-to-school-board-meetings-and-complain thing." I gave them my school e-mail address. I said, "Talk to me. I'm here to work with you. We work *with* parents, not *against* parents."

Two weeks later, Friedman e-mailed me and Roger Dailey an article from the *Tampa Free Press*, which is not a reputable news source. MediaBiasFactCheck.com places the *Tampa Free Press* at the reddest point along their partisan metrics and gives it a "mixed" review for "Factual Reporting."[7] The article was titled: "Parent Chokes up After Reading Vile Excerpts from Florida School Library Novels." In the interview, Friedman describes himself and Roger Dailey as "two brave men" who are trying to save the children here.[8] The article goes on to say, "He [Friedman] stated that a media specialist for Ridgeview High School" – that's me – "admitted during the June 30 School Board meeting that she had put a book on the shelf because she liked the first episode of a series and had reviewed it, and the second one came out and she was sure everybody would love it and just put it on the shelves. But she didn't read it first." The reporter quotes Friedman saying, "I'm not looking to get gallows built to see her swing. I just want the process to be revised so that she doesn't do that anymore."

I was astounded and very upset. I remember sitting on my couch, shaking, wiping away tears as my husband tried to console me. When I called Mr. Dailey the next day to ask what could be done about it, his response was, "You are under no obligation to respond to that gentleman." I was like, "Okay, but he mentioned *gallows* for *me*," and that was after I'd had a nice, cordial, 45-minute conversation with him at the school board meeting. He *e-mailed* the threatening article *to me*. It was incredibly unnerving.

The only local group who showed concern was the Clay County Education Association, our teachers' union. The CCEA president asked me to form and chair a new committee – a Media Specialist committee – in response to the growing spotlight on district libraries and censorship. My role would provide me with a bit of protection when speaking to people about what's going on because I'm speaking as committee chair as opposed to speaking as a media specialist at Ridgeview High School. In December 2022, I agreed to be interviewed in that capacity by Judd Legum, an investigative journalist for *Popular Information*, an online newsletter published through Substack. He also interviewed Friedman.

When the article appeared in *Popular Information*, the last paragraph read, "The goal, according to Friedman, is to use Clay County library to 'set a good example for what a clean library looks like' for Florida and the country. If anyone gets in his way, Friedman vowed to 'run them over like a dead body.'"[9]

I'm the only media specialist in our county who has spoken up publicly about what's going on, so I'm very much in the crosshairs. Early on, back in the summer, I reached out to our former district media specialist, who's been retired for years. Her daughter is a media specialist at one of the elementary schools in the county. I said, "Things are getting really bad. We need some people who know what they're talking about to reach out to the board about the problems with these new policies. We need people to speak at school board meetings." She said, "I really wish that I could, but I just can't because my daughter still teaches in the school system, and my granddaughter attends school there." I was dumbfounded. I thought, "Okay, so it's fine for me to do it, knowing that my job is on the line?" I'm on an annual contract, so I can be let go or reassigned to a completely different position without reason.* But I can't just stay silent. I speak up because it's the right thing to do.

These kids don't need a sanitized library. They need access to information and to books they enjoy. And they should be able to step into someone else's shoes. Regardless of why these people are trying to exclude these books, they are, at the very least, removing opportunities for students to learn empathy toward people who are marginalized. If you look back over the years, there weren't books available about kids that weren't white, that weren't straight, that weren't cisgender (not that we had that word). All that was available for teens was *Sweet Valley High* and Judy Blume's *Are You There God? It's Me, Margaret*. All kids deserve to see their experiences reflected in books. Do we want them to read, or do we want them just to disappear into TikTok?

---

* Since 2011 in Florida, teachers can be dismissed without cause under Senate Bill 736, known as the "Student Success Act." Those not already on professional contracts (as of 2011) must be rehired annually. Mrs. Miller was on an annual contract because she changed districts in 2009, and a professional contract requires three years of effective teaching in one district.

How is nobody raising this question of "Really? You think library books are the problem? Library books? Have you seen what they can access in their pockets?" School libraries are an easy target. These groups can't go after YouTube, TikTok, or Snapchat because they're too big. There's too much money involved.

At the end of the day, these groups are not the grassroots efforts of concerned parents. This has never been a case of "My child checked out this book from the library, and they brought it home, and I am appalled at what they read." That's not what's going on. At our school board meetings, I've never seen more than eight to 10 people who are there on the side of Moms for Liberty or No Left Turn.

These book-banning groups have very deep pockets because they're funded by conservative political groups. Moms for Liberty, which came out of Brevard County, Florida, has been making a concerted, well-organized effort to mobilize people all around the country to take over school boards. They've just taken over ours.

In Florida, for about 20 years now, legislators have been working methodically to undercut public education. Evidently, their end goal is to privatize education so that they can monetize it. Some of the charter schools in our state are legit schools trying to meet unmet needs in the community, but many are shell corporations owned by legislators or by their fat-cat friends. They would like to see public education collapse entirely so they can make money from private and charter schools: "We're spending $7,000-plus per kid in taxpayer dollars? Every year we're just giving that to public schools to operate? Wow. What could we do with all that money?!"

You wouldn't believe how many people in this community have no idea what is going on. And most of the people who *do* know about it either don't care enough to go to a school board meeting or write a letter, or they're fearful of speaking out because we're in Trump country.

This has only been a problem for a year, but it's been a godawful year. I've had to start medication to treat the stress hives on my neck. I've had to up my antidepressants and add an anti-anxiety drug. I'm losing my hair. My insomnia has gotten worse, and I've gained weight. And, yeah, my blood pressure has never been higher.

I stay in this job for the kids. I'm not going to quit because if I'm not here to fight for the kids in this county, no one will. The lack of action from my colleagues over the last year has made that clear. There are other high school media specialists and junior high media specialists who are outraged, but they're not willing to speak at a school board meeting during public comment time.

In September, I spoke at another school board meeting because we were being blocked from purchasing academic research databases. A month earlier, Roger Dailey had asked the district media specialist to gather information from us about what databases we use, what classes use them, and what content they are accessing. I'm talking about JSTOR, ABC-CLIO, Gale. I said, "I don't understand what the problem is here; the students are accessing peer-reviewed journals, newspapers, and magazines." I provided e-mails from teachers at my school about how their students utilize academic databases and… radio silence. Five weeks went by. Other secondary media specialists and I were getting concerned. Some of our subscriptions were expiring. I was contacting vendors and telling them, "Hey, our district is blocking us; they're just holding onto our purchase orders because we're not approved to renew the subscriptions." All of the vendors were great. None of them cut off our access, but I had to go speak at the school board meeting to explain what databases are and why we need them before the district would unfreeze purchasing.

The day of the meeting, I was co-teaching a research workshop for an advanced class full of seniors, and I had to tell them, "Hey, guys, I just want to make you aware we're not 100 percent sure that we're going to be able to continue having JSTOR and Gale databases for you. You can still access them for now, but I don't know what the future holds." The students were highly concerned because they understood how vital access to databases would be for their papers. Five of them showed up at the school board meeting that night. I didn't invite them; I didn't even know they'd be there. One of the students signed up to speak.

He explained how he needed access to databases in order to meet the requirements to get an IB diploma. International Baccalaureate (IB) is a prestigious academic diploma program, and this student is slated to be this year's valedictorian.

I received a call from the superintendent the following week, letting me know that the database situation would be handled. I wish I could say that he thanked me for bringing the issue to his attention and advocating for students; instead, he expressed disappointment that I had not informed him about the problem directly instead of publicly. I still find it ironic that he was upset with me when it was his colleagues down the hall from him at the county office who didn't keep him in the loop.

Way back in March of 2022, before I had even heard of Bruce Friedman and No Left Turn in Education, the superintendent and Mr. Dailey called all the media specialists and principals together to update us on the new laws and how they affected us. At that meeting, they informed us they were freezing all library book purchasing for the time being. So, we haven't been able to purchase new books for our libraries since March of 2022. This is *still* true, almost a year later. They don't want to hear from us, and when we do speak out about it, they tell us to sit down and be quiet.

* * * * *

Update: December 2023

In June 2023, I received an e-mail from my principal telling me that I was being reassigned from my library position to a classroom position in a subject I had never taught. Despite the horrific stress I had been under for the last year and a half, I was completely devastated. Shattered. I loved being a high school librarian, and I loved my students. I thought I would stay in that position until I retired.

Viewing the reassignment as retaliation for speaking up, I filed a grievance with the county. In the meantime, I chose to accept a position teaching English at a different school, my husband's high school, rather than accept the reassigned position so that I could work for a principal who we knew and trusted.

For nearly four months, the grievance process escalated through several meetings with the union, me, the principal, and the district. In October, we were about to go to arbitration with an outside legal party when, instead, I accepted an academic library job outside of Clay County. It's less stressful, but it doesn't fill that hole in my heart. Some days, I feel like I live on the verge of tears.

Clay County's district reconsideration list has expanded to over 700 titles as of December 2023, with nearly 250 titles being removed permanently and over 200 more titles being limited to upper grades.[10] According to the district, 94 percent of our challenges have come from one man: Bruce Friedman. Oh, and the libraries still haven't been allowed to purchase any new books.

People who ban books never fall on the right side of history. They get mad when we bring up the past, when we bring up Nazis and how they burned books. But it's like, "Well, you know, sometimes the truth hurts."

WILLIE EDWARD TAYLOR CARVER JR.

IF YOU'RE A TEACHER IN THE STATE OF KENTUCKY AND YOU'RE FOLLOWING THE LAW, YOU'RE CAUSING PEOPLE HARM.

"I faced harassment and my students faced threats because we dared to be queer in a conservative school that would not defend us."

'm an advocate for Black, brown, LGBTQ+, Appalachian, and rural students, a poet, and the 2022 Kentucky Teacher of the Year. I'm a professional gay, meaning: I speak to mental health advocates, social workers, government groups, and anyone else who will listen about LGBTQ+ mental health, civil rights, and education issues.

I'm gay as a Belgian duck. I have a husband with whom I have been married for fifteen years and three cats with whom I have lived slightly less time. I grew up in the mountains of Appalachia. In Appalachia, there are hard-working people trying to make it, but hard work is not always enough to make it in Appalachia. To put it plainly: Failure is not an indication of a lack of work ethic in Appalachia and probably not in a lot of America.

What that looked like for me as a child was that despite how hard-working my parents were, there were times when we didn't have basic resources: food, water, and electricity. School was a place where all those things were always bountiful. School always had running water. School always had heat. School always had food. For that reason alone, I always thought the magic within those walls was why I was drawn to school.

Even in kindergarten, I remember feeling like it was magic. Here we were, just a bunch of random kids who didn't know much of anything yet, sitting on a little brightly colored reading carpet, and none of us knew what the "B" sound was. And this person, the teacher, would stand up in front of us and say, "By the end of this day, all of you are going to know the 'B' sound." And we would. If that's not magic, what is?

I remember feeling that the people in front of me, these people teaching the letter B, photosynthesis, and algebra, cared deeply about me as a human being. I remember vividly being a tiny body in those classrooms. I remember thinking, *They see something that I am not yet, and they're willing to feed that so it might grow.* From the earliest moments of my life, I wanted to be a teacher.

I ended up at the University of Georgia. At first, I thought my future as a teacher was going to be at the university level. I imagined myself lecturing at whatever university offered me a tenure-track position. In my dreams, that was always some liberal, coastal place. But then I had a moment where I was sitting in a linguistics course, watching my classmates and my professor talking about the weakening of voiced glottal fricatives or something like that, and I thought, "My sister is smarter than everyone in this room, including me, and including the professor." My sister has a high school diploma. Where we're from, that puts her *above*, in terms of education, a great deal of people. I thought, "Why is my sister not in this room? Why are more people like my sister not in this room?"

That single moment of realization inspired me to make the switch to K-12 school teaching because the real work I wanted to do, that I needed to do, wasn't French linguistics. Whatever I happened to teach, that's just the vehicle. The real work is getting people like my sister into rooms like this one. That meant no liberal coastal cities for me. So, I switched to a master's in teaching and moved to rural Montgomery County in Appalachian Kentucky.

I was proudly and openly gay that entire time. My teaching was my advocacy. I taught French and English in a rural high school for 15 years, and it was a beautiful experience for which I am grateful, the sort of beautiful experience most people might never get to have. I will always recognize this. I saw kids that statistics might suggest aren't going to do great things, but I spoke to them as if they *were* going to do great things and had phenomenal results by just sincerely believing that they were going to do something. After two years, my French students, none of whom had any connection to France, took our assessment, the STAMP Assessment, which looks at holistic skills in the second language.[1] Ninety-three percent of my students were proficient in French.

To my English students, I said, "I see burgeoning philosophers, sociologists, and teachers, so you're going to be writing and understanding research." We were a college course taught in high school. Eighteen percent of my students were writing above the average of on-campus college students two years older than they were. I knew the trick that's not a trick, which is, namely: If you honestly believe, good things will happen.

I ran a positivity group called Open Light, a school club where we invited students to talk about issues they thought we could work on as a school.

One of the first things the students wanted to do was rename the group the LGBTQ+-Affirming Club. I'm very ashamed of the fact that I pushed back. I said to myself, "I'm not tenured. Just saying the word 'LGBTQ+' will likely get me fired." I talked them out of it. Instead, we listed a whole bunch of perspectives, and we threw LGBTQ+ in there, like, "at least you get to exist."

But I felt guilty. The next year, they talked to me again, and I said, "Let's do it." So, we called it Open Light, an LGBTQ+-Affirming Club. It was the closest thing the school had to a GSA.* The students tried to work on positive change at the systemic level. They wanted queer and Black history taught at their school, even though a school in rural Kentucky is not going to do these things, obviously.

---

* According to Wikipedia, GSAs (gay-straight alliances or gender-sexuality alliances) started being established across the U.S. and Canada in the 1980s as community-based or student-led organizations within universities, colleges, high schools, and middle schools to provide a supportive and safe environment for all LGBTQ+ youth and their allies.

So, these students *wrote their own curriculum*. They took turns *teaching themselves* queer history and Black history. It's embarrassing that our children have to teach themselves because people who are paid to teach won't or can't legally teach them. But I was very proud of them because, every Tuesday, these kids would pick whatever topic was interesting to them – "This week we're talking about the queerness of ancient holidays" – and that's how they would decide their curriculum.

Eventually, they caught the eye of Eric Marcus, host of the *Making Gay History* podcast.[2] He interviewed a couple of these students, and they ended up in *Time* magazine, talking about their advocacy around narrative approaches to gay history and their commitment to learning about it.[3]

The school didn't mention Open Light or any of its accomplishments, activities, or initiatives in its weekly newsletter, on its social media pages, or in its e-mails. A history teacher who was an ally shared the *Time* article in her class since no one else would even mention it, and said she was proud of the students. But another teacher mocked the article and read it aloud in front of students in his class in a lisping, feminine voice. When enough of us complained, they suspended that teacher for two days. And from what I understand, with pay.

So, that was the environment. Up until 2016, there was a deal-with-able amount of pushback at my being openly queer, not just because I was doing things that related to queerness. By "pushback," I mean I'd get called into the office on a Friday because a parent was upset that we were reading *As I Lay Dying* by William Faulkner, which had a "cuss word" and the parents "were good Christian people" who were "concerned" that their child "was in class with me." I happen to be Christian, but people would say these sorts of things about me to administrators who took them seriously – because I'm gay. They had already decided what was true about me before I got to speak.

After Trump's election in 2016, though, the dial on bigotry of all kinds got turned up. Suddenly, hatred became protected political speech. When students would say the f-slur, for example, the school would respond, something to the effect of, "Well, they have the political right;

they can believe whatever they want to believe," and send them back to class. When a parent would blatantly say something like, "Well, we don't want our children reading that Black stuff," we would be asked to please pick a white author, and not always just for this particular family but for the whole class and curriculum.

In response, in 2022, I wrote a policy meant to govern the entire school. It was, I thought, a very straightforward policy. It simply said, "If a parent objects to any given reading and the basis of their objection is the identity of the author, then no teacher will be required, against their will, to replace that text."* Because it's a heavy lift for me, morally, if a parent says, "Well, I'm not reading a Jew," and then I have to find a text that's not written by a Jewish person, because that would make me complicit in their antisemitism.

In 2022, the state legislature had passed Senate Bill One (SB 1), which dissolved the powers of school-based decision-making councils that the State of Kentucky had created in the early 1990s in order to give parents and teachers control of the curriculum.[4] The idea was to democratize the curriculum at the local level. The councils were inspired by a judicial decision in a case that suggested Kentucky schools were not being run fairly, and that more parental input would remedy that.[5] Here's how the councils worked: Parents were elected by other parents to represent them. They were voting members, alongside teachers. The councils controlled the curriculum. They were majority teachers, though parents got a say. They were created to ensure that those who had a vested interest in the students at a local level – the parents and the teachers – could prevent outside forces from making too many decisions (though they were still bound by law).

So, the state dissolved those councils in 2022 and gave all those powers to the superintendent. Parents and teachers lost all ability to make decisions. In a place like Kentucky, the good-old-boy system means that the superintendent is likely much more conservative than parents or teachers – and schools lost any and all ways to balance their power. The irony is

* Here's a copy of my address and policy request: https://docs.google.com/document/d/1vSQO-SZVZ5sIAaCgW9oArkhJikvB8jjC-AsP_5j_6t_A/edit?usp=sharing.

that this right was taken from parents under SB 1, which was presented under the guise of being a "parents' rights" bill.

In 2018, though, the majority of superintendents teamed up with teachers to fight Senate Bill 151, which was legislation meant to take away teachers' pensions. Though the bill was passed by Republican legislators and signed by Republican Governor Matt Bevin, it was eventually overturned by the Kentucky Supreme Court.[6] The effect that was felt, then, was more cultural than anything dealing with our pensions: there was suddenly, for the first time in a long time, an example of otherwise conservative, good-old-boy superintendents widely teaming up with educated teachers, mostly women who were moderate to progressive, against Republicans officials.

The superintendents' open support for teachers created conflict between them and Republican officials. And so, by no small coincidence, SB 1, which appeared only a couple of legislative sessions after the pension bill fiasco that caused superintendents to side with teachers and not with elected Republicans, gave additional powers to the superintendents – who were suddenly again on the side of the legislation. SB 1 took power from teachers and parents and gave it to superintendents, who greedily took it. These same superintendents, just a year before, were mostly helpful to teachers. Now, however, they were very quiet in the face of legislation harming students.

That's when things started to become unbearable. It was an assault. Every week, a teacher was crying because they'd been asked to do something they felt was immoral or inappropriate. Banned lessons. Books removed during class. Teachers' social media accounts spied on. A brown student was removed from a class he wanted to be in because white boys *had been bullying him*. To whom could anyone appeal this? A teacher was told she couldn't teach a novel written by a Native American. To whom does she appeal? The councils no longer existed in a way to check the powers of the good-old-boy system.

It is in this climate that I won the 2022 Kentucky Teacher of the Year award (which is conferred at the state level and has nothing to do with local schools). A big gay Appalachian teacher of the year in rainbow glasses who said the words *Black, brown, rural, Appalachian,* and *LGBTQ+* every time he spoke. At that time, a group of conservatives started coming to our school board meetings. People started paying attention to me, and not in a good way. My face, because of my Teacher of the Year award, was on the news. Immediately there was a conspiracy theory online that our Democrat governor had chosen me because I was gay. "How unfair is it that there were so many good teachers, and they've chosen some gay person just for being gay?" someone wrote on Facebook. "Why else would they make the choice in September when it's not even 2022 yet?" The fact of the matter is that they choose the Teacher of the Year on the exact same day every year. But facts don't matter anymore. Not when anger and hatred are the prevailing modes used to understand the world. And they were angry and hateful.

Then, this group of community members connected to a church with ties to Moms for Liberty and a history of extremist views starts coming to board meetings and saying, in so many words, that it's inappropriate for me to be around children. That I'm a groomer. That our LGBTQ+ group, Open Light, is a cult. That I'm leading students into other pro-gay cults. I will admit I didn't hear everything they said because it was so obscene and insane; I shut it out of my mind. Of course, if people believe it, it doesn't matter if it's insane.

The group started going online with the same sort of smears about my being sexually inappropriate. They would do strange things like write out conversations they imagined me having with imaginary students. They would write it as if it had really happened and share it. They would share pictures of me and say I was grooming students. I repeatedly begged the school to intervene. They wouldn't. I told them I was afraid. The superintendent's response was, "Then call the police." That was it.

Things came to a head when the group started sharing pictures of the students who were in Open Light. We're talking 18-, in some cases, 17-year-olds. They shared their faces, their names, and their after-school jobs and suggested that these students were harming other students. That they were grooming younger students at, say, the middle school. It was very unsafe. The police had to get involved because one of the threats was deemed serious. The police had to remove a young girl from her home because they felt the threats were so serious, they couldn't guarantee her safety. I don't know where she had to go, but the trauma of it caused her to eventually leave the state. Other students' parents begged for help and received nothing, not even a conversation with these vulnerable children. One parent shared how scared his child was and then went on to explain the risk of suicide and the need for intervention. The school did nothing. One parent sent a plea to the superintendent: "Please do something." The school did nothing. They eventually decided to pull their child from the school system.

This entire time, I'm working behind the scenes, sending e-mails to the superintendent and calling board members, begging the school to talk to these students, offer them some support, or even just say something nice about them through official channels. They could easily have posted a single comment about Open Light to say what the group really did, but they didn't. I knew that our school had a Bass Fishing Club, but only because the school posted *once a week* about the Bass Fishing Club. Open Light existed for *five years* while I was there, and not *once*, as far as I can remember, did the school reference them, not even when they were written about in *Time* magazine, not even when the nation's leading LGBTQ+ historian wanted to talk to them for his podcast. So, at no point did the school intervene on my, or the students', behalf to protect me or the students from this hateful, threatening mob. That was the hardest part for me.

Later that year, another queer teacher, someone I'd worked with in Kentucky in my high school – in the same department – and who'd been targeted multiple times for similar reasons, wrote me to say that she'd been suspended and wasn't allowed back on campus for the next two weeks. She'd made a TikTok, and there was a cuss word in the song she used. That was it. From what I understand, it wasn't even an open TikTok. She had a private account that was only accessible to her friends. None of that mattered. Despite how benign the TikTok was, despite how common the song is, and despite the fact that the account was set to private, the school labeled her as unfit to be around students. Plenty of teachers had social media accounts – accounts referencing drinking, cursing, and even containing jokey sexual innuendo. But none of those people had to worry – they were straight, white, and Christian. My friend was queer.

There came a moment when I realized: I can't go back to a situation where, soon enough, there'll be laws asking us, in effect, to harm students. I can't go back to a situation where I am hounded by this district that, every day, in some new way, is trying to harm me or my students. And I can't go back because my very presence is putting these students in danger.

It was a lot to wrestle with. Part of me thought, "Am I running away and abandoning them or am I doing the right thing?" But my presence was making people share students' private information. So, I decided to leave.

I can't imagine a world where I'm ever in public education again. I don't think public education is a good choice for queer people these days. I would tell any young queer person going into teaching, "If you're doing this, think of it as military service." We need people like us to show up for a few years and fight. But you can't make this your life's calling. It's simply not a good choice in terms of mental health: no one is strong enough to put up with the sorts of problems they'll face as a queer person and be able to be mentally healthy.

It's a very sad place to be. I worry about these kids every day because I know the statistic, according to a 2022 Trevor Project survey, that school is where students felt safest.[7] Thirty-seven percent of queer students felt that home was a safe and supporting place, but *55 percent* felt that school was. That same survey reminds us that trans students feel less safe than LGBTQ+ students in general in both places. By making schools unsafe places, we're effectively doubling the suicide rate in certain communities. We're doing this in communities that are already among the most vulnerable to depression, anxiety, and suicidality.

* * * * *

The day I realized I couldn't go back to school I was sitting in a hotel room in Washington, D.C. The Teachers of the Year were meeting the president. It was the day before I was supposed to meet President Biden.

The Department of Education had encouraged me to create a Twitter account. I didn't have any social media before then. So, I signed up and got something like 200 followers. I mostly tweeted encouraging things about education. But on this day, the day that my friend had called me to say she had been suspended over a TikTok, something in me just broke. I felt so very alone, so very tired. I tweeted something like, "I'm a proud gay man. I'm the 2022 Kentucky Teacher of the Year, but I'm exhausted, and I can't do this anymore. I'm sorry."[8] I was so tired.

Then, I fell asleep. I had planned on getting a massage and having a day alone in D.C. before everyone got there. When I woke up, there were 55,000 responses to that tweet. Among them was an invitation to come testify before Congress.

I went back to D.C. in early May and testified before the United States Congressional Committee of Civil and Human Rights about what was happening at my school. After that, I basically couldn't move without a lawyer. My superintendent e-mailed me to say something like, "We're very concerned that someone working at the school may have violated your Title IX rights. We would like you to meet with this independent third party." I showed the e-mail to some friends with legal connections, and one of them said, "That's not an independent party. Do not respond to this." What was sad and almost funny is that my congressional testimony cited *verbatim* e-mail exchanges, only without referencing names – so the idea that the school needed to investigate anything was ludicrous. Whatever this "third party" the school hired was doing, there was plenty of evidence to suggest that it wasn't to care about my rights. An investigation suggests an inquiry for evidence to discover the unknown. This information was widely known. For my part, I didn't need an investigation to believe that the school didn't care if my or my students' rights, dignity, or safety were violated. I had seen evidence for years, particularly the last one. I had learned that I had no reason to trust this investigation and every reason to believe this was some new tool to harm. I took the advice of the friend and remained silent.

After I spoke before Congress, however, one of the many lawyers was like, "Now, you can speak." But one piece of advice they gave me was, "You need another job before you resign, not just for financial reasons, but because these homophobic people are going to twist whatever happens. If you don't have another job, they're going to say that you resigned out of guilt or that you did something wrong. Sadly, that's how the world works." Two days later, I started a new job at a university as an academic advisor. I resigned from Montgomery County High School in eastern Kentucky, where I'd taught for 15 years.

Once my situation had risen to the level of Congressional attention, I knew I needed attorneys. When the school didn't act in response to these random people attacking me, I said, "Okay, I need help." I didn't know if I was going to need to sue the school. It was the invite to Congress that made me reach out to a legal team.

I'm a member of the American Federation of Teachers and during all of this they were incredibly supportive. So was Dr. Marty Pollio, Superintendent of the Louisville School District, which is in Jefferson County, not located where I am now, but in the most open-minded district in the state. One of the sweetest moments that year was so unexpected you couldn't have made it up. Someone texted me and said, "You need to be watching the Jefferson County board meeting." I was like, "Why would I watch that?" I was in Montgomery. Dr. Marty Pollio was in Jefferson, where Louisville is. The next text doubled down: "You need to watch it." So, I turned it on, and the superintendent is doing his monthly state-of-the-schools thing. He says, "I'm supposed to do this report, but instead, I'm going to read an op-ed written by a Mr. Willie Carver." So, he read my op-ed in the *Northern Kentucky Tribune*,[9] and at the end, he said something to the effect of, "Willie, I don't know how much they're paying you at Montgomery County, but I guarantee you I can pay you more. You have a job here Monday if you want it." I felt like the pretty girl in the movie, and there's a boy holding a boombox over his head, like in the '80s movie *Say Anything*, beckoning, "Come over here, please."

I considered moving to Louisville to work with this superintendent at Jefferson County Schools, an open-minded district. However, I realized that even liberal districts are not safe, even if they make overt signaling to the contrary. A queer journalist asked me about this. I almost felt he was frustrated with me, like, "Why didn't you move somewhere else?"

I said, "The legislation's coming. I mean, we're already in a situation where racist parents have some control of our curriculum, and that's going to harm African American students." Florida had already passed its "Don't Say Gay" law.* I knew that if I was stuck in the classroom and one of these bills took effect, I'd have to walk out of the classroom. If you abandon the classroom, you lose your license to teach. It came down to that.

As a teacher, you're only as safe as the legislators controlling the classroom allow you to be. In the past, there's been lots of legislation pointed at harming teachers. The attacks have always been about pensions, about teacher unions – taking money and power and a collective voice away from teachers. In SB 1, we saw legislation that for the first time was targeting *students*, at least indirectly, by effectively making it impossible, under the rubric of opposing critical race theory, for African American history to be taught truthfully.

This anti-CRT approach will have a clear effect on students and make it much easier for parents who are, say, racist or homophobic, to challenge materials. SB 1 forces teachers to teach from a conservative standpoint that blames African Americans for the discrepancy between their experiences and those of white people, claiming that anyone who is poor is choosing to be so because everyone in America has an equal chance to succeed. The bill concedes that "the institution of slavery and post-Civil War laws enforcing racial segregation and discrimination were contrary to the fundamental American promise of life, liberty, and the pursuit of happiness" but goes on to say that "defining racial disparities solely on the legacy of this institution is destructive to the unification of our nation."[10] This is something I know to be false based upon not only my life experience but upon countless sociological studies from the past century. The bill is forcing teachers to teach one perspective – one that the legislators who wrote the bill know – or should know – is wrong.

---

* Florida's House Bill 1557 constrains instruction on gender and sexuality in all grades. In part, it states that "Classroom instruction by school personnel or third parties on sexual orientation or gender identity may not occur in kindergarten through grade 3 or in a manner that is not age-appropriate or developmentally appropriate for students in accordance with state standards." Classroom conversations and counseling services related to gender identity and sexual orientation are also prohibited.

SB 1 also requires the teaching of 24 texts, some of which are quite long, the reading of which will dominate the history curriculum and leave room for little else. Seventy-five percent of these texts were written by white men. Only a single text, "The Declaration of Rights of the Women of the United States," written in 1876, was written by women, and it focused on women's rights. Of the few texts written by people of color – and only by men of color – all are about slavery or the Civil Rights Movement. The required texts view non-white, non-male people only through the lens of struggle while demonstrating the agency and creative power of white men. Neither LGBTQ+ people nor Native Americans were given a voice at all. Governor Andy Beshear would go on to veto this Bill, stating that this list "excludes the full spectrum of diverse voices that make up our history" … and that it "tries to police classroom discussions on topics such as race."[11]

The legislators would go on to override his veto, making this white supremacist approach to history the law of the land in my state.

There are other caveats of that bill that are clearly tied to fears that conservatives have about what progressives and liberals do. Things like, no teacher will tell a child that they're completely defined by their race, or that schools can't require stereotyping, or force students to engage in political views against their will. But I really don't care about those sorts of things because no one's doing that, and they shouldn't be.

Senate Bill One got me involved in politics. We were fighting back pretty hard. Before then, I didn't do much outside of voting. When SB 1 was in the news, I started going to meet with senators and representatives to try to get some clue as to what was happening.

After reading some house or senate bill being voted on that day, I met with a senator to say, something to the effect of, "Hey, are you aware that this particular bill that you're voting on today has a caveat that says that if any teacher is anxious about teaching anything, they don't have to? Have you thought about the repercussions of this? Any teacher can now refuse to teach anything that even touches on African American history. Any teacher could refuse to talk about religion, even if it was part of a standard required for their curriculum area."

It was obvious that this senator hadn't read the bill. I watched the bill go to a committee where it was obvious that *no one* who was voting had read the bill. One member of the Republican senate committee stood up and told everyone in the room that all of the teachers' unions were in support of this bill, which was a blatant lie because I knew teachers were unhappy with it. For the first time, I saw, "Wow, even the legislators don't know what's happening." That bill passed a committee that had not read it.

This year, we knew – had known, a year before – what was coming in the 2023 spring legislative session. There was already talk about Kentucky's version of the "Don't Say Gay" bill being the most destructive in the country. I saw the writing on the wall; I knew it was going to pass. I knew it was going to be brutal. It was.

They released that bill, Senate Bill 151, our state's anti-LGBTQ+ education bill, at 11:00 p.m. to go into committee the next morning and be voted on at 11:00 a.m.. There was a 12-hour window for anyone to read it. I stayed up that night, tweeting journalists who were there, asking them, "Hey, can you show us what this is," trying to get an advance copy of it.

I was so scared for these vulnerable LGBTQ+ kids targeted by the bill, kids around the state who were just like the members of Open Light for whom I had been fighting for years, that I went into my home office the next morning and said, "We need some amendments to protect them." I didn't know what I was doing, but I knew how to Google. So, I Googled "amendments," looked at how they were worded, and just wrote two amendments and sent them to everyone I knew who was in the building – every representative, every advocate, every parent protesting with a sign begging to be heard. I don't even know who put them up, but both of those amendments were voted on as the first two proposed amendments.

The first version of Senate Bill 150 would have allowed teachers to misgender students.[12] My two amendments would not force any teacher to do anything that goes against their personal beliefs.[13] We thought, if you're already giving teachers the right to misgender, then let's at least give teachers the right not to be *forced* to misgender. My other amendment to Bill 150 was that if a teacher was using a pronoun that a trans student's parents didn't want the teacher to use, the school would accommodate the child by moving him, her, or them to another class. The bill was already giving teachers the right to misgender – so I knew that basing the bill on the child's right wouldn't work. The idea was that in those cases in which a parent wanted their trans child's pronouns respected, and the teacher went against their trans child's pronouns, then the school would try to move the child for safety to a teacher who respected the parents. I thought some Republicans might be on board for "parents' rights" or, at the very least, not want to vote against them.

I wrote that amendment because I've worked in districts that would *intentionally* pair a trans student with an anti-trans teacher. They move trans kids into an anti-trans teacher's class to punish them for being trans. Many of my previous evangelical, white, conservative administrators thought that being LGBTQ+ was a sinful choice and they were angry over the "misbehavior" of it – and would want (1) to punish it, and (2) to "correct" it through misgendering.

Of course, the Republicans on the senate committee voted against both my amendments, which is ironic because my proposed amendments are based on a "conservative" principle: "Let's give individuals the power to choose." Of course, we have conservatives who might make the counter-argument, "We want parents' rights." But this isn't about parents' rights. If it were about parents' rights, I can point to the anti-trans Senate Bill 150. It *takes away the parents' right* to name their own child. Let's say my child is, like, "Hey, I know that my birth certificate says Greg, but Monica is the name I feel comfortable with." Now, I've been calling my child Monica for 10 years, and we've legally changed her name to Monica. Senate Bill 150 says that teachers have the right to use the name on the child's original, unaltered birth certificate – even if the parents prefer another name and even if the parents have legally changed their child's name. It gives ultimate rights to the school, not the parents, in this particular situation.

The same is true for health care. I have a friend who lost her trans child to suicide. She is a superhuman being. Her response was to take in trans children who are homeless, usually because their parents can't have legal custody of them. For example, if a child's only parent goes to prison or a hospital or is arrested and there's no one else to take them in, the foster system usually kicks in. But many foster parents refuse to work with trans kids, so my friend gives them a home and gives them somewhere they can be safe in an otherwise unsafe and hostile world.

A lot of these children are 17 or 18 and have been on blockers to prevent the onset of puberty, which actually *prevents* them from having to have surgery or even think about surgery because it prevents those secondary sex characteristics from developing. Blockers give them time to figure out what they want to do with their lives. An unintended consequence of Senate Bill 150 is that preventing any of those children from having access to that medication and forcing them to go through puberty *increases* the likelihood they might have to have surgery later. For example, a 17-year-old trans girl who wants to have feminine features might fear puberty because it could cause facial hair and other masculine features to arise. Forcing her to go through puberty makes it more likely that she'll have to have surgery later to undo the changes brought on by puberty. (I want to add that this is just offered as a single example. There is no monolithic experience of being a trans girl or any type of trans person.)

And again, the parent has no say in this. The doctor has no say in this. The more than 30 major medical associations that all believe this is good medicine, that blockers help these children, don't get a say in this.[14] The only people who get a say are the legislators.

That's why I say this isn't about parents' rights. What all of this is about is drumming up as much fear as possible and creating legislation that codifies, legalizes, and weaponizes that fear. In this case, that fear is being used against queer people.

Before this, the far right had abortion. Abortion was the single easiest topic they could use, especially in red states where you might have had a swing voter who would say, "I'm with you on every other issue, but abortion matters so much to me that I'm not going to be with you." Now they need something else. Queers are the new monsters.

It's the same argument, really. The right uses the abortion issue to claim that progressives, democrats, and liberals want to harm children. Governor Andy Beshear is a genius – he's our governor in Kentucky. As Kentucky Teacher of the Year, my advocacy point was standing up for Black, brown, LGBTQ+, and Appalachian students and trying to give them a voice. In the early days of my time as Teacher of the Year, Governor Beshear said to me something to the effect, "What you're doing is very difficult, Willie, because people are being told that people like you are trying to harm their kids, and this gets to the reptile part of their brain. At that point, words like justice, equity, and love don't matter; all that matters is protecting their kids. You're trying to get people to see you as a human being, even if only momentarily. I love what you're doing. I just need you to know it's going to be very difficult."

That's exactly what's happening now. The abortion issue is no longer a talking point that they can use because, in Kentucky, abortion is now illegal; the new talking point is that LGBTQ+ people are trying to harm innocent children. It's the exact same approach, and it has the exact same effect, which is getting people who might otherwise vote for a progressive policy to swing right and vote Republican.

In April 2022, the Republican legislature rewrote the final version of Senate Bill 150 – at lunch, on the last day of the legislative session, while the building was empty. Then they voted on it. It was so very long, with words stricken out and ambiguous sentences, that we had to read it five or six times to even try to begin to understand. I was seated with someone who had a copy of it, and we were reading it as fast as we could. My friend who had lost her trans child, who fostered trans children no one else wanted, was with me. We were reading through tears as we began to realize the implications of this bill: death. Given the fragile mental health of so many LGBTQ+ youth because of constant harassment, this bill would mean depression, hopelessness, and suicide. They voted before we could even finish reading. They passed Senate Bill 150 with an emergency clause, meaning it's an emergency and so must be passed and go into effect immediately without due consideration, including public input. Most bills in Kentucky go into effect on a very specific date, but if they add the emergency clause, then it's immediate. It's pretty common for fascist regimes to use such a strategy.*

Our Commissioner of Education actually resigned because of SB 150, saying he couldn't in good conscience enforce this law because it would be harming children.[15] It's a horrific bill. It bans any trans child from using any facility used by their cisgender classmates – no bathrooms, no P.E. locker rooms – if the facility involves changing, or using the bathroom, or something like that. Even if they're alone in the bathroom, they can't be in it, so if any cis classmate is entitled to use it, they aren't.

It also prevents schools from letting students have access to any mental health resource without first contacting the parents, including even *telling* them about the existence of such resources. If a student is suicidal, the school's not allowed to tell them about that resource without first contacting the parents. So, the bill is deadly.

Then there's also a caveat that bans the instruction or presentation of gender identity, sexuality, orientation, or gender expression – obviously, everyone has all four of those things, so it's not actually, on first glance, about LGBTQ+ people. It presents sex and gender as something inherently sinful, inappropriate, or wrong, and the only people whose gender identity is visible are trans people. The only people whose sexuality is visible are queer people.

We've already seen, across the state, that majority-white schools are choosing to interpret the intent of the law as the ability for schools to out students to their parents if the teacher becomes aware that the student is LGBTQ+ and to entrap the students by not letting the students know of their disclosure to parents beforehand. As I heard multiple people at a school district meeting verify, one particular school district official said, "If these students think they're LGBTQ+, then they need special help and counseling, so we need to trap them early on."

---

* Gordon Silverstein states: extraordinary powers are "invoked as a means of resolving a crisis or protecting a political regime." Gordon Silverstein, "Emergency Powers," Encyclopedia Britannica, accessed November 27, 2023, para. 1, https://www.britannica.com.

Now, I'll give the new law some credit. It *does* say something to the effect that "If a teacher has a reasonable and substantiated suspicion that outing a student would cause the student to become abused or a ward of the state, i.e., homeless, then the teacher does not have to out a student." The bill doesn't actually *require* outing. In fact, it states, "Nothing in this subsection shall prohibit a school district or district personnel from withholding information from a parent if a reasonably prudent person would believe, based on previous conduct and history, that the disclosure would result in the child becoming a dependent child or an abused or neglected child."

Obviously, conservatives don't want schools contacting Child Protective Services (CPS) because parents hate their gay kid. That wouldn't be a good look, politically. But many teachers will find themselves, by virtue of the law (which requires them to answer parents if the parent asks if their kid is gay), in an uncomfortable position. They're given the right not to tell the parents if they think telling them would be dangerous, yet they're not required to turn these dangerous parents in to CPS. The GOP didn't want teachers resigning, so they put this caveat in so teachers don't have to out queer kids – but they also didn't want teachers reporting parents for hating their LGBTQ+ kids since haters are the GOP base.

Nonetheless, some of these schools are forcing teachers to call CPS if they think the parents will harm the child when they discover their kid is trans or queer or whatever. This means that if you're an LGBTQ+ student in some counties in Kentucky and you say out loud to your teacher, "My girlfriend and I were at the movies," so the teacher now knows you're gay, or if the teacher finds out you're trans by hearing your friends use a trans pronoun for you, then they're either going to call your parents or, if they think that your parents will harm you, they're gonna call CPS, to say, "Hey, we're afraid the parents will harm them, but we will need to document that this child is LGBTQ+." Who knows what will happen then?

Once implemented into law, Senate Bill 150 allows every district to interpret the law however they want. In southern Kentucky bordering Tennessee, which has deep south values, they're using the law in extreme ways. In northern Kentucky, on the outskirts of Cincinnati, where we have a pretty big enclave of KKK and Moms for Liberty groups, they're using it to their advantage, too.

As a general rule, however, the Appalachia Region is actually doing pretty well when it comes to *not* using this new law as an excuse to harm children. Jefferson County does a fantastic job of resisting the bill as much as possible in order not to harm queer kids. Fayette County, where Lexington is located, does a *somewhat* fantastic job. I think a queer teacher would be okay-*ish* there.

That said, a single shift in the administration can shift everything about your working life. Let me use myself as an example: in 2010, during my first year of teaching in Montgomery County, I was pulled into an office before the first day of school even started and told, "Oh, you're openly gay." I said, "Yes." A vice principal said, "You will be crucified, and no one will protect you, including me."

The way the Kentucky system works, your first year is an internship. Even if you've completed your KTIP (Kentucky Teacher Internship Portfolio), your degree, and everything, you're not awarded a teaching license until the superintendent and principal sign off at the end of that first year that you've been a successful teacher. The assessment itself is highly subjective. Anyone could look at the same person's performance and come to a very different conclusion. It occurred to me, "I have to go back in the closet for the first time in my life." After that first year, I left and moved to Vermont with my husband for two years. Here, I taught in much more progressive places and had a chance to feel like a free, normal human being whose queerness wasn't important.

Then I got a call from a new administrator at my former school, who said, in so many words, "I've heard your story. I've heard from other teachers what they did to you. If you would ever consider coming back, we want you." I had a wonderful few years with him. Then, they replaced him with a hyper-conservative, anti-queer person whose district policies of erasure and frequent banning of Black, brown, and LGBTQ+ topics and dismissal of their importance created a racist and anti-LGBTQ+

atmosphere. As a result, I was fighting for the kids but slowly realizing, "This is unattainable."

Unless you can look at a school and be reasonably sure that the school isn't going to become hostile to LGBTQ+ people, look at your legislature and be reasonably secure that it's not going to become hostile to LGBTQ+ people, there's really no way to function as a teacher, knowing there's the potential that you're going to be asked to harm students. The question is not, you know, should you be a teacher or not be a teacher? The question is, how do you reconcile what you want to do with what you're doing? If you're a teacher in the State of Kentucky and you're following the law, you're harming people.

* * * * *

Recently, I've been thinking about this a lot, especially in terms of the after-effects of Senate Bill 150 becoming law. I'll give one example. We had a school district that was doing the calling-home-and-outing-students thing. The stats are real: just under 30 percent of trans youth say that they're supported at home. Of those who don't feel they're supported at home, the likelihood that they're going to die by suicide has nearly doubled.[16] Roughly 20 percent of trans youth are sent to conversion therapy and another 20 percent are threatened with it. It's legal in 26 states, and Kentucky is one of them.

The best study that's been done on conversion therapy shows that even if we're looking at 23-year-olds, LGBTQ+ youth who had experienced conversion therapy were more likely to attempt suicide.[17] You are engaging in something that is going to cause someone to die. Effectively, trying to rewrite someone's basic human wiring and making them hate a part of themselves they can't undo makes the person permanently hate themselves – so much so that they may decide to end their lives.

How do you reconcile who you are with what's happening? You can't. I think what a lot of teachers want to do as an out, is say, "Well, I am not a part of this. I didn't do the law." But you're enacting it. It's like saying, "Well, I'm a Nazi who doesn't hate Jews. But I have to be a Nazi to feed my kids, so I'm the good Nazi...." You're not a good Nazi. There are no good Nazis. There can't be. I'm not saying all teachers who don't leave the profession are Nazis. But the conundrum is: the teacher who says, "Wouldn't you rather have me as an ally teacher there, than a non-ally teacher there?" is, in a sense, complicit. If the law's forcing you to act like a non-ally, what's the difference? I don't know that there can be a difference unless you're willing to break the law.

I now work as an academic advisor. I do lots of outside advising, working with groups like Progress Kentucky, the Kentucky Law Project, and Campaign for Our Shared Future. I'd rather my advocacy not be connected to my paycheck, because it frees me to do what I want to do.

What I'm seeing across the state is what I call the Great Resignation, people saying, "Well, my hands are tied." A group I do advocacy work with was working with a journalist who wanted to speak with any teacher in a certain district who would talk. They were assured they'd have complete anonymity – neither their name, nor their gender, nor the school that they worked at, nor the subject they taught would be revealed. Yet I couldn't find a *single* person, not *one*, who was willing to speak out.

I get how difficult this moment is. I've been fighting this fight forever. And now the law is here. I imagine it would be pretty easy, when my superintendent says, "Hey, take down the pride flag" or my superintendent says, "You're going to have to document if a student is LGBTQ+," to say to yourself, "Well, there's nothing I can do." I can sympathize with that.

But there are ways to find joy. Advocacy helps. A good example: on one of my last days as the director of Open Light (or liaison or whatever I was for the kids), right before I went on sabbatical, one of them gave me this box of books. It was a really sweet moment. I was, like, "What are these?" They told me that in middle school, they were all so miserable that each of them would get their parents to buy these books and their parents didn't pay attention to books. This was before the rise of Moms for Liberty and the subsequent legislation and school board fights. The kids would pass all of these LGBTQ+-themed books around and, for a moment, feel normal. These weren't licentious books, just sweet little romance stories, like *Heartstopper*, written for a teen audience. They said to me, "Now that we're here and we have Open Light, we don't need the books; will you find someplace where people could use them?"

I love student initiative, so I said, "Hey, why don't you all think about some ways you can give books to other groups?" They wrote a grant to the It Gets Better Project: they won $10,000. $4000 of that was earmarked for books. They heard about the suicide of an LGBTQ+ student in another school district. They decided that they were going to buy that district $2000 worth of exact copies of every book they had. They were buying them for the students of that district.

We found a local bookstore and a young-adult curator who is familiar with YA books and can create curated book lists. This bookstore even gave us 20 percent off all books so we could buy more books than we'd planned. We sent this list to the school district and said, "If there's a single title among any of the books on this list that you have an issue with, let us know, and we will replace it." We wanted to give them the opportunity to look the list of books over so that we could be sure they would accept all of them.

The district rejected all of them. Every single title.

There's joy in filling the gaps, too. Because school's not the place where LGBTQ+ kids are going to be safe anymore. So, other places have to be. We found a local art center that was ecstatic about the book idea, and we put out a little feeler online, and said, "Hey, we are really excited to have this, the Rainbow Freedom Library. But not every student in the county lives close enough to walk to it. There's some rural kids. We would love to have some funds to help those kids get access to these books." Within 24 hours, we had $7,000 to do this work. We spoke to seven news stations about it.

That reminded me of something RuPaul talks about: other people want you to succeed. Even in this moment, there are lots of people who want these LGBTQ+ kids to have access to these resources, who want good things to happen. They just live in a state where they can't because of gerrymandering or because they have other concerns that cause them to vote in a way that doesn't align with this interest. Over 70 percent of Kentuckians were against Senate Bill 150.[18] But that didn't matter, right? Because corporate interests were involved. Any bill that weakens K-12 education increases the likelihood that people will turn on public education, causing charter schools, which the GOP has been pushing for, to have firmer footing. Charter schools are for-profit corporations; they make money for private investors which donate to the GOP, which then leads a never-ending attack on K-12.

A lot of the advocacy work that I do, these days, is tied to my poetry. The first poem in my book, *Gay Poems for Red States*, is called "Minnie Mouse Car." I was sitting down to write an angry e-mail to my superintendent and this memory came flooding back to me. I remember going into a McDonald's with my mom. My mom ordered a Happy Meal and then asked for the Minnie Mouse toy. The cashier looked me up and down, and then said to my mom, "You're going to ruin him." I watched my mom's face fall; I saw the pain in her face for the rest of this little time we were together in that McDonald's. I remember being ashamed of the toy. I was probably four or five. This memory returned to me from when I was maybe four years old, before I'd started school. That moment – sitting down to write an angry e-mail to my superintendent and remembering that incident – inspired me to write almost every day. Every day a new memory would come. It all started with that.

Toni Morrison says we often have these floods of emotion and it's our body going back to that primal place where something started. I think, from that moment in McDonald's in 1988, part of me knew, "You don't fit in; you're not the same, and you're never going to be." Even right now, I'm flooding back to that moment, remembering the pain of that kid.

I think what that kid is trying to tell me is, "None of this has changed. Where you see beauty, others see evil and ugliness. The things that bring you joy and the things that make you happy, other people are going to try to prevent you from having."

I've been researching queer childhood. A lot of queer people are just lucky to survive it. Those aspects that are most painful, we don't want to revisit. But there are all these lessons that this kid that was me learned so he could survive long enough for me to be here, and I'd tucked them away. Writing my book of poetry was my way of re-learning all those lessons that kid learned so I could get to where I am now.

MISTY L.C.
A WELL-FUNDED, WELL-BACKED PUSH
TO PRIVATIZE PUBLIC EDUCATION.

"I was the recipient of a sabbatical award in 2020 to help create more equitable conditions for all students in schools. Then, school-board candidates aligned with the right-wing culture war spread misconceptions about my work."

This story is about my experience working on a sabbatical award I received during the 2020-2021 school year, where the goal was to promote equitable educational opportunities, which means providing people with what they need to learn and be successful. I was working with my state and local affiliates for the NEA – the National Education Association, the largest labor union in the country. I'm in my 24th year teaching middle-school social studies at a public school in New Hampshire. I've been active in my local union for close to two decades. Knowing that an organization will have your back if problems arise is crucially important, given the complexity and risks of what we do. I started to get more engaged and involved with the NEA around 2010 when I noticed more and more attacks on the teaching profession.

In 2019, I was tapped to join a group of teachers for a conference in San Diego called Leaders for Just Schools. The NEA, with support from the W.K. Kellogg Foundation, brought together teachers from all over the country, along with international participants, who shared the goal of making schools more just and equitable spaces. It was a life-changing experience. I came away from it thinking, "Finally, this is something I really want to spend my professional time on."

In my district, professional development for teachers had been primarily focused on testing and scores. Meanwhile, I've watched students become more disengaged as a result of programs geared toward their perceived weaknesses instead of focusing on making school more joyous, a place that relates to their humanity. The mental health crisis of our students and the problems they were dealing with were losing the spotlight needed to make school more transformative and their lives more enriching.

At the Leaders for Just Schools conference, I met teachers from all around the country and got to hear their stories of what's been happening in their districts and the efforts they were putting into improving the culture and climate of their schools. If the historical climate of the school is resistant to change because there have been too many initiatives that staff could not rally behind, it's challenging to change the school's culture. That attitude becomes institutionalized, locked in. Leaders for Just Schools tries to focus on making school more inclusive and, in addition, more joyous – positively affecting both the immediate climate of the school and, in the long term, its classroom and workplace culture.

People really opened up. By the time you'd finished your first coffee of the morning, people were already crying, sharing meaningful experiences about the state of education, talking about concepts that needed more attention, like trauma-informed instruction, which considers how trauma affects learning and behavior, social-emotional learning, which fosters social and emotional skills; and the importance of bringing the issues of racial and social justice into the classroom, further developing ideas for how teachers and students can embrace fair and equitable treatment of all people.

In San Diego, I experienced a rare professional development that showed basic respect for the humanity of both teachers and students. Most teachers I know feel that there's often a lack of understanding for what we face, working with 100-plus students every day. The conference was a coming together; it allowed for open conversations and teacher-to-teacher connections that nurtured a feeling of respect for our work as educators. It was therapeutic to know that other people are facing many of the same professional challenges and insults I face and to be able to share possible solutions on our own, without school boards, administrators, or legislators deciding for us or without us.

After the conference, I was motivated to do more. I joined the Human & Civil Rights Committee of the state affiliate of NEA. I was ready to do everything I could to build a New Hampshire Leaders for Just Schools movement to further the organization's goals in my state.

At the same time, I realized I needed to learn and to reflect on everything I'd taken away from the conference. Somebody told me, "Hey, why don't you apply for the Christa McAuliffe Sabbatical for exceptional public school teachers? They'll pay your salary for a year-long leave of absence. You'll be able to take on a project that could benefit the public school students of our state." The Christa McAuliffe Sabbatical, which the New Hampshire Charitable Foundation administers, offers the recipient teacher time and funding to explore a self-designed project to enhance teaching in schools. So, I hunkered down over my December vacation, working on the application.

On March 13, 2020, the same day the world was shutting down because of COVID, I got word that I'd been awarded the sabbatical. Many people wanted me to have a solid idea of one thing I would do to solve problems of racism or inequity right at the beginning, but it was not at all possible or realistic to think one lone person had those answers. I knew my learning was going to be a significant component of this. I'd been in the grind for so long that I needed time to step back and get a bird's-eye view of my profession and its impact on so many people's lives.

The announcement that I'd received the Christa McAuliffe Sabbatical was carried worldwide by the Associated Press; longer articles appeared on the New Hampshire Charitable Foundation's website and a free, local newspaper that was easily accessible through its website. The media coverage gave people a general overview of the project and my goals for that year of service. I said that there would be educational equity work and that it would have a racial and social justice component to help students grow to their fullest academic and social potential.

On top of the budget provided by the Christa McAuliffe Sabbatical, I helped to secure a $40,000 grant from the National Education Association to run a summer conference and start my own Leaders for Just Schools effort that following summer. I had a huge responsibility not only to meet that grant's goals and requirements, but also to plan an event for 40 teachers. It was an unbelievable amount of work, but my passion for the project kept me going. Through Zoom, I was able to connect with people around my state and all over the country that summer, networking while sharing my experiences from the Leaders for Just Schools conference in San Diego.

It was eye-opening for me to connect with educators from all over and hear what they had gone through at their schools, in some cases as students and now as teachers. It gave me a better sense of where I needed to put my energy. For example, I met a teacher from another state whose middle school had a jail cell right in their building. So, not even a *subtle* school-to-prison pipeline experience for those kids.* It was used to punish students and to hold them until the local police could intervene. The school environment was unsafe; the cell was the administration's solution to dealing with the problem.

These dismal and dehumanizing discipline practices really shocked me. It's hard to understand why people wouldn't embrace restorative practices that could provide students with a way to solve conflicts and deal with the difficult situations they might face with their peers and teachers.

In a way, the teachers were subject to dehumanizing discipline practices, too. I spoke with teachers from Texas and Florida who were living in fear because they had to get rid of books or restrict what they were teaching. This is their profession. This is how they feed their families, and they have people threatening to investigate them for teaching a particular text to students, and people in certain Facebook groups threatening to

---

* The "school-to-prison pipeline," a concept introduced to mainstream media by the civil-rights activist and attorney Michelle Alexander in her 2010 book, *The New Jim Crow: Mass Incarceration in the Age of Colorblindness* (New York: New Press), refers to policies and practices that, by prioritizing punishment over education, push schoolchildren of color into the criminal justice system.

make it difficult for them to support students and still do their job – people who, unlike them, haven't gone to school to be teachers.

My sabbatical work on educational equity and racial and social justice wasn't risk-free either. There were fearful moments for me, like if I went to a school board meeting, for example, I had to have somebody walk me to my car for my security because of what people said and posted against me personally.

That summer, with the murder of George Floyd and other realities replayed on national television, the country went through a racial reckoning. Racial and social justice were at the forefront of everybody's mind. In the schools, people were more open to discussing the school-to-prison pipeline and ensuring that DEI (Diversity, Equity, Inclusion) programs were getting more attention and funding. DEI encompasses conceptual frameworks intended to promote the full and fair participation in the educational experience of all people, particularly historically underrepresented groups without equal rights.

That meant there was more opposition, more resistance from conservatives. Whenever there's a movement toward racial and social justice, it's always paired with backlash. My project got caught up in the backlash against Black Lives Matter protests and the far-right outcry over what they claimed was the teaching of critical race theory (CRT) in schools. This new conservative outrage began to spread into our community – into our politics, our social media, our school board meetings.

In November 2020, I got a call from a colleague in a partner organization I was working with on the project, who said, "Hey, just wanna let you know that we got a nasty message at the office today. I wanted to give you a heads-up that people are threatening our funding if we continue to support programs like yours. We fully support you; I just wanted to make sure you were comfortable continuing, in light of this phone call," or something to that effect. I said, "Absolutely." I'd never assumed my initiative was going to please everybody.

Fast forward to the end of January 2021. A friend of mine called and said, "Misty, you might want to take a look at the town education page on Facebook," which typically lists school-related posts for the community, by the community. Somebody had posted a flier they'd received in their mailbox. It said, "A teacher in our town, who is on sabbatical, has promised to teach critical race theory, a Marxist ideology, to our students upon her return. Also, she'll be advocating for eliminating grades and lowering academic standards," or words to that effect.

I was like, "Oh, my gosh, I'm pretty much the only teacher on sabbatical." It was obvious that it was me. I was shocked. The flier looked expensive; it was well-crafted – professionally designed and printed. I started monitoring the page, following the discussions as they popped up. I researched the two names on the flier. It was a couple who was running for the school board. The wife in this couple was already a state legislator, so she already had a position of influence, and now she and her husband were running for the school board. (Unbelievably, it's legal to be both a state legislator and a local school board member.)

On the same town education page on Facebook, parents were jumping in to defend me, saying, "What problem, exactly, do you have with her trying to improve as an educator, trying to do something important for her students? She won a major award. Leave her alone. It's twisted that you would do this to her." There was a lot of defense, which was great, but there were also voices supporting the couple and attacking me, though they didn't know me and didn't know anything about my project. None of these people ever contacted me directly, even through my school account.

People criticized my work, saying it would make white people feel guilty about the past or racial inequities. I don't know if it was the right thing to do, but I chimed in and said, "Listen, I'm only just now learning about critical race theory, so if you think that I've promised to 'teach it,' you'd be wrong. I'm just trying to be a better educator for my students, and I won't apologize for that. I wish those of you who have questions had reached out to me directly because I'm proud of the work I'm doing, and I'm always open to talking about it." But the chatter continued, with strange accusations from other legislators aligned with the one who'd sent the flier.

The gist of the accusations was that if I wasn't advocating for CRT, I was advocating for something *like* it, perhaps without even being aware that I was promoting CRT or Marxist ideologies. These people have been known to use their positions of influence to fearmonger about racial and social justice being discussed in school settings. Even though none of their accusations were really about me and the accusers didn't know anything about me, they were making accusations to try to whip up the conservative parents.

Instead of retreating into myself and getting upset about the fact that most of my colleagues were largely silent, not immediately defending me or the work or even reaching out to me privately, I took heart in the parents and community members who stood up for me.

At the same time, I realized I needed to understand what was happening. I discovered that the legislator who had authored the flier was also on the New Hampshire Board of Moms for Liberty. I realized that groups like No Left Turn and The Heritage Foundation were funneling a lot of money into local parent groups involved in this effort to attack educators and public education.

It was also connected to the nationwide patriot education movement to embrace the 1776 Curriculum* from Donald Trump's President's Advisory 1776 Commission, which consisted of conservative appointees, including then-Housing and Urban Development Secretary Ben Carson and Charlie Kirk, founder of Turning Point USA. They claimed their goal was restoring American education to the founding principles of American unity and confidence. Most education leaders I knew in the social studies world laughed at that curriculum when it was released because, from what I remember, much of it was not based on anything seriously academic or well-researched. When Joe Biden was elected, one of the first things he did was eliminate the 1776 Curriculum initiative and take it off the White House website.

---

* For more information on this initiative, please visit "The Hillsdale 1776 Curriculum," Hillsdale College, K-12 Education: An American Classical Education, https://k12.hillsdale.edu/Curriculum/The-Hillsdale-1776-Curriculum/.

I realized I was up against a well-funded, well-backed force with an agenda ramping up in New Hampshire. The legislator in Moms for Liberty was one person also supporting or co-sponsoring a couple of bills, including "parental rights," "loyalty oaths," and one that specifically called for not teaching "divisive concepts." The final version of the unpopular bill, added into the budget to help it pass, was purposefully vague as if to still please the people fighting for the Divisive Concepts Bill and to throw those opposed to it, of which there were many, off the scent. The numbers *against* these bills far outweighed the people pushing for it.

The proposed legislation restricted what teachers could and could not do. Initially, it would apply to businesses, colleges, and public schools alike, but after some debate and conferencing, the legislators agreed it should only affect public schools. Coincidentally, this was happening when we had an un-precedented push for privatization and vouchers such as EFAs – Education Freedom Accounts. These programs divert funds from the public schools for parents to use toward private and homeschooling costs. Even religious education, which could *literally indoctrinate* students.

This effort to privatize education and destabilize the public school system coincided with conservatives expressing extreme opinions about how educators were tackling topics of race and, supposedly, critical race theory in the classroom. Later on, issues related to gender identity took center stage.

Some of the organizations that were trying to privatize education saw this as their moment because a lot of parents were dissatisfied with the experience that their children were having in the public schools during the pandemic. They saw it as a burden on their households. So those trying to privatize education saw parental dissatisfaction over how COVID was handled – the school closures, the mask mandates, the online learning – as their moment to mobilize parents against public schools and toward private education. They moved as swiftly as possible to whip up as much fear as possible about what was happening in the schools.

For example, our Commissioner of Education, who appears to be no friend of public schools and has pushed for the use of partisan materials from PragerU – a collection of videos and documentaries promoting conservative viewpoints that Florida has adopted for its public school curriculum – would post things on his blog like a supposedly damning photo of a poster in a classroom with the word "Socialism" on it. What he didn't say was that it was part of a set of 10-plus economic systems that could be discussed as part of the social studies curriculum in a class that may (or may not) touch on comparative economics. He was part of a growing assault on public education that used social media as its platform, accusing teachers of pushing "alternatives to capitalism." He didn't seem to care that comparative economics had been written into our state standards for as long as I'd been in education.

While all of this is happening, my name is getting brought up every time there's a school board meeting for a while. More community members are starting to ask questions about my sabbatical and make strange accusations concerning my project. For instance, one legislator came up to the microphone at a board meeting and, incredibly enough, started crying, saying, "The people of this town should be aware that the Leaders for Just Schools program is linked directly to Black Lives Matter. I know a lot of people like Black Lives Matter, but they don't realize it's a Marxist organization. I promised my friend, a survivor of the Cambodian genocide, that I would talk about these things publicly." Somehow, my sabbatical was being compared to the Cambodian genocide!

One man, who was part of this group called NH Patriot Hub,* went up to the microphone and said that I was using my time to raise money for Leaders for Just Schools and that this was all financial. He found the link to the Communities for Just Schools Fund on a fundraising website. What he said was totally false. I hadn't even heard of the Just Schools Fund as it was not connected to the NEA Leaders for Just Schools.

These people seemed determined to try to crush me and my career. Luckily, the school board told them, "That's not what's happening here. She's on sabbatical working on a social studies project. You don't have to worry about this." That was great, but nobody on the board really explained the work I *was* doing or why I was doing it. Instead, they just tried to shut

---

* For more information on this group visit New Hampshire Patriot Hub, https://www.nhpatriothub.org/.

down or ignore what community members were saying. So, I wanted to go to a board meeting and explain what I was actually doing, but I wanted to avoid making a big spectacle, which is what my critics wanted. Also, my mental health started to take a turn for the worse because I felt conflicted all the time. I wanted to fight back, but I didn't want to give red meat to people trying to get on Fox News. I say that because there *were* some people from my community whose primary goal was getting their 15 minutes of fame on Fox News. Some succeeded and even made up stories about teachers from my district.

I continued to feel more dispirited about the future and about what the outcome of all of this would be. Nonetheless, I pushed on with my summer learning conference and dealt with the lingering issues of the pandemic and the controversy in our state and our country over racial and social justice. We had a wonderful three-day summer learning event, and the teachers seemed energized to connect with each other on issues of educational equity.

Luckily, the couple who put out the fliers about me lost the school board election. Sometimes, I wonder if it was actually a *good* thing that they sent that mailer out because people got to see their values and understand their true feelings about public schools. They had a lot of negative things to say, and people in our community love our schools, for the most part.

To be sure, things aren't perfect. We still have a long way to go when it comes to improving support for mental health and for students who are traditionally marginalized, but I'm not seeing a complete retreat into the type of education that forced me into needing to step away and reflect on my career and what I provide to students day in and day out. That gives me a lot of hope.

My principal and one of the guidance counselors leaned into a new program to bring students, teachers, and administrators together in what was called the Student Change Committee. It tried to empower our students to have a voice in the school community and talk about the things that they thought needed to be changed to reshape post-COVID education at our school.

When it was time for me to give my school board presentation to explain the sabbatical at its conclusion, it was the first time I'd surfaced at these meetings. It was wonderful because my principal put together a group from the Student Change Committee and gave them a chance to speak at the meeting. The students were there not just as window dressing but to give their raw assessment of how they viewed education and their experience at our school.

A conservative news webpage alerted everybody that I was going to be appearing at the school board meeting. After I spoke, someone posted on their page, "Well, she doesn't seem to be teaching CRT based on her presentation, but she's definitely an activist and wants to turn the students into activists." I thought, "Hmmm, that's an interesting charge, considering the people who are going up to the mic time and time again are activists themselves." I assumed they were proud of *their* activism within the community, although they didn't seem to value student activism.

Then, the conservative activists shifted their focus to another teacher at our school because of an art project where students could choose whatever they wanted to create. They focused on one poster displaying a student's concern over reproductive rights and the limiting of those rights. Some people became very vocal; I think they were hoping to whip up more outrage. In response, many parents were strongly supportive, saying, "That's the student's choice. Students are allowed to express themselves. They have First Amendment rights." So, the argument fizzled out.

When I returned to the classroom to teach in the Fall of 2021, it was a bit of a difficult transition because I didn't want to lose the connection I had begun while working with various organizations in the state and around the country. I was now teaching full-time, raising two kids, and volunteering many hours to continue working on behalf of what I felt were the right kinds of school reform efforts – the sort that valued progressive ideas, equitable educational opportunities, and, I suppose, human betterment. Leaders for Just Schools is definitely one of those initiatives. As a mother of a child in a special education program, I understand the benefit of protecting public education where parents have significant rights. I wish I had even more time to dedicate myself to making important changes while protecting access to public education. Still, I am really just contributing when and where I can.

I now spend a lot of time in Zoom meetings at night, connecting with like-minded people who also care about these meaningful improvements to our public schools. I have been interviewed for education-related articles and podcasts. I have spoken at rallies against legislation discouraging teachers from teaching truth or censoring materials just because people don't ideologically agree with their content. In the Fall of 2022, I spoke at a conference titled "Trust the Teachers" at Yale, where Kimberlé Crenshaw also spoke and made an excellent point that the conversation should be less about how we aren't "teaching" critical race theory but more about why it is a truly important study for our society and not feeding into the narrative that it is somehow wrong or divisive. I appreciated hearing many perspectives that day on the dangers of fascism and the frightening parallels to other times in history when teachers were villainized for cheap political points. That is what education is all about – teaching people to solve problems and providing examples for them to become critical thinkers. It was never about indoctrination, despite what many right-wing folks have been accusing teachers of.

We, as teachers, have to hope that the efforts that people made to discredit us backfired and, hopefully, brought all of us, the educators and the community, a little closer together and strengthened our sense of purpose – why we support public schools; why teachers are there every day, showing up for the kids; and why we, as teachers, will continue to educate in a way that benefits *every* young person in front of us.

GAVIN DOWNING
I'M STILL HAVING PANIC ATTACKS BECAUSE OF HOW EVERYTHING WAS HANDLED.

"I'm a middle school librarian who was harassed by my administration for refusing to let my principal unilaterally ban books from my library."

The story begins when I was starting my fourth year at Cedar Heights Middle School, which is part of Kent School District, a suburb about 20 minutes outside of Seattle. It's a very large school district.

I'd been the librarian there for three years and had made the decision to focus on expanding my LGBTQ+ books. We had an active Gay-Straight Alliance club, and there were a lot of students who identified as non-binary. I wanted to make sure they saw themselves represented in the library and knew they were supported. So, I looked into what books I should get.

I was specifically looking for books to enhance our LGBTQ+ material, and the book *Jack of Hearts (and Other Parts)*, a queer-themed Young Adult novel by the gay author L. C. Rosen, came up in my searches as a new book. It was highly rated, I noted, with strong positive reviews in *Kirkus Reviews* and *School Library Journal*, among others. It addressed mature topics, but they were topics that some of our students were dealing with in real life. After reading a number of reviews, I decided to order the book and read it over closely before placing it on the shelves. I read the first few chapters, then browsed the rest of it, paying particular attention to the sexual advice columns that appear throughout.

Jack of Hearts is about Jack, a sexually active gay teen who gets stalked after he writes an advice column for his peers. Any time the characters are about to engage in any sort of sexual activity, the scene fades to black. So, there are no sex scenes in the book, but there is talk about consent, condoms, and safer sex practices.

The advice columns throughout *Jack of Hearts* are based on questions from actual teens. The author worked with sex educators to make sure the answers were medically accurate and that they stressed the importance of consent and safer sex practices (both of which are part of our sexual health education in Washington state). It was my professional opinion that this book was appropriate for some of the students at Cedar Heights on a self-selection basis. Of course, I realized that, eventually, someone would likely challenge the book, but that isn't a reason to exclude a book from the collection, so I made the choice to include it.

I looked at that title very carefully before I decided to include it. It wasn't one that I was gonna recommend for most students since it might not be content they would connect with. But having *Jack* available for those who needed it was an important option, I thought. There is a portion of the student body for whom that book could be lifesaving, and that's why it needs to be on the shelf. If it's not for you, there are literally thousands of other books in that library, and you can just walk on by. I try to have my collection act as mirrors (where students see themselves represented), windows (that open them up to new insights), and doors (that expand their worldviews).

This is a seventh- and eighth-grade middle school, so the students range from 12 to about 14. According to a 2019 Youth Risk Behavior survey by the CDC, 19% of students have had sex by the time they enter ninth grade. Another study, the 2018 Washington State Department of Health Healthy Youth Survey, noted that 17% of 10th graders said they'd had sex before the age of 13. So, the reality is that many of the students at the eighth-grade level are starting to experiment with sexual practices and are developing their attitudes and opinions surrounding such behavior. Making sure that students are exposed to sex education that equips them with the knowledge to make the right choices is really important.*

Unfortunately, LGBTQ+ teens are often left out of discussions in sex education classrooms in the United States because of discriminatory curriculums, ignorance on the part of some teachers and students, or fear of retribution from conservative political and religious activists. They have the right to age-appropriate sex education, and libraries have the duty to serve their needs.

LGBTQ+ young-adult novels such as *Jack of Hearts* offer safe spaces for students to explore sex and sexuality free from the oppression of homophobic peers and adults, which is perfectly in alignment with the role of a school library. Supportive schools and resources relevant to the needs and interests of LGBTQ+ students have been shown to reduce the risk of suicide attempts among adolescents, helping them to grow into healthy adults with positive self-images.

In my state and district, we weren't yet experiencing widespread book challenges, so I wasn't necessarily *expecting* any challenges. In any event, I wasn't afraid of pushback because I'd done my professional best in selecting materials for my library collection.

So, I placed my book order in September. It probably wasn't added to the catalog and everything until early October. On December 9, my principal, Mrs. Erika Hanson, came in carrying the book. She went up to my aide – not to me – and shoved it at her, holding it open to a particular page. She said, "Read this page and tell me what you think about it as a parent," because my aide was a parent of a student in our school.

That's when I stepped in and said, "Well, I'm familiar with this book. I vetted it very carefully. If you feel it's inappropriate, there's a challenge

---

* In regard to sex, I wrote the following in my 20-page response to the (eventual) book challenge for *Jack of Hearts*: The exact statistics for American teens have not been recently formally studied, but Andrie et al. (2021) suggest that "The prevalence of any online exposure to pornography (for 14-17-year-olds) was 59% overall and 24% for exposure at least once a week." As a result of exposure to actual pornography, it is all the more important to ensure that students have access to medically accurate sexual education that stresses the importance of consent and safer sex practices.[1]

process to go through, but I'd ask that you read the book first – in its entirety." She replied, "Well, I'll read it, but if I don't like it, it won't be on the shelf."

The next day, she called me into a meeting. She had a second book, *If I Was Your Girl*, by Meredith Russo, that she wanted me to remove. Then, on January 19, she had a *third* book – *All Boys Aren't Blue*, by George M. Johnson – that she wanted removed. On top of that, she wanted me to bring her all the other books in the library that had "sexually explicit material."

For the record, none of these books contain "sexually explicit material," according to the state definition of the term. For example, *Playboy* or *Hustler* are considered sexually explicit because they contain photographic or pictorial works that are sexually explicit and meant to arouse. I sent her an e-mail quoting Washington state law RCW 9.68.130, which defines "sexually explicit material" as "any pictorial material displaying direct physical stimulation of unclothed genitals, masturbation, sodomy (i.e., bestiality or oral or anal intercourse), flagellation or torture in the context of a sexual relationship, or emphasizing the depiction of adult human genitals," with an exception for "works of art or of anthropological significance."

I added:

> Below, please find all items currently in the library catalog that meet that definition, starting here:
>
> Nothing. I have nothing in the library catalog which meets the RCW's definition.

Jack of Hearts, I told her, wasn't sexually explicit. It was recently challenged in Texas and, even by their particularly stringent standards, it didn't fit that definition.

If I Was Your Girl by Meredith Russo is about a trans girl at a new high school who develops a relationship with a popular boy and is concerned about what will happen if their relationship progresses to the point where he discovers she's trans. My principal felt that this book was inappropriate because, in one scene, a guy puts his hand up a girl's skirt. As she told me in our meeting, there should be absolutely nothing beyond hand-holding and, maybe, kissing for relationships at the middle-school level, as far as she was concerned.

One of the things she mentioned about *Jack of Hearts (and Other Parts)* was that it talks about taking nude selfies and sending them. It treats that as a thing teens do and doesn't make any judgments, although it does talk about being cautious about how you take and send them. She asked me, "How can you have a book that talks about nude selfies when you know that's a problem at this school?" I thought, "Because it's a problem at this school!" It's something these students are talking about and doing. So, let's have some discussions about it in the library.

As I pointed out to the principal, cutting off any references to sexual behavior does not protect students. If anything, it makes them more likely to be victimized. A head in the sand does not stop bullying – and it doesn't protect people from things like being trafficked or from the sexual grooming the far right is so worked up about, these days. If we shelter students from accurate information, they'll just get their information from other sources, such as pornography, which is an unhealthy, distorted choice. There's science on this. There are studies on what causes harm and what reduces harm. When kids have more sex education, they wait longer to have sex and tend to wait to have consensual relations – given the tools to make better choices.*

I brought her books that other people had accused of being sexually explicit: A pregnancy book, a human biology book, the Bible, *Are You*

---

* As I included in my rebuttal to the book challenge: Leung et al. noted that comprehensive sex education (CSE) "incorporates a range of prevention strategies on contraception to prevent STDs and unwanted pregnancy and highlights the importance of safe sexual practice. (...) [CSE] aims to equip students with knowledge, values/attitudes, and skills to facilitate students to make informed decisions that promote sexual health. Research supports the implementation of CSE. For instance, the United Nations Population Fund reported that CSE does not lead to earlier sexual debut or risky sexual behaviors which may be a misconception held traditionally. Rather, approximately two in three CSE programmes evaluated showed reductions in risky sexual behaviors. 60% of the CSE programmes yielded positive effects such as increased condom use or reduced teenage pregnancies. In addition to the aforementioned effective outcomes of CSE, the authors firmly believe that healthy sexuality plays a crucial role in holistic positive youth development. Without healthy sexual attitudes and behaviors, adolescent development will be adversely affected."[2]

There God? It's Me, Margaret. I also told her, in writing, that I would not arbitrarily remove what she might consider "sexually explicit material" or LGBTQ+-related books from our library because doing so would stigmatize "the interests and concerns of students who read and utilize those resources" and stymie my efforts "to achieve inclusive and equitable access for all our students."

That meeting was after school on a Friday, December 10, about a week before we went on break. Let's just say it didn't go well. For most of the meeting, Mrs. Hanson appeared highly emotional. She interrupted me repeatedly, wouldn't give me an opportunity to explain myself, and dismissed my responses. Much of the time, she seemed on the verge of crying or screaming.

I don't want to speculate on the political or religious beliefs of Mrs. Hanson, but I do know, from public records, that she was sharing posts from *The Daily Caller* (a far-right news and opinion website) and articles from conservative sources about why the YA queer memoir *All Boys Aren't Blue* wasn't appropriate for school libraries. She held preconceived notions and found alleged evidence to back them up in my library. Yet she repeatedly insisted, "This isn't a book ban." She made it clear to me that she doesn't agree with book banning and didn't want to be known as a "book banner," but she was comfortable using homophobic-adjacent language and forcing the removal of LGBTQ+ books from our library.

And what's gonna happen is, in removing these books in the guise of protecting students, their educational experience will be incredibly white-washed. The existence, much less the contributions of minority groups – you know, the BIPOC community, the LGBTQ+ community, the disabled community – are all going to be removed completely.

When I brought up the American Library Association's Reading Bill of Rights, my principal said, "Oh, well, that's for public libraries, not for school libraries." I said, "Actually, that's not true." But she had already moved on. She wasn't listening to anything I was saying.

After the meeting, I reached out to union leadership. From that point on, I worked with Christie Padilla. She and I spoke on a daily basis, almost. The union filed two grievances on my behalf, based on how I was treated and my principal's and district's refusals to follow established book-challenge procedures. My union said, "There is a process for this. Your principal can't just remove books because she wants to," even though by that point, she had removed two already.

My principal sent an e-mail in early January, telling me, "Here's what I expect from you, and these are all the things we're going to do." She wanted to set up a panel to advise me on age-appropriateness – composed of members of her choosing, of course. She wanted to be able to remove whatever books she wanted to and make sure I wasn't ordering anything she didn't approve of. When I responded with a very long e-mail that broke it all down and talked about the legalities and the importance of these sorts of books, she never responded.

Then, she pulled a third book that I'd ordered – just pulled it out of the incoming mail without even letting me know she'd pulled it. It was *All Boys Aren't Blue* by George M. Johnson, which is a "memoir-manifesto," as the author calls it, about what it's like to grow up queer and Black. My principal didn't feel it was appropriate because the author writes about losing their virginity!

My union representatives reached out to the district to say, "Hey, she's not following the process," and the district responded, "Well if she's the principal, she can do what she wants." We replied, "Not legally, she can't. There's been a whole First Amendment case that went before the Supreme Court on that." I cited that in my responses, but the district wasn't listening; they were just ignoring the law.

The district was not budging. My principal was not budging. In fact, I started hearing from other librarians in the district that she was reaching out to other principals, encouraging them to do as she'd done, pulling books they didn't want from their shelves.

At that point, after we weren't making any headway and with my union's okay, I took my story to the media. Christie even warned the district that I would be going to the media, and their response was, "No one will care."

There was an article in *Book Riot* and another in the *Seattle Times*. The *Book Riot* article got a lot of attention, particularly after the bestselling author Neil Gaiman retweeted it, saying, "Hey, this is a really horrifying story." Once it went public, the school got a lot of angry phone calls, and the district suddenly changed its story.

The books ended up back on the shelves – quietly. They were returned to the guest teacher when I was out for a couple of days. So, I didn't realize they were back until I saw a statement from the district saying, "The books are still on the shelves." I was, like, "Really?" I took a look in my system and, "Oh, look at that: They are there."

The district reached out and told me, "This is where we stand in the process of the book challenge." I said, "No, that's not where we stand because none of these steps have been followed." Then they claimed that a student had filed the complaints, but they weren't gonna tell me who the student was. The principal was handling it all for the student, they said, which hadn't been their story up to that point. I replied with all of my evidence (at this point, I was keeping notes), and the district finally wrote back, saying, "Well, okay, the process hasn't been followed up to this point, so all of the complaints are being dropped."

Within half an hour of that, I received a *new* challenge to *Jack of Hearts*. This one came from a community member who didn't even have kids who were students at our school. (I later learned she had worked with my principal in the past, and was informed that they attend the same church, I believe.) I followed our district book review policy, which stated that I had to meet with the community member bringing the complaint. From our first meeting, she showed no interest in finding common ground and was not pursuing the process in good faith. She wanted the removal of the book, full stop. This is not normal. Typically, the parent and I should be able to find ways to ensure that the book in question isn't found by a particular student. But, again, this community member didn't have a student in the school.

When this same community member was speaking at the June 8 public hearing on the book challenge, she engaged in personal attacks on me, suggesting that, because I obey library privacy law, I am somehow fostering inappropriate relationships with students. The board allowed this to happen. According to two individuals who saw it, Hanson and her husband were quietly but enthusiastically cheering on the personal attacks.

Using terms like victimizing or grooming to accuse the very people who are trying to protect students is grotesque because it's a one-two punch: it takes people who are protecting students from that kind of predatory behavior and frames them as predators, and it puts them in danger as a result of that accusation. Once you've been accused of endangering students by your boss, no less, you're in danger, and no one is going to protect you, certainly not the district. My home address was provided by the district to this community member, the one who wanted *Jack of Hearts (and Other Parts)* removed. Even now, months after the final decision of the ban, I'm very cognizant of windows and blinds, of doors being locked, of being alone when I'm in my home or the school library. The library was the closest room to the entry of the school and the easiest way for threats to access the building. I talked with security, and they were supportive of my safety concerns.

When the formal book challenge finally came in, I replied to it with a 20-page response that included a letter from the author. My reply is now being used as an exemplar for responses to book challenges. When the principal first brought her concerns about the book to me, I reached out to several of my LGBTQ+ friends and said, "Hey, would a book like this have been helpful for you, specifically in middle school?" One of my friends read the book before answering and, after reading it, said it would absolutely have transformed their life in positive ways if they'd had it in middle school. They wrote a letter to that effect, which I included. I doubt my principal read it – or anything else in my 20-page reply.

The process ended up before the school board. The Wednesday after school let out in late June, the board finally made its decision. They decided not to ban the book. It was a close call. I received a lot of e-mails of support, applauding me for championing LGBTQ+ students and their right to read material reflecting their experiences, but I also received a lot of e-mails that were definitely not supportive, with some demanding that I be fired. On April 20, I received a threatening phone call at 9:13 a.m. from an unknown number that mentioned my wife, Michelle, by name. The individual asked, "Gavin?" and when I replied, "Yes," he said, "It's your turn now. From behind a computer screen, you've insulted some good people. You and Michelle are going to answer to me." Then he hung up. I reported this to the office, then to the union, and then to the police. The police informed me that they didn't consider it a threat as it was too vague.

Abruptly, people I'd been friends with at Cedar Heights Middle School no longer spoke to me socially. They barely spoke with me professionally. Some of them, specifically most of the front office staff, didn't even do that. Instead of communicating with me on a human level, many would be blatantly rude to me at every opportunity. I'd get glares from the staff whenever they saw me. They changed the locks on my office without telling me, shut doors when I came through spaces, and pointedly ignored me when I greeted them in the hall. It became a very hostile working environment. I even heard from another teacher that one teacher read sections of *Jack of Hearts* aloud to the Science department teachers, specifically to get people upset about the book and be against me.

I'll be honest: for most of those last six months, I stayed in my office with the blinds closed as much as I could. I'd come out for the students because they deserved my support, but as much as I could, I'd be in my office with the blinds closed, especially when my aide was there.

I was waking up in the middle of the night, unable to breathe or get back to sleep. I blew through all of my sick time. In all the years I'd been teaching, I'd almost never taken sick time because I loved my job so much. I have a healthy immune system, but I went through so much sick time during those six months when everything was happening that I had none left at the end of the school year. None.

Then, I learned that one of the high school librarians was retiring. I reached out to her and said, "I'm thinking about applying for your position," and she said, "I think you'd be a great fit."

We reached out to the district to see if we could just reallocate me because I was in an unhealthy environment. The district hemmed and hawed for months. I think they were hoping I'd quit.

We have a pretty strong union, thankfully. The district can't really fire any teacher at will. There's a process for any teacher they want to remove, and the union makes sure they follow it. Without union support, mine could've been a very different story.

Finally, after four months of sitting on my request, they approved my move to Kentridge High School. And that's where I've been ever since. I love it. It's so much better. My staff is great. The students are great. My administration there is great. I'm just so thankful to be there.

Even now, though, I sometimes wake up in the middle of the night, short of breath, thinking, "Oh, my gosh, I have to go back there tomorrow." Then I realize, no, not anymore, and I'm able to get back to sleep. But I'm still having panic attacks because of how everything was handled.

It's very rare that a challenge comes from the administration. When a principal does that, it's an attack on students' First Amendment rights. Usually, librarians feel the need to quietly let the principal get their way. The reason I didn't is that I was a teacher in 2008 when my wife was getting her Master of Library Science degree, and I sat in on her online classes when they were talking about what to do when there's a book challenge.

So, when that happened in 2022, I was ready. I sprang into action. Right off the bat, I was already going, "Okay, I need to call my union reps. I need to call the ALA." Being prepared really helped.

If you're doing your job as a librarian, someone *will* be upset with one of the books you've got. If you don't get challenges, you're not getting books that are serving all your patrons. However, these challenges are trying to prevent students from experiencing the world by locking down their definition of what the world should be. There's a lot of evidence to suggest that this is part of an organized attack on public education in general.

I had a lot of community support. There were plenty of parents who reached out to me and were very supportive. The kids almost never spoke about it, but I had some pins that I allowed students to take if they wanted them, little lapel pins that said, "Queer books save lives."

There was a moment in June, just after I had been told that I was going to be able to transfer schools the next year. It was Pride Month. My principal had raised the ally flag in front of the school herself, which is pretty ironic. In my initial meetings with Mrs. Hanson, she said, "This has nothing to do with LGBTQ+. I'm not homophobic." Just like she doesn't believe in book banning and wouldn't want to be considered a book banner, she didn't want others to think of her as homophobic. But her actions speak for her: her abuse of power in demanding the removal of books from LGBTQ+ perspectives is brazenly homophobic.

I had a very quiet student come up to me that month. He was often in the library but didn't say a lot and kept to himself for the most part. He came up to me and said, "Mr. Downing, I just wanted to thank you for always having such *great books* in the library." He put that emphasis there. He looked around to make sure no one was looking.

Then he raised his fist, and he said, "Happy Pride."

In that moment, everything I had gone through was worth it. For that young man to feel safe and comfortable enough to open up to me as much as he did makes it all worthwhile because that's who I do it for. My students.

ELLEN BARNES
I PROMISE TO SPEAK THE TRUTH.

"I'm an 8th-grade social studies teacher living in a state that has a law intended to discourage teaching true history from diverse perspectives."

As of June 2021, we have a new law in the state of Censoria. It was the second draft. The language in the first draft, HB 544 – the "divisive concepts" bill, which didn't pass – strongly resembled passages in the 1776 Project, an initiative of the Trump administration. It was as if they'd pulled the exact wording from it.

HB 544 states that the state of Censoria "shall not teach, instruct, or train any employee, contractor, staff member, student, or any other individual or group, to adopt or believe any of the divisive concepts defined in RSA10-C:1, II." RSA10-C:1, II is an annotation to the law that defines "divisive concepts" as those in which "(f) an individual, by virtue of his or her race or sex, bears responsibility for actions committed in the past by other members of the same race or sex" as well as the belief that "(h) meritocracy or traits such as a hard work ethic are racist or sexist, or were created by a particular race to oppress another race." Teaching topics that "challenge or diminish" the traditional version of American history – in other words, the white-centered, exclusionary narrative – is deemed "divisive." The notion of "unconscious racism or sexism" is divisive, too, as is anything that triggers feelings of guilt or anguish caused by "distress on account of his or her race or sex."

Holding educators accountable for the feelings and emerging awareness of students is unreasonable. Number one, that's incredibly subjective, and number two, it's revisionist history, which is inaccurate and unhealthy. For example, there absolutely *are* connections between post-Civil War Black Codes (laws limiting the rights of Black people), Jim Crow, and our current incarceration rate. If we, as a society, erase the experiences of an entire group of people – their victories, their pain – by denying that those historical events ever happened, then we're not able to look honestly at things that are occurring today.

What HB 544 was really proposing was the idea that you need to censor yourself because there's only one story, one answer, one approach to society. Also, it promotes this disingenuous idea of "color blindness," which is highly problematic 'cause it's an erasure, a denial of people's experiences of everyday life in America. The idea that our identity is attached to our skin color has real force, even though it's socially constructed.

There were severe objections to the first draft, not just from educators but from businesspeople and elected officials as well, because there were very pointed restrictions put on freedom of speech and First Amendment rights. The business community pushed back especially hard on that aspect of the first draft of HB 544, arguing that they couldn't run internal programs and trainings that represent their values, attract the kind of employees they want to have, and articulate how employees should treat customers and still comply with the law. It was government overreach, they said.

So, the law was renamed, rebranded, and, interestingly, they were able, somehow, to attach this new version to the budget package, which put the governor in a very awkward position. He would've had to veto the entire budget in order to kill that provision (although I don't think he would have; he pretends to be a centrist but he's definitely right-leaning). So, the new law, HB 2, passed.

HB 2 says no one can be taught that one group is inferior or superior to another on the basis of sex, race, religion, et cetera. It purports to promote the right to freedom from discrimination in the workplace and in educational settings – which is redundant since there are already laws on the books prohibiting workplace discrimination.

My interpretation of the redundancy is that the passing of HB 2 was part of a national wave of anti-CRT legislation that demonized educators and framed teaching about non-white and nontraditional identities or accurate history as an affront. If you're participating in public education, there's a certain amount of acceptance of the painful realities of American history and American society that's required. People who don't see a purpose behind learning about, say, the genocide of indigenous peoples because they feel it diminishes a more glorified narrative of history resist this. This law gives them the right to claim discrimination when, really, what educators who teach history as it really happened are doing is addressing discrimination and bolstering rights.

HB 2 focuses on the language of equality as opposed to the idea of equity, which raised flags for parents of children who receive special-ed services. Within education, there are protected classes, one being Special Ed children. The way the law is written, it appears to remove the provisions for protected categories of students. You could interpret the wording of this law to argue that a child who *doesn't* receive additional assessment time is "unequal" to one who does, so all children must have additional assessment time. Say there's a student with a specific impairment of short-term memory, we might allow them to have math formulas on a card during a quiz. Another child could go home and complain to their parents, "I never get to have the math formulas. I want the math formulas," though that child is capable of studying the information, retaining it, and applying it. They just may not have done the work. But based on the wording of the law, the parents could file an official complaint, claiming discrimination, because it's "not equal."

With HB 2, we get into a very odd space of what's equity and what's equality. There's a saying that fair isn't always equal. Equality means everyone's treated the same; equity means individuals receiving what they need. Equality is everyone in the school getting a computer. Equity looks like students with dyslexia getting special software loaded on their computers: highly sensitive voice-to-text software that enables kids to use dictation to speak the words instead of writing with a keyboard. Equity is removing obstacles to performing, to engaging, to having the maximum opportunity to learn. In the education world, we're focused on equity, not equality: looking at a student's unique needs and meeting them. Not all children need the same thing.

Many of the things that are good for the student with a learning disability are good for all students, like breaking things down in steps and additional assessment time. While these were created for children with learning disabilities, educators often provide these allowances for all children as part of classroom procedure. So, to be truthful, in my day-to-day experience, the fear about equity and the concern in the law hasn't come up because many of the provisions are common sense approaches that are just good for all students and we do them for everyone. The real problem is a lack of understanding or empathy about the needs of Special Ed kids.

With HB 2, the tricky part is the vague nature of the language, which leaves the law open to interpretation. And when it's not vague, it's erroneous. Parts of the law are written as if educators routinely teaching kids about who is inferior and who is superior is a problem that actually exists. It doesn't.

HB 2 is one more expression of a systemic cultural issue in America of not trusting teachers, assuming the worst intent, and not recognizing credentials and the professionalism of education. There's always this double-speak of educators as professionals while at the same time implying that we're not capable of making classroom decisions. The way our school boards are set up, with community members who think they know how education works because they were once students in a classroom, is part of the problem – because they *don't* know how education works.

As a white middle-class lady in America, I live with a lot of privilege. But, overall, educators have a giant, systemic problem of respect. There's a duality of "education is the most important thing, and educators are heroes." But state or local districts are unwilling to put any money into schools. The amount of labor behind teaching is tremendous, and we aren't paid for all of the time we put into it. The amount of free labor teachers perform is wildly inappropriate. There's very much a culture within education of martyrdom – you know, self-sacrifice. I've been on my own journey of pushing back against that.

I teach Early American History at the middle-school level, so HB 2 was deeply offensive to me. Not only offensive but seriously problematic because it's creating a threat for teachers. Teaching early American history truthfully and authentically requires pulling together multiple narratives that might make people feel sad or bad about what happened in the past. History isn't always a victory story for everybody. Under HB 2, though, if I don't teach it in a revisionist way, I run into the possibility of someone feeling discriminated against. I know teachers who have pulled back from teaching certain topics because they might be accused of doing harm.

One of the provisions of HB 2 is that you can have training around equity, inclusion, diversity, and social, racial, and economic justice, but you can't mandate that training. The logic behind that provision is: "Someone might feel bad." My stance is, "People are not that fragile. Furthermore, we need to ask: What is the moral and ethical dilemma we're really dealing with here?"

It's about race. In the state of Censoria, around 95 percent of our population is white. Within our school district, about six percent of our student population falls under the demographic umbrella of Southeast Asian and Pacific Islander, and about one percent of our students identify as Black or African American.

But despite the whiteness of the state and the tiny percentage of students of color in our district, ours was the first school district in Censoria to write an anti-racist policy. I'm super proud of that. If someone really wanted to get down to brass tacks, it probably conflicts with HB 2, but no one has really put the two together. So, we're doing this strange dance where we're expected to abide by HB 2, but our school board has approved this anti-racist policy, which I often look at as sort of like our Constitution. It's something I fall back on if someone questions why I'm doing something, but, to me, it's also part of my mandate to rise to that policy.

For a long time, we've had policies around identity, particularly gender identity. We were on the leading edge on that front. In that regard, I have it much easier than other teachers in other school districts. Also, I'm very privileged to have district leadership with vision – a superintendent and an assistant superintendent who really support teachers. We've received very specific advice from our district lawyer about documenting difficult conversations and keeping a handwritten record of who said what in a personal notebook rather than in digital form because things that are digitized can become part of an official court record.

Often, though, things feel like, one step forward, two steps back. Take the actions of our commissioner of education, Conrad Bosegeist. We've had a human rights commission in Censorborough for quite some time, where people could file a complaint to receive justice or restitution if they felt discriminated against in the workplace or in an educational setting. But after the passing of HB 2, Commissioner Bosegeist created a shortcut through the Department of Education website to make it much easier for people to document perceived violations of HB 2 and file complaints – which was a very strange thing to do. The purpose of the Department of Education is to put structure and systems behind educators, to provide guidance for administrators and superintendents, and to equip all of us with resources. The fact that they would create, on his initiative, this super streamlined opportunity to destroy careers is the antithesis of what they should be doing.

It felt like teachers were being targeted. It was very alarming because the most severe potential consequence, if the state Intake Coordinator from the Department of Education finds the complaint to be legitimate, is losing your license and, therefore, losing your job. So, there was a big uproar among teachers across the state about that, but Bosegeist's shortcut is still there, undermining the usual process.

In tandem with that, we have one of those fake grassroots organizations. They have different names, like Moms for Liberty, but they're all cookie-cutter groups that are probably getting their guidance from right-wing organizations like The Heritage Foundation. So, a very tiny chapter of Moms for Liberty opened up in Censoria. Just a few months later, Moms for Liberty offered a bounty of $500 for the first family that successfully filed a complaint and proved, to put it bluntly, how racist and terrible public educators are – you know, let's finally out those teachers and administrators who have devious intentions. Which, again, is a fiction. I don't know anyone who would bother going through the hassle of being a teacher if they didn't have good intentions. You can make so much more money doing something else!

I like to make what I think of as good trouble. I have this contact, a producer who worked for National Public Rumble and now works with *Planet Podcast.* On a whim, I texted her the article about this bounty on teachers. Three hours later, she texted me back and said, "Would you be willing to go on the podcast? We'd love to talk to you about it." So, even though Censoria is a tiny state with less than two million people, I was excited to bring a little light to this and, to be perfectly honest, a little shame and embarrassment to these people – because they *should* be ashamed to be targeting teachers like this.

A lot of us in the teachers' union feel that Censoria, because we're small, is being used for target practice; Moms for Liberty wants to see what it would take to topple public education. So, I went on *Planet Podcast* and they wrote up an accompanying article. They had contacted our commissioner of education, and he pretended to know nothing about the bounty. He said something like, "You can't believe everything you see on social media," acting like it was all just a rumor when, in fact, it was 100 percent legitimate. A couple months later, a photograph released on Facebook by Moms for Liberty showed him at one of their events. So, our commissioner of education and that group are connected.

It's bizarre that Bosegeist is head of the Censoria Department of Education. He home-schooled his children. Before his political career, he worked as an auditor and accountant. If he had worked in a school in any capacity, he could provide some insight into public education, but he has no background in education whatsoever. He was the second runner-up in the Republican primary for governor. The Republican governor appointed him to lead the Department of Education as, what many of us suspect was, a consolation prize, something to persuade him to stay in that inner circle and deploy a conservative agenda. It's shocking that a person with no work experience in a school setting is running the

Department of Education. It was cronyism that put him in his position. He's quite clearly not invested in what we educators do and what we're looking to accomplish.

In any event, the Moms for Liberty bounty is still out there, but there have been no successful complaints, which speaks for itself.

But Moms for Liberty isn't our only headache. In 2021, there were public rallies across the country in support of the Howard Zinn Project's "Pledge to Teach the Truth"; I went to one of those rallies in Censoria. The Project is based on the premise that teaching history should help students deal with and challenge ideas deeply ingrained by our culture so that we can overcome racism, sexism, and war. The Zinn Project shifts the perspective of history from the owners to the workers and considers the interests of individuals rather than a "national interest." Educators are morally and ethically encouraged to teach complete narratives.[1] The pledge promotes teaching factually accurate history, warts and all. A couple of my colleagues signed the pledge that summer. It's really just, "I promise to teach the truth."

But a small group of conservatives in our community reframed it as a pledge to be racist and hate white people. There's a couple of blogs in Censoria that pose as news sources, but they're really just rumor mills. One of the sites data-mined the Zinn Project's website and doxxed the people from Censoria who signed the pledge. ("Doxxing" is when you publish identifying information about someone with malicious intent.) Censoria bloggers scoured the list for educators from this state, published the names of educators, and characterized them as willing to "break the law" and "willing to go to jail" for teaching racist ideas. A Censoria high school teacher who signed the pledge was subject to online harassment, threats, and obscenities, which required support from local law enforcement and the FBI. Teachers rely on their professional reputation to establish a relationship, founded on trust, with their community. This smear campaign undermined that trust and put teachers in danger.

After the list became public, a parent lodged a complaint against a teacher with the principal of one of our elementary schools. The parent said something like, "I will not allow my child to be placed in this racist teacher's classroom. I'm outraged. They should be fired." Fortunately, we're in a supportive space so that's not what happened. But it was scary. We were still working on understanding HB 2 and what people could get in trouble for, and that's still not totally clear. Anyway, the school made sure that child wasn't placed in that teacher's classroom, the complaint blew over, and people carried on.

Then, *another* parent filed a formal complaint, using the shortcut link on the DOE website, against a high school teacher who had signed the Teach the Truth pledge. Our school district went through a process, which included a questionnaire. She signed the pledge, but she teaches a subject that isn't in the humanities. So, there's no overlap with the content concerns in her classroom. As a result, she was able to answer "no" to all of the questions on the questionnaire. Ultimately, the complaint was deemed invalid. As it happens, the complaint came from a person who doesn't even have children in our school district.

* * * * *

I'm a little bit privileged because I have a lot of social and professional capital in the school district that I'm in. Nonetheless, I think very carefully about providing a well-rounded narrative in my classroom. What I've doubled down on is the social/emotional lens that I bring to the classroom. I've consciously made emotional safety my primary objective when I teach about challenging topics that may trigger feelings of shame or discomfort. This is the art of teaching where I build relationships between me and kids through non-academic experiences like students submitting a pet photo to share on the classroom screen or "guess-who" questions, such as "What is your fondest childhood memory?" or "What's the worst injury you've ever had?" We learn about each other and build trust.

What educators call the "social-scaffolding" aspect of learning might involve explaining that race is a social construct or reminding students that feeling sad or bad is normal when discussing painful history. We unpack issues around slavery because, logistically, I think the students need to learn about generational wealth or lack of generational wealth and complex questions of freedom. For example, what does it mean to be "free" when you've been denied the capacity to build wealth? But I also remind students that they're not personally responsible for a historical legacy. In adulthood, they can deal with acknowledging how they fit into the historical picture, whether they support the idea of reparations or make a point of supporting Black businesses or whatever. But, right now, they're not capable of taking this on.

The wording of HB 2 has a lot to do with how certain people – conservative white people, if I'm gonna be honest – feel, not what teachers actually do. There seems to be a fictional idea, in some quarters, that some public school teachers relish shaming, blaming, and othering children. While educators who shame children may exist, there have always been laws and policies to protect children from that sort of thing.

What I *actually do* is teach thorough, accurate history while making space for students to wrestle with ethics and their personal stances. This involves asking critical-thinking questions; having students read historical fiction (for example, books that highlight the value African cultures held before exposure to colonizers); using cause-and-effect frames to examine the triggers that lead to larger events (such as the role played by the Kansas-Nebraska Act, which allowed states to determine the question of slavery, in sparking violence that led to a preview of warring factions in the Civil War).

I work hard to foster dialogue. Conversation is the most meaningful learning experience for kids because they're doing the heavy lifting, wrestling with a question, and confronting disagreement. I have my students look at comparative studies of the way different groups report on a historical narrative. For example, impoverished European immigrants who benefited from land grants during the 1862 Homestead Act may not have known of or considered how their settlements were made possible by the corralling of indigenous human beings into reservations. It's disruptive to find out that atrocities occurred to get these grants. I spend a lot of time making allowances for diverse perspectives to be equally true at the same time, while centering the value of humanizing other people.

My students' ability to wrestle with hard truths and confront disagreement is only possible because I make a very overt effort to make it clear that my classroom is a safe space. We spend a lot of time discussing and debating societal norms. I make it clear that we can all respectfully disagree and that it is not my position to tell students what to think, politically. But it *is* my job to teach you *how* to think, and to seek evidence that's legitimate.

HB 2 makes it tough to teach critical thinking and historical truth. Because of HB 2's nebulous language and the lack of guidance from the state, the union pressed the attorney general to provide guidance. That "guidance" amounts to about a page of vague text that mostly replicates what the law says. It's frustratingly unclear, leaving administrators to figure it out at a local level. Someone who teaches 20 minutes down the road from me was told by her curriculum coordinator that when she teaches about enslaved people, she must be crystal clear with kids that it's her *opinion* if she calls it a bad practice. *Yeah.*

We *must* take a stand when it comes to certain topics. When discrimination or someone's humanity is on the line, where are we if we pretend that there's some level of acceptability with topics such as slavery or antisemitism? In those cases, I'm not gonna practice "both-sides-ism."

I just did a lesson around Kanye West and "what is hate speech?" and "what are the limits of First Amendment rights?" Because if I don't address it and kids are wrestling with it by themselves, they may not have the language to discuss and debate it, even though they know where their values are around these issues. Discussing Kanye's antisemitic comments gave them an opportunity to unpack the controversy from a legal standpoint, from a language standpoint, and why people are objecting to things he said. My hope is that they'll walk away feeling empowered. I have to be willing to adopt a moral stance on a question but then allow students to be where they are. I'm not gonna come at them and challenge them. But I would argue it's a moral and ethical failing when we're afraid to take a stance on controversial issues. It creates confusion in the students' minds.

* * * * *

I feel a little ashamed that it took George Floyd and Breonna Taylor to inspire a movement. But it did. We began this work before HB 2, in response to their murders by police. HB 2 and the anti-critical race theory movement reeks of Reconstruction backlash. During "Radical Reconstruction," the pace of social progress was shocking for white Southerners; sharing a statehouse or senate seat with a formerly enslaved class of people terrified many white people. The rise of Black Codes and Jim Crow Laws correlated strongly to a fear of losing power and status. Today, exposing systemic racism also exposes the racial biases of supposedly merit-based systems in our communities. Maybe we haven't actually "earned" all our privileges. I mean, that's what we're dealing with here.

A friend who teaches in a nearby school district wanted to use excerpts from *Stamped: Racism, Antiracism, and You: A Remix*, Ibram X. Kendi and Jason Reynolds's book about the historical roots of racism, which was written for middle- and high-school students. She wanted to use it simply to compare how historical events are framed and described in that book in comparison with standard textbooks that might describe, for example, Lincoln's presidency or the cause of the Civil War quite differently.

Thanks to HB 2, *Stamped* was seen as threatening because it includes often-suppressed details of American history. The students weren't even reading the whole book, just some excerpts. But one of the students who was assigned this book was instructed by their parent to walk out of the classroom when the topic came up or if the book was even mentioned. So, this child walked out of the room and told the front office that they felt unsafe. I have no problem with students interrogating my own authority – students asking me "Why?" – since I should be able to answer their questions. But telling your child to do that as soon as a subject is brought up is dismissive of a reasonable conversation and an intellectually engaged relationship with your teacher and disregards the possibility of mutual understanding. It's unhealthy problem-solving and disrespectful to the learning environment.

I think administrations are unnerved. Many school districts are afraid and worn down. You know, they've been through the pandemic and the emotional trauma that went with it. They don't have the resilience to deal with these sorts of complaints. The very common response is, "Just don't use the book." Like, "We're just not wrestling with this." Also, as a society, we've confused discomfort with tough subjects with the lack of safety. If I had to pick one overarching problem, that's it. We haven't allowed adults and kids to wrestle with dissonance; to ask themselves, "What does that mean?", and then pause for a minute and sit with that discomfort.

ELISSA MALESPINA
I REFUSE TO BE SILENCED.

"I'm a high school librarian in New Jersey who was fired for promoting racially diverse and LGBTQ+ books to students."

'm one of the only librarians in the nation who is also on a school board. There might be one or two others, but I know I'm the only one in the state of New Jersey. So, I bring to the issue of censorship the unique perspective of being someone who is writing the policies against censorship and, at the same time, was censored. It's been a very interesting experience.

In April of 2022, I was working at Verona High School, which is in Verona, Essex County, New Jersey. It's only seven miles from South Orange, New Jersey, where I live and where I'm on the South Orange-Maplewood Board of Education, but it is a world away politically. I'd started at the high school before COVID and had been there for three years.

The COVID lockdown happened in March of my first year in the district. During that time, I ran a lot of outreach to students, including driving books to kids' houses. During my time in the district, I worked hard to build relationships with the students, teachers, and administrators. I never got a bad evaluation, never had any disciplinary actions, or any other indication that anything was wrong.

When it came time for my final evaluation of the school year, at the end of April 2022, I expected to be hired back because, again, nothing had been wrong. Instead, I was told – not in person, but via an e-mail – that I was *not* going to be hired back. In the evaluation, the principal, Mr. Josh Cogdill, said that part of the reason I was being let go was because my book displays focused too much on LGBTQ+ students and racially diverse topics and, supposedly, nothing else. He wrote, "Mrs. Malespina does a nice job with creating collections for displays about equity, specifically regarding the themes of race and LGBTQ+. However, the selections never seem to go beyond those two topics. This has created the perception that the library is about only two things and not necessarily about promoting a variety of different books centered around a variety of different topics." Which was not only false because I'd done a wide variety of book displays, but it was so hurtful of him to say that I didn't make the library a place where everybody could feel like they belonged because I'd worked hard to do just that.

I was completely shocked. I had a full-on panic attack. I was diagnosed with severe anxiety and depression and had to go on medical leave for the remainder of the school year. For a while, I was not in a good place.

I was blindsided, but I started to talk with people. As I did, I began to realize that there was a vocal minority of parents who were against anything related to diversity and inclusion. This group of parents did not want Verona to hire a Diversity, Equity, and Inclusion consultant, but they ended up hiring them anyway. The parents were saying we were teaching the kids "critical race theory," ya know, all the talking points we're seeing everywhere now. They started talking about some of the books in the library, but none of their complaints ever reached my level.

I did a different display every month: Hispanic Heritage Month, Women's History Month, Black History Month, Native American History Month, that sort of thing. Instead of autism awareness, I had a neurodiversity display. You name it, we did a display on it.

Whenever I chose books for my displays, I made sure to pick titles that represented a wide variety of people. So, even though the school was mostly white, I didn't want every display to be a display of all-white books. So, I mirrored the diversity around us. In the nonfiction area, I had books on LGBTQ+ topics, such as *Gender Queer* and *All Boys Aren't Blue*, and I had Art Spiegelman's *Maus* out – some of the books that are now banned. But I also had books about Republicans such as Newt Gingrich and libertarians like Elon Musk and a book on the history of policing in America; all sorts of topics were displayed.

In addition, I always had a banned book display up. I had one sitting in the hallway for a good portion of the year, that year. Another teacher and I did a whole project about reading banned books. Banned books are part of the New Jersey curriculum on the teaching of intellectual freedom in the language arts curriculum, but this group of parents was starting to question the curriculum, too, especially a new course curriculum called *Race and Identity*. Students had the option of taking it, and their parents were getting annoyed with the books chosen for the class – books such as Ta-Nehisi Coates's *Between the World and Me* and *White Teeth* by Zadie Smith. I was like, "The class is about race and identity; what do you expect?"

This vocal minority didn't want any diversity and inclusion books, any race and identity curriculum, or any DEI consultants in the Verona schools. They named themselves the Verona Watchdogs. They started coming to board meetings and fighting against having the DEI consultant, whose role was to suggest changes to the historically all-white, all-straight, cisgendered, mostly male-focused curriculum in order to diversify it. Anyway, that vocal far-right minority didn't win the war. Despite their protestations, the administration hired a DEI consultant. But the principal, maybe to appease these parents, decided to get rid of me. I was not renewed.

In New Jersey, we have a tenure law: you work in one position for four years and a day before you get tenure; if you're a non-tenured teacher, you can be let go for anything. You know, if they didn't like the color of my hair, they could fire me.

I'm on a school board, so I know exactly how firing and hiring works. I knew that, in my case, not much could be done for me. The union wrote a letter to the superintendent and the board, condemning what had occurred, calling it "chilling" and saying this would lead to teachers not wanting to participate in the new DEI initiatives they were developing. Perhaps that's exactly what the anti-DEI brigade wanted: to shut us up as educators.

The only thing I could've done is, I could've gone in front of the board and fought for my position, pleading my case as to why I should have been renewed. I didn't want to do that because I didn't wanna be in a place where they're okay with firing me for my efforts to support our diversity and equity initiative and my commitment to making kids of all kinds, not just white kids or straight kids, feel they have at least one safe space in our school. Because, then, what? I get my job back, but I have to worry about every book I put on the shelves or display. I couldn't live with that; the stress would've been too much. I could have fought. I might have won; I had a good case. But it wasn't worth it.

Let me give you an idea of how horrible the whole process was: they waited till the *last* day – literally, the last day – to do my evaluation. I was out sick because I'd just been exposed to COVID. The principal didn't even call me. He just e-mailed the evaluation to me and said we're not hiring you back. I *still* have never had a conversation with him from that day forward. I never even went back into the building. I just broke down. I had a complete panic attack.

One of the first things I did after finding out was to call my friend and fellow New Jersey librarian, Martha Hickson, who'd also dealt with book challenges and, as a result of the stress, was forced, like me, to go on medical leave. She was like, "You need to go to your doctor to-morrow." I called my doctor, whom I have known for years as a friend, and he took one look at me and said, "You're not okay." I couldn't stop shaking. He's like, "We're gonna up your meds. I'm gonna check on you in two weeks to see how you're doing. You tell me if you wanna go back, but you don't need to be in that situation."

I was expected to go back for the end of the semester, but I just couldn't. I could not get myself to go back into that situation with a principal who'd said those horrible things about me. I felt awful about it because my kids were e-mailing me, asking me why I wasn't in school.

As part of the negotiations for my medical leave, the district tried to get me to sign a non-disclosure agreement (NDA), which I refused to do. They were trying to buy my silence. The trade-off would have been that if I'd signed the NDA, they'd have paid me for the remainder of my time out of school. (I had used up all my medical leave and was out of sick days, but I still had about 10 to 15 days when

I would've had to come in.) So, I said, "No, I'll take the no-pay option, thanks." The NDA would've prevented me from speaking about any of it, ever. I had legal counsel, representation from the New Jersey Education Association (NJEA), and they were like, "Yeah, you're not signing that NDA." They agreed that what happened was wrong but said that, because of how the tenure laws are written in New Jersey, a lawsuit was a long shot.

Ironically, the DEI consultant that Verona hired, who was in the district while all this was going on, recently published a report and it completely vindicated me. I mean, I was bawling when I read it. One, because it was so uplifting to be exonerated of all these trumped-up allegations, but two, because I was so sad for the children, reading about what has happened to them and their feelings since I was forced out. It's heartbreaking.

In the report, the consultant talks about how my library was one of the best spots in the school, how it was a safe spot where the children felt welcomed, and they didn't understand why a staff member wasn't there anymore. The report talked about book displays as something we need to see *more* of. Basically, the consultant told the principal, "What you did was wrong." Here's the exact quote from the section on "library, and other school-wide displays":

> It was noted that the librarians throughout the district worked hard to create culturally responsive, sensitive, and inclusive displays, and these practices are to be commended. It is also noted that the high school library included many books on issues critical to the underrepresented students with differing abilities, cultures, and immigration. Students reported that because of these displays, they perceive the library as a safe space in which to look at literature and have discussions with library staff. It is strongly recommended that the library continue these practices. Others noted that the libraries have also been successful in celebrating important cultural events of students and community members from diverse cultural backgrounds, and it is strongly recommended that the libraries continue and, when possible, enhance these practices.

In contrast, here's an excerpt from my principal's letter, the one that accompanied my final evaluation: "Mrs. Malespina has some relationships with the students. However, by and large, the students do not seem to warm to her." That got me worse than any of the other things he said because I try really hard to make everyone feel welcome in my library and when he tried to say I didn't, I started to believe that I'd failed. But this is what the diversity consultant wrote in her report:

> Many high school students, in particular, noted that they had formed close ties over the years with staff who later left the district. For some of these students, that teacher or staff person was their safe place within the school. Students, particularly students of color and LGBTQ+ students, noted that the changes were not only disruptive to the educational environment but also particularly disruptive to their emotional well-being. These same students noted that there was very little, if any, communication from school leadership about the changes, leaving the students to wonder why their safe person was gone. This lack of official communication to the students also resulted in increased speculation as to the reasons for the employee's departure, and the speculation merely served to increase the anxiety for many students.

After my breakdown, I needed to find a new job. I thought about leaving teaching altogether, but I was so close to the 25 years I needed to retire that it didn't make sense financially. Luckily, one of my friends was looking for a librarian in her district. She knew my work and reputation and took a chance on me. I became the librarian at Union High School in Union, New Jersey. It's a much more diverse district. Very inclusive. The administration is truly supportive, the kids are amazing, the staff is great, and everyone, from my supervisor to my principal to the superintendent, has been encouraging about my initiatives to focus on diversity and inclusion in the library.

After I'd settled into my new job, where the administration had my back, I decided it was time for me to speak out about what had happened, not only because it's a form of therapy but also because I was in a position where I knew I had a platform that many other people don't have. So, I've been speaking out about what happened to me because there's a lot of people who don't feel they can.

A lot of librarians are so scared right now. I've gotten so many e-mails from people, other librarians, some of them my dearest friends, who are going through horrible things but they're afraid to talk about it because they need their job, they need healthcare, they need all these things, and they're worried about speaking out against censorship and becoming targets. They're scared, and I totally understand why. I've gotten death threats. So, I'm like, "Hey, if I can use my voice to help others, I'm gonna do it, and I'm gonna try to do what I can to be there for them if it happens to them."

After January 6, 2021, we started to see parent groups like the Verona Watchdogs rise in their power. I mean, there was always talk, but once the January 6 insurrection happened and Moms for Liberty became more popular, everybody started using the same talking points. The Verona Watchdogs group was using them, too. They look at the 850 titles on the book list published by Texas Republican Matt Krause, they take one line or one picture out of context, and then they use that to say we have porn in our libraries.

While all this is going on in my professional life, I'm also an elected member of the South Orange Maplewood School District. There are nine of us on the school board. We don't always agree on everything, but South Orange and Maplewood are very diverse towns and have always been leaders in the state in terms of diversity in race, religion, and sexual orientation. Then, our school district was targeted by right-wing organizations. We made Turning Point USA's Watchlist. Turning Point is a right-wing hate group that targets school boards that focus on diversity and inclusion. While it's scary to have your name on these hate-group websites, I'm proud we made their list because it tells me that we, as a district, are doing something right.

Nonetheless, I spoke to my school board, and I said, "Guys, we are seeing districts that have parents and community members and even people who don't live in the community coming in and challenging books. Our policies stink. They're old. They're outdated. Our policies aren't gonna hold up if we're faced with challenges. For once, let's be proactive instead of reactive." They said, "Okay, Lis, have at it. You're on the policy committee. Revise these policies however you think they should be."

So, I spent time talking with other librarians throughout the state and tried to craft a policy that dealt with some of the issues we were facing. Our new policy states that you can only challenge a book if you're a student, a parent, or a guardian of a student in the district in order to weed out those community members who don't have a stake in the district or far-right activists like Moms for Liberty, who are going to try to come in and stir things up.

Our new policy talks a lot about inclusivity in terms of not only race but gender, ethnicity, and all that. We talk about the Library Bill of Rights and the First Amendment. We talk about how we in New Jersey have a very diverse curriculum that we must teach in our schools; it includes materials on the Holocaust, the New Jersey Amistad Curriculum (which is one part of our official Black history curriculum, which we're mandated to teach in New Jersey schools), an LGBTQ+ curriculum, an AAPI (Asian American and Pacific Islander) curriculum.

I wrote the policy in such a way that ensures that anyone trying to challenge a book or other resources is gonna have to be able to prove how they don't meet those curriculums. Well, you're not gonna be able to do that because they do. The policies and regulations I wrote are now being modeled by districts around New Jersey and across the nation. I'm immensely proud to be able to provide school districts with policies and regulations that they can use to help combat the rise in book challenges that we're seeing.

Don't think that the right-wing hate groups have left me alone, though. Because I'm a school board member and because I've spoken out about what happened to me, I've gotten death threats. I had to file police reports. I have security at conferences where I speak. I have people that my security at school knows to look out for. I've been called every name in the book and had vicious lies written about me. I have people who have written my employer and tried to get me fired. Luckily, the district and my administration don't believe their smears and baseless claims, but it's hard to deal with. It's all done to silence me, but I refuse to be silenced.

This far-right assault is moving beyond just attacking a librarian or teacher for offering students a book. It's moving towards trying to go after their livelihood and their personal safety by making stuff up about what the person is doing. Because they can't easily attack the book anymore, they're going after the person.

I thought things would get better by speaking out, but the numbers show that things are getting worse. Lots more books are getting banned. Lots more librarians are being called pornographers, pedophiles, and other vile slurs. But librarians are starting to fight back. We must continue fighting these bans because it's not about the books. LGBTQ+ and students of color are already the most marginalized kids in our schools. Taking those books away from them only reinforces the idea that they don't belong. Everyone deserves to feel like they belong, and for many students, the library is the only space in the school where they feel accepted and safe.

MELISSA GRANDI STATZ
I COULDN'T BELIEVE THE THINGS PEOPLE I'VE KNOWN MY ENTIRE LIFE WERE SAYING ABOUT ME.

"I'm a 4th-grade teacher who was threatened and attacked online, then forced out of teaching social studies, after I facilitated conversations and readings about racism and the Black Lives Matter movement with my students."

Everything that happened was during my first year in Burlington, Wisconsin. This is my fourth year teaching fourth grade here. Before moving to Burlington, I taught fourth and fifth grade in Chicago Public Schools. I grew up in Burlington. It's my hometown. I went through the school system, so I knew, coming in, that it's a small, white, conservative community.

I had taken a few years off from teaching to be a stay-at-home mom while I raised my toddlers. I hadn't planned on going back until my oldest was in kindergarten, but after COVID and all the social unrest following the murder of George Floyd, I felt this calling to come back to the classroom. I needed to try to do some good, to do my part to make things better.

One of the principals in my school district called me right before the school year and said, "I need you to come in. We just lost a fourth-grade teacher." She knew that was the grade I wanted. So, I ended up accepting the position of writing and social studies teacher for the fourth grade.

Within the first couple days of school, Jacob Blake was shot in Kenosha, which is about 30 minutes away from us. A lot of kids have family or friends in Kenosha. One of my students had just gone to a dentist appointment there and saw boarded-up buildings, so the kids were starting to talk about the shooting, the protests in Kenosha, the plywood planks covering storefronts.

I was just about to teach my first social studies lesson when I thought, "We need to talk about this." Kids were already discussing it. It's something they had questions about. So, I went home and worked on a lesson. I already had *A Kid's Book About Racism* by Jelani Memory, which I'd bought for my own children. *The Kid's Book* series also includes *A Kid's Book About Feminism*, *A Kid's Book About Divorce*, and many others. They take topics that are hard to talk about and put them into kid-friendly language.

I knew I was going to start with that book and have a conversation on race and racism before going into the Black Lives Matter movement and what had been happening all summer. In class the next day, we had a great discussion.

This was still during COVID, so we had really small class sizes and our kids were broken up into a bunch of different groups. I taught the same lesson five times that day to groups of about 10 kids at a time. The weather was really nice at the beginning of the year, so we sat in a circle outside, where we read and discussed the book.

Maybe 10 percent of the fourth graders that year were students of color, which is pretty high for our district. A few kids in each group shared their family's experiences with racism – you know, uncles' and aunts' experiences – as well as their own. We had a lot of kids sharing, which was really awesome, especially for the first week of school when most kids are still finding their social footing. The kids that were sharing were very excited to talk about what we were discussing. Other kids were upset when they heard some of the stories that their classmates told them. One student of color shared a story about his uncle getting pulled over by the police when he was in Milwaukee, even though he hadn't been doing anything wrong. He talked about how the police treated him –

how they made him get out of his car and patted him down. Some of the white kids were really surprised by that story.

It was obvious that some kids had already had conversations about race and racism at home. One girl raised her hand and said, "Uh, all lives can't matter until Black Lives Matter." It was amazing to hear. It was very powerful. We then had a conversation about the Black Lives Matter movement, how it started, and what they had been witnessing all summer.

I didn't want to have a conversation about the BLM movement solely from my perspective, so I found an article on *TeachersPayTeachers*.com, a website where teachers can post classroom materials for other teachers to access and use in their own classrooms. At the time, there was no textbook that talked about Black Lives Matter. The article I found was a comprehensive, kid-friendly worksheet with facts about the movement – how and when it began, who started it and why, and the goals of a protest generally. The worksheet was created by a teacher. I liked that the article addressed the murders of Trayvon Martin and George Floyd and the protests our country had seen over the summer, putting these events in the context of a bigger circle of protests over the past decade. I could connect that with what we were seeing in Kenosha, asking my students, "How is this similar to what you witnessed all summer long?"

I used that reading with my five student groups to get us started, reading a paragraph, then discussing what they had questions about, using the text as a jumping-off point. Some groups of students only read a couple paragraphs; other groups made it through the whole thing; it depended on where the conversation went. Some groups talked about protests as something that we don't have to be scared of. Some kids brought up Martin Luther King Jr., pointing out that this is not the first time people have needed to protest for their rights and noting that this is the history of what we're living through right now. Students who I had barely heard talk in the first few days of school were raising their hands and sharing their thoughts. They were very engaged and had a lot to say.

One Black student shared some racist slurs he'd been called before. Another kid, one of his white friends, was so upset for him. He said, "Oh man, I didn't know people said that kind of stuff to you." It was really great to see such empathy from nine-year-olds.

When we got up to leave, one of the boys, that same kid who had shared his story about the racist slurs, came right up to me, gave me a huge hug, and said, "Thank you." This is a student who's not super affectionate, usually, so it obviously meant something to him. His mom e-mailed me that night. He rode his bus home that day. It takes him about 45 minutes to get home on the bus. His mom said he sprinted into the house, gave her a huge hug, and told her, "We got to learn about the Black Lives Matter movement at school today!" She said he was just so excited about this, even hours later.

Another student, a Black girl, came up to me and said, "Thank you so much for teaching our class about racism." Many of the students of color made comments about being happy with the discussion. The next day, one student asked, "Are we gonna keep talking about that?" They really did enjoy it.

I left feeling good about everything. It felt like a really good day. That night, when I was giving my kids dinner, my co-worker, another fourth-grade teacher, called me and said, "You gotta get on Facebook. Someone posted something about your lesson, and people are going crazy." The comments were in a Burlington-based Facebook group with 40,000 members that encompassed our and other surrounding communities. Typically, the majority of the posts on the site are about items to buy/sell/trade, but people also post random things happening in the community. During COVID, the group was dominated by a vocal minority who used it as a forum for venting about masks and stay-at-home orders and complaining about the mayor's willingness to follow the mask mandate and ranting about boycotting businesses that followed the mandates.

So, I think they chose to post about me in that group because they knew it'd hit the biggest audience with the loudest bunch of conservatives. Someone had posted a picture of the handout I'd used with "NO" written across it in really big red, or maybe black, letters. That same person posted a comment that said, "This is the indoctrination that's happening at our elementary schools. This was from one of the fourth-grade teachers at Cooper Elementary," which is where I was teaching. Even though it had just been posted, there were already hundreds of comments and reactions. I started reading through the comments. People were saying I was "a Marxist," I was "a terrorist," I was "mentally abusing children," I was "indoctrinating" them.

Like I said, I'm from this community. It's not very big. We have about 12,000 people in our town. I have three sisters who grew up here as well, and my parents still live in the community. We're pretty well known and liked, or so I thought. I couldn't believe the things people I've known my entire life were saying. I only looked for a few minutes 'cause it was too disheartening.

I thought I might get a couple e-mails from a few parents. But I definitely didn't expect a huge public reaction. Because I would've taught that lesson in Chicago and thought nothing of it, I definitely underestimated things.

No one from my administration contacted me that night. I went to school the next morning, and no one talked to me, but I knew that I was going to get in trouble in some way. I walked outside to pick up my kids and saw our superintendent outside, and I was like, "okay, he's definitely here for me." He doesn't just stop by for the morning drop-off. I taught for a couple hours, and then, during my prep, he came in with my principal, and they sat me down. They told me they just wanted to have a conversation, and it wasn't going to be confrontational. They just wanted to understand why I did this. I told them that the kids had been asking about the shooting and protests in Kenosha.

Ultimately, they weren't happy with my decision to teach the lesson, but they didn't reprimand me. My superintendent said, "I wish you hadn't said the words, 'Black Lives Matter.' It's become political; we've never had this many people contacting us about something. So many people have called and e-mailed, we need to make a statement." He asked me to write my own statement to be included in the official response that they were going to send out to everyone in the district.

I spent my lunch hour writing a statement explaining my decision to lead a class discussion on racism and the Black Lives Matter movement. I included information about our class discussion and the resources I used for the lesson. At the end of the day, the superintendent didn't include anything from my statement in his letter. It only included his words and was very poorly written. He said it was an individual decision that the district did not approve of. Teachers are supposed to use material that is unbiased and shows both sides, he claimed, and which isn't controversial or political in nature. He wanted to put out the fire. Instead, he made it so much worse.

After that, I really started getting harassed online. People started posting pictures of me and my kids on social media. They would post the pictures and write nasty things about me. They started a Facebook group about me. It was called Parents Against a Rogue Teacher. The whole point of the group was to get me fired. I had a few friends who were able to sneak into it, and they would send me screenshots. People were starting rumors: that I had been fired from my school in Chicago, that I didn't deserve to be near any children, including my own – all these nasty things. Their big decision was, "Okay, we're gonna go to the next school board meeting. We're all gonna show up, and we're gonna speak during public comments and get her fired." We see this a lot now, but at the time, I had never seen anything like this and didn't know what to expect.

At least three different people posted pictures of their guns on the Rogue Teacher group. One wrote, "I'd suggest everyone use their Second Amendment right. Get a concealed permit. If you aren't comfortable and need some assistance, just ask me. I'll be glad to help." And then others replied, "I'm working on getting mine now!" and "I'm good…. Flavor of the day lol Being a firearms and certified dnr [Department of Natural Resources] hunters safety instructor has its perks."

They made it clear that, with concealed carry permits, they could bring their gun with them wherever they went. They talked about wanting to protest outside of my classroom every day at my school until I left. I tried to distance myself from some of the things they were saying and pretend, "This isn't real." Just to be able to function and go to work every day. I managed to distance myself from most of the threats by thinking of them as muscle-flexing. But this post really creeped me out:

You all do understand that there are other ways that you can show Ms. State [sic] that she is not welcome in the Burlington School District, right? You don't need the school board to fire her. Don't do anything illegal like fire bomb her car or vandalize her house by spraypainting graffiti all over it, (you're not ANTIFA or BLM!). Usually districts have pages where you can contact teachers by email, (or two, or 10), explaining that you don't appreciate her curriculum and that you would like to see her move on to a district that may be more receptive to that kind of thing, like Chicago or Milwaukee. You are all smart enough to figure out where she lives, what her cell phone number is and which social media she is on.

That was seriously unsettling.

When my sisters, parents, and then-husband read the posts, they were very concerned for my safety. They found a crisis manager through a friend who's a judge in Chicago. He wanted me to take a leave of absence from work for a month until things died down, but I didn't feel like that was the right answer. We did other things he suggested. We got motion-sensor lights for our house and alarms on our doors so that if a door was forced open, a loud alarm would go off in the house.

Together, we wrote a statement that I posted on my Facebook and Instagram pages, along with two pictures of some of the hateful messages people had sent me, so that people in my circle would know what was going on. And then he had me go off social media to minimize how visible and accessible I was.

I tried to talk to my superintendent. I said, "I need to make a statement. I don't feel like you made a statement on my behalf, so I need to say something." He advised me not to say anything, not even to the parents of the kids in my class. He didn't want me to make any type of public statement; he said it sounded defensive. So, I didn't, and things just got worse.

Luckily, I'm part of the Burlington Coalition for Dismantling Racism, an anti-racism group in my town. A friend of mine, a Black woman named Darnisha Garbade, started the coalition. She has a blended family of Black and white children. When she saw the way her Black children were treated compared to her white children, she started working with the district, saying, "You know, my kids are experiencing all this racism. What can we do?" She worked with them for years and nothing was happening. After a couple of years, Darnisha found that the district wasn't really doing anything to change things. So, four or five years ago, she founded the coalition with a local Black pastor and a white couple who were pastors at another church in our community. I wasn't one of the founding members, but I'm now one of the longest-active members. Our goal is to make Black people in Burlington feel welcome and safe in the community.

At first, we focused on the school district because, at the time, they claimed there was no racism of any kind in the district. It didn't exist. They would say that a racist incident was "bullying" or call it something else. So, we had zero reports of any racist incidents, even though Darnisha had been fighting for her kids for years and saying, "Hey, this happened … and then this happened."

We went to school board meetings, we worked with the school to create an anti-racism policy in the school handbook. We filed complaints for families of color because a lot of people don't understand how the complaint process works in school districts. We host community events like Juneteenth and "nights of understanding," where teachers or speakers who are knowledgeable about Burlington's history teach about our multiple stops on the Underground Railroad, Frederick Douglass's lecture in a church in Burlington, and our town's history and abolitionist history.

Eventually, Darnisha and the Coalition, along with the ACLU, filed complaints with the Department of Public Instruction, asserting that reports of racism weren't being handled appropriately. She won. The DPI said our district was a hostile environment for students of color and put our school on probation. The district had to make a plan to train teachers and it had to create an equity committee.

So, I had some people in my corner. They started trying to get some public support for me, getting people to send e-mails and make phone calls on my behalf, addressing our superintendent's language in his letter.

Right before the school board meeting, the superintendent approached me. We had another meeting, and he made it clear that he'd realized the error of his ways. The language he used was terrible, he admitted. I think a lot of the families of color in our district had told him how harmful and offensive his words were and how hurt they were by them. Our district had recently hired the National Equity Project to help us work on equity because it has been an ongoing issue in our community.* So they called him out: *what you said was not good.* He told me he regretted his choice of words and was going to put out a new statement that was much more supportive. I waited for that statement. It never came.

Finally, a reporter from a local newspaper reached out to me. At first, I said, "No, I don't wanna talk to you" because that's what I was told to say. But finally, I'm like, you know what? They're not doing anything to help me; I'm just gonna do it. I need some support at this school board meeting. I need people in my corner. So, I agreed to an interview, and it made it onto the front page of our local paper right before the school board meeting. At least I was able to tell my side of things.

I think that article and the support of the Burlington Coalition for Dismantling Racism really helped. The school board meeting had about 300 total people there. It had to be moved to our school gym because it was too big. We had about two hours of public comments with people lined up to go talk into the microphone and share.

It started off with people who were against me, yelling. They were angry. A police officer came in 'cause someone wouldn't give up the microphone. But then we started to have a lot of people in support of me

---

* The National Equity Project is a national education reform organization that works with school districts to address leadership development in education in order to address systemic bias, such as racism, classism, and language bias.

come up as well. By the end, it was at least 50 percent, if not more, of the people in support. It felt really good to leave there and be like, okay, maybe our town's not as terrible as I thought.

At the end of the meeting, the school board made a statement. It said, "A teacher doesn't deserve to be fired for this. She is going to remain employed."

I thought it was over. But some local stations in Milwaukee picked it up, and the controversy spread beyond our community. I started to get hate mail in my Inbox and social media messages from people from all throughout Wisconsin – Green Bay, Madison, Appleton, etc. I continued to get harassed, to the point where even my then-husband started sleeping with a baseball bat next to his bed. One of my sons' bedrooms was on our ground floor, in the front of the house, and we had to move him into his brother's room, which was upstairs, because we didn't feel comfortable with him there.

It got really bad. Our school district started to be targeted by hate crimes as well. Someone came to my school and wrote "Black Lives Don't Matter" and the "N" word in the woodchips on the playground. The kids couldn't go outside for recess because the police blocked off the playground. A new middle school was being built in the district, and someone came in and spray-painted the "N" word on the floor. Things were escalating.

My school resource officer, a city police officer appointed as a liaison for the school district, told me to go to the police. But the young male officer who met me there was rude and said that the screenshots I showed him didn't add up to harassment. It wasn't "enough." He wouldn't take my statement. I had gone all these weeks, through all this stuff, and I had never cried. And then, that day, I started bawling.

At the time, my dad was a city alderman and close with the chief of police. He reached out to him and told him how I was treated by the officer. The chief told me that I should definitely come back in, and he would have a different officer take my statement. On this second visit to the station, I met with the female school liaison police officer who had originally told me to go in, and she took my statement. She was much more empathetic and helpful. The police said they would "keep an eye on" one of the more vocal members of the Facebook group, and they tried to increase police presence in my neighborhood, but that was about it.

Around the same time, I called my assistant superintendent and set up a meeting. I told her, "I had to go to the police, and I wanna document this with you as well. You guys have done nothing to support me. You have done nothing to speak out on my behalf. If something happens to me, I want it documented that you guys did absolutely nothing to help me, your employee."

The next day, the superintendent finally put out the statement he'd promised to issue. In this new statement, he was much more supportive. He said, "Black and Brown Lives Matter to the Burlington Area School District." He said, "I would like to begin by apologizing to the families of color who were negatively impacted by my previous statement in regard to the Black Lives Matter curriculum and my perspective concerning neutrality. Upon significant reflection, I see how my perspective was offensive and understand that there is no neutrality when pursuing equity." He said, "Valuing the lives of people of color is a basic human right and should not be treated as political or religious, just as valuing the lives of white people isn't treated as being political or religious." He quoted human rights activist Desmond Tutu and Holocaust survivor Elie Wiesel's statements that taking a position of "neutrality" when there's an injustice is, in effect, siding with "the oppressor."

He made a very strong statement. That was a turning point. Him putting that out finally got people to back off. It made people in the community realize, "Hey, we're not gonna win this. Maybe we need to leave her alone," because after that, I would get maybe one or two hateful e-mails a month. It was no longer a daily thing.

That said, a lot of my students' parents continued to harass me throughout that year. That was the year Ruth Bader Ginsburg died. We read her picture book, and *that* made people mad at me. There were so many things happening in the election, but if I talked about anything that related to current events, I got nasty, nasty e-mails and phone calls from parents. On the day of the Trump/Biden election, my students and I talked about how the Electoral College works. We set up a mock election with two kids as candidates to see how the numbers work and that someone can win the popular vote but not win the election. I gave them a map so that, that night, they could color it in blue and red to try to figure out who was going to win. It was really fun. But one parent wasn't happy about that. She said I told her daughter's class that Trump and his family are bad people, and they shouldn't be allowed in our country. It was a blatant lie that had nothing to do with the lesson at all. So, I got called into the principal's office for that.

It was uncomfortable having to go into the principal's office and explain everything that I did. She never said, "I support you. I'm going to tell these parents to leave you alone." She never vocally stood up for me. At the same time, she didn't reprimand me or tell me to stop teaching any subjects. She would just suggest that I take certain students out of the room for some lessons and have them do an alternative assignment. But I only had one parent who asked me to do that: to remove her daughter from the room if we discussed any current events, no matter what they were.

I'm not going to ask parents' permission to teach what's right. When people say, "You didn't teach the other side," I'm like, what *is* the other side of this? Racism is real. It exists. The Black Lives Matter movement exists. These are facts. We did have a conversation about police officers because I know people leap to the assumption that a conversation about the BLM movement is anti-police. I wanted to be sure we had a discussion about what good policing should look like. Some students shared that family or friends they know are police officers. One of my best friends from college is a police officer. I shared that with the kids. We had a conversation, like, there are officers that we know in our community, officers we trust. But discrimination by law enforcement and police harassment and brutality is a reality for people of color in our country. This is happening, and we need to talk about the fact that Black people in our country are being murdered by police officers and why it's wrong.

That's as close as I could get to both sides of this. I do think, when it comes to human rights, there are certain issues that don't have two sides.

At the end of that first school year, my superintendent told me I wasn't allowed to teach social studies anymore. He claimed it was for my own good. I love teaching social studies, so that was really upsetting. He left at the end of last school year, though, so I'm hoping maybe I can teach social studies again.

For now, I'm teaching ELA: reading and writing, grammar, phonics. Which is funny because we still have the same discussions and read the same books; we do all the things we would've done when I was teaching social studies. Whatever the subject, you can always find opportunities to talk about what's going on in the world. For example, we do opinion and persuasive writing, so we always get into social issues and their opinions. I have kids who are talking about the LGBTQ+ community not being treated fairly and why our world is racist.

When all of this was going down, a handful of teachers reached out to me, but not many, maybe three. One of my former English teachers told me, "Hey, I've gone through this, too. You're gonna make it through it." One of my former high school teachers sent flowers. And my immediate team was really supportive. The other two fourth-grade teachers and my special ed teacher were my core support team. But everyone else in the school shunned me the whole year. One teacher wouldn't even look at me when I tried to say hi in the morning. I felt very isolated. It didn't help that they didn't have a chance to know me before this happened. It was a really weird year as a new teacher in the district because I felt like a pariah.

Because of all of this, I lost the core group of friends I'd made since moving back to Burlington. A lot of parents with kids the same ages as mine were really against what I was doing and either no longer wanted to be friends with me, or I no longer wanted to be friends with them because of their views and actions. We lived in a small neighborhood community that had been friendly and close. During the summer of COVID, we would have outdoor happy hours, and the kids would run around.

Well, they stopped inviting us. Our backyard was attached to our next-door neighbors' yard, and we didn't have a fence, so we could see each other's yards. One day, during that first year, the entire neighborhood was over there, sitting in their backyard in plain view of ours – and we hadn't been invited. I thought, "You know what? I'm gonna go water my flowers right in front of them just to make them feel awkward." And I did. And no one spoke to me. One of the kids ran over and talked to me, but none of the adults would. Seeing different sides of people that you don't know, it's sad, like a breakup.

In 2021, our administration restructured our district. A new elementary school opened, and they put some of us – teachers from the other five elementary schools – together at this new school. It seemed like they pulled the people that were "problems" at the other schools and put 'em all together. I was one of them.

I've gotten a lot of support from the people I'm with now. Teachers I'd never met introduced themselves and said, "By the way, I really support you" or "Awesome job, what you did." I feel much more accepted now.

Teaching is just an uphill battle right now. Our district pays so poorly, and we have terrible benefits. Some of our class sizes went up by 50 percent this year. I keep being like, "I guess it's time to leave." But I can't imagine another job that would make me happy. I feel fulfilled as a teacher, and I don't think I could do a job just to make money. In spite of everything, I still really love teaching.

CAROLYN FOOTE
THIS ISN'T ABOUT BANNING BOOKS.
IT'S ABOUT TRIGGERING PEOPLE.

"I'm a recently retired librarian who started a 'freedom to read' coalition, the Texas FReadom Fighters, to fight extremist book banners after Governor Abbott claimed children were being exposed to pornography in schools."

I retired in March of 2021 because of COVID (and how Texas was handling it), as well as health issues. I was just like, "Okay, that's it for me." I hadn't really decided what I was going to do in my retirement. So, I made a list of some ways I could still be active in the profession. One of 'em was advocacy.

Well, in October of that same year, 2021, then-Texas state representative Matt Krause – a Christian-oriented, ultra-conservative Republican – sent out his infamous letter to superintendents around the state, asking them to audit their school libraries for any books from the list of 850 titles he'd singled out. At that time, Krause had aspirations to run for Attorney General of Texas, and the release of the letter seemed to be motivated by a play for attention. But, a year later, in November 2021, he dropped out of the election, presumably because it was a crowded primary with at least four other Republican candidates. Perhaps with his explosive letter, he was attempting to "build name recognition" since he was not polling well.[1]

Many of the books Krause singled out, like Ta-Nehisi Coates's *Between the World and Me* and Isabel Wilkerson's *Caste: The Origins of Our Discontents*, were books about race and racism, books about LGBTQ+

history or issues, books about sexual abuse, books about the medical facts of abortion. Before Krause's letter, I noticed that the attempts to restrict diverse curriculum and books were more focused on "critical race theory." But 30 to 40 percent of the titles on Krause's list were about LGBTQ+ topics. Honestly, I fault his list with bringing the LGBTQ+ titles into the whole conversation and planting the seed that spread the effort to ban books like these, nationally.

At the time, I had a few colleagues around Texas who were creating conference presentations on how to be prepared for book-banning attempts. (We'd seen a slight uptick relating to race and racism in the spring.) Being librarians, we knew many of the books on the list and immediately realized how slanted it was against race and LGBTQ+ people. Four of us started texting each other, saying we should do something. While we were discussing this, Greg Abbott, our governor, doubled down on Krause's effort to have these books removed from school libraries with a statement asking the Texas Association of School Boards to "ensure no child is exposed to pornography or other inappropriate content in a Texas public school."[2] He asked school boards to find and remove all such material from their schools. The Texas Association of School Boards doesn't have the authority to regulate anything and that was their response to him. But, basically, Abbott called out pornography in libraries without naming specific titles. Of course, he was misrepresenting the kind of content we actually have on our shelves.

It was so offensive, and we were afraid it would take hold. We wanted to highlight stories about censorship but couldn't find a common hashtag in use, so we brainstormed and started our own: #FReadom. My colleague Becky had seen people talking about doing Twitter takeovers, so she texted me, "What if we did a takeover of the Texas legislative hashtag?" I loved the idea. The Texas legislative hashtag is #TXLege, and it's followed by reporters gathering news about the legislature.

We, and a few other colleagues, made an info sheet with tips about how to participate, reminding them that Twitter is public, advising them not to post during work hours, and asking them to use our template to post about a diverse book that mattered to them, using the hashtags we suggested. Then, we secretly notified authors, friends, and our librarian networks, asking them to participate on November 4. Then, on November 4, to our surprise and amazement, 13,000 tweets went out.

I was in California on vacation, and I got up at, like, four in the morning so I could retweet things as they came in. We ended up sixth on Twitter's trending topics, and we were like, "Wait, what just happened?" After that, we were like, "Maybe we should make a Twitter account and a website." We coined the name the Texas FReadom Fighters and started a Twitter account (@FReadomFighters) and a website (https://www.txfreadomfighters.us/).

We started to do weekly #FReadomFridays, using that hashtag to tweet things for people to share, like, say, articles on the power of diversity in literature, the importance of sharing books about people who don't look like they do. We asked people to share a book that was a gift in their lives. We asked authors to share letters they had received from students about what their books meant to them – heartfelt letters from kids that showed why these books are needed. We were worried about school boards complying with Krause's letter, even though it had no official weight, so we did a month-long campaign to get anyone following our Twitter account – students, teachers, parents, community members – to write their school boards. We encouraged them to use our template letter to explain how libraries give students access to information, and why that matters.

We designed a shirt, sold it on Etsy through a third party, and donated the proceeds to the Texas Library Association's Intellectual Freedom Fund. Today, we have 17,000 plus followers on Twitter, and we're getting national media attention for stories because people can't fight stuff they don't know is happening. We've been on CNN. I've done interviews with Swiss TV and the news in Tibet. It's been a mind-boggling journey.

This fight is taking place at the school board level and the state legislative level. We've had the most impact on the local level, inspiring people to show up at their school board meetings to fight back, to vote, and to publicize things their districts are doing. Our group was the model for the Florida Freedom to Read group and for a Texas Freedom to Read group as well. Those are both parent groups. There are organized non-profits like PEN America in this fight but no national grassroots group fighting censorship. There's not an opposite to, say, Moms for Liberty or Mama Bears Rising. We began with a Texas focus but now we get contacted by people all over the country to connect them with resources and help with library policies at the school board level.

So that's where we are today. A lot of our role is sharing articles on social media, spreading news, alerting people to incidents and issues related to the freedom to read.

Our primary goal in the Texas FReadom Fighters is to provide hope and uplift librarians, teachers, authors, and students. We do that by providing information on our website about what librarians do and information for community members – how to speak at a school board meeting, how to be an effective advocate for the freedom to read age-relevant books with diverse viewpoints and for the First Amendment right to read. We have templates for letters to the editor. A student wrote a how-to on what students can do when books are removed from their libraries or policies are proposed or changed.

One of our main goals is shining a light on what's going on. We've become a conduit for the media because people will tell us, "This is going on in our district." So much of what's happening, like the soft censorship going on in a lot of school districts, people can't speak up about. Because there's no teachers' union in Texas, people are fearful for their jobs because each district handles things differently and there's no union protection. Teachers and librarians are out there on their own.

Everyone in our group has had negative feedback in our school districts – even me, who's retired. I've been accused of being a "groomer" of students, although I haven't been in a school for almost two years now. The first time I was called a sexual groomer and a pedophile, I was shocked. It made me very anxious and nervous. "Is this a hate group?" "Is someone gonna come after me?" That kind of thing. Now, I'm just like, yeah, whatever, I'm grooming my dog, 'cause it's just so overused at this point. Still, it's very scary when somebody says that to you.

Librarians are used to being appreciated by parents. Teachers, on the other hand, are used to a certain percentage of parents being upset with how you graded their child's paper or what grade their child got in your class. But, as a librarian, you tend to get a lot of positive feedback and very little negative feedback. So, it's a hard transition to suddenly become an "enemy."

"Pedophile" is a common accusation. That we're tryin' to sexualize their children. "Indoctrinate," that's another common one: we're tryin' to indoctrinate kids. That we're "activists." When we won the 2022 Intellectual Freedom Award from the American Association of School Librarians, there was a headline in *Texas Scorecard*, a conservative online news site. It said, "Activist Librarians Win Award."[3]

Another thing they do is file multiple Freedom of Information requests – a list from your library catalog, any books about this subject, e-mails between the librarian and the principal. It's harassment. Across the country, we're seeing this attempt to inundate districts with requests to gum up the works. Districts don't have enough staff-hours, money, or attorneys to keep up with it. In our view, they're sabotaging the school system so that it's bogged down and can't work effectively, then using this as evidence to convince voters that public schools are failing.

When we started this, we knew there might be some censorship, but we had no idea that, after minimal changes in policy for 30 years, districts are rewriting their policies around library materials – specifically, what materials can be purchased – and creating internal review processes that aren't transparent to taxpayers. Some districts have added more barriers. Like, a book has to be mentioned in X-many review journals before it can be purchased. Or a librarian has to read every book in its entirety before it's purchased. I mean, try that on for size. If you're a high school librarian and you purchase Barbra Streisand's biography, you have to read all 970 pages, in total, first. I mean, that's absurd. Or that books being considered have to be posted online for parent comment before the order goes out to be purchased.

In some states, they've expanded "Don't Say Gay" laws through grade 12. We had no idea that the harassment and the attacks on LGBTQ+

students and their families would get this bad. We had no idea how radically states would change laws to restrict curriculum or library content, as they've done in at least 23 states, such as Florida, Texas, South Carolina, and Oklahoma. States like Tennessee, Iowa, Oklahoma, and Arkansas have passed laws that say librarians can be fined or *imprisoned* for distributing obscene materials. We're seeing schools in Florida not being able to have book fairs, students not being able to bring a book from home to read in class.

We had no idea it would get this bad because it felt like someone would file a lawsuit or existing Supreme Court rulings would stop it. But everybody's afraid to sue because they're afraid of the current Supreme Court. They don't wanna have *Island Trees School District v. Pico* overturned. Even if the ACLU gets involved, they file civil rights complaints because that goes to the Department of Education, which they told me they believe will usually be a more successful route.

The *Island Trees School District v. Pico* suit is from 1982. A student, Steven Pico, sued the Island Trees Union Free School District in Nassau County on Long Island, New York because they had removed a bunch of books, including *Slaughterhouse-Five* by Kurt Vonnegut, *Black Boy* by Richard Wright, *Soul on Ice* by Eldridge Cleaver, stuff like that. The Supreme Court ruled in a split decision that libraries are voluntary marketplaces of ideas and that students had free speech and, as such, they should be able to pick the materials they read. So, while school boards can't include materials that don't meet community standards in terms of explicitness, they also can't just remove materials because they disagree with the ideas in them.

But that's obviously happening. States have passed these "critical race theory" bills, and school librarians and teachers don't know exactly what they can and can't keep on their bookshelves. Even though books about racism are not explicit in any obscene sense, which might violate community standards, they're still being challenged on those grounds and removed. In the past, these suits have typically been resolved in favor of libraries. Court cases are still supporting libraries but that's not preventing the censorship or the chill factor.

An important distinction is that the *Pico* ruling only protects school libraries. The Supreme Court decided that libraries are meant to offer broad "access to ideas" to prepare students to participate "in the pluralistic, often contentious society in which they will soon be adult members," whereas classrooms are "compulsory environments."[4] So, whereas students are free to choose materials in a library, every student in a class *has* to participate. So, instructional materials in classrooms aren't considered voluntary and aren't protected by *Pico*. This means that if you're just some random art or math or social studies teacher whose instructional materials are challenged, you don't have any support. Unless your whole department stands with you, you're on your own. Librarians are more willing to go, yes, this is a violation of civil rights, and reach out to the ACLU, whereas an individual teacher is much less likely to even try to take an action, 'cause they don't feel like they have that much power.

There's a bill pending right now in Texas to remove the protection in the penal code that protects educators. Currently, librarians, educators, museum professionals, physicians, and others "acting in their capacity as employees" are exempt from prosecution under state obscenity laws for "legitimate scientific or educational purposes."[5] A legislator providing testimony during a sexual assault case or an educator teaching sex education is doing so in the course of their job, so they're shielded from any potential penalty because the law assumes positive intent on the part of the educator or that materials with sexual themes have literary merit (or other valuable content) and aren't meant to be prurient. If this bill passes, we're gonna see devastating amounts of censorship. I mean, that's what happened in Florida and Missouri where they passed that criminal penalty.

Now, this particular part of the penal code is really about more mature material. So, if you were teaching *The Bluest Eye* by Toni Morrison, which includes a rape scene, a parent could say, "That's explicit! This educator gave this prurient material to my child to read in English class!" and bring charges. And while the code still says the material has to be prurient in nature and be meant to arouse, if those protections are removed, that parent could file a lawsuit. In conservative areas, they're gonna overreact. Ultimately, those parents may not win, but it's not gonna prevent them from filing charges. Sometimes, the school district is penalized – like, fines or withholding money from the district – but at least one state has a jail penalty for teachers – like, up to five years.

The amazing thing is, I worked with conservative librarians, and while everybody thinks of it as a partisan issue, lots of conservative educators are against book banning, too. They don't think of it as a partisan thing. I just think it's in a librarian's DNA that we believe kids should be able to read books about people who look like them or are living lives like theirs. And if you believe that, then you don't think those books should be removed. We feel protective of our students, and we wouldn't want the needs of our most vulnerable students to be denied. Also, librarians, whatever their partisan stance, are readers. We know what books are being withdrawn when people put out these lists. And while there may be a couple of books on a list that maybe someone thinks, "Oh, that's too much for my district or for me," there's lots of books on those lists that shouldn't be on *any* such list, and librarians of all stripes get that.

A lot of this stuff is politically driven. In Virginia, there was a controversy over the book *Beloved* that became part of the governor's race. The Democratic candidate muffed his response and said something about parents shouldn't decide or whatever. Well, the gubernatorial candidate just took off with that, raising the banner of parental rights, and he won. So, then, Republicans everywhere said, "This is a winning issue."

Also, in 2021, we were coming out of George Floyd and people around the country felt, for the first time since the civil rights movement, that America was coming to a racial reckoning. They were going, "I need to read more. I need to learn more. I'm not doing as well as I should in how I speak about race." People were forming book clubs; I was part of one at our public library. Black Lives Matter came along, and then all of a sudden, that became political, and white conservatives started pushing back about Black Lives Matter. And then they started pushing back about books about race. And then that got melded with Christian-nationalists' anti-LGBTQ+ rhetoric in Texas, and Matt Krause's list of 850 books was part of that.

The thing that's so hard to get across in our messaging is: it's a political tactic. This isn't about banning books; it's about triggering people. They're going after suburban schools, primarily, because they're trying to get the suburban-mom vote. At the Texas-Mexico border or in the inner cities, they've had hardly any book challenges. Book bans aren't a winning argument in an urban school or a more multicultural school, but it's an argument that works in the less integrated suburbs. If they really cared about this issue, they would care what kids in *every* school in the country were reading, not just what kids in certain schools are reading. So, it's pretty disingenuous.

It's also about racism. You can't remove books about how Roberto Clemente suffered racism in his career and say, "Well, that book can't be in a school because it's racist against white people." I mean, it's what happened to him. You can't just say his life didn't happen the way it happened. Or that we aren't gonna look at that part of history. I find it really disturbing.

Now, when I was first a librarian in the '90s, there was a wave of anti-occult stuff. I remember reviewing our books on the Salem witch trials because someone was concerned about them. But we didn't really receive any complaints to speak of. I think it's partly 'cause social media didn't exist then, so this stuff couldn't spread like wildfire. Back when things were normal, there might be three to 400 books challenged nationally in a year. This year, I'm sure it's gonna be over 2,000. Last year it was like 1,600 or so.

It's a phenomenal, unprecedented moment that we're in. We may not be able to prevent what's happening, but we can at least tell people what's going on. It gives you a sense of empowerment if you can at least do that. It's surprising how many people don't know what's going on. I talk to reporters who have no idea this is going on. And they're *reporters*.

I keep thinking: our kids are going into the global marketplace, especially now, when half the students will be working on Zoom with people from across the country. They could be working from anywhere, for anyone, with anyone. We're not doing them any favors by putting them in this protective bubble as if they're never going to leave their isolated suburban islands. They need to know about American history and how to get along with people different from them – and to have empathy with those people. We're depriving them of that knowledge, that experience. It's a really sad and unprecedented moment in this country.

JILL JAMES
I SEE THE KIDS THAT NEED TO FEEL SEEN.

"I'm a 7th-grade teacher who was accused of 'promoting an LGBTQ+ agenda' in my classroom through the books I offered students."

The January 6 insurrection was hard. It was during COVID, and we were teaching in a hybrid format, with some days in school and some days from home. The day of the insurrection was a teach-from-home day, so I knew many students would likely have seen what happened on TV while it was happening. When we went back to class the next day, I opened up space to talk because many of the kids had seen something terrifying and were stuck at home. Students shared what they'd seen and the conversations they'd had with their parents; one child shared that her father was supposed to be there and decided at the last minute not to go. What do you say to that? So, I just said, "Well, I'm glad your dad's safe." That was all I could say at that moment.

We're a small rural community in New England. We have about four hundred students in our school. We're overwhelmingly white. We've sort of been this last holdout that tends to vote blue in a sea of red, but that seems to be changing. There are some strong advocates, in our town, for a very conservative way of being, and their number seems to be growing.

For the first five years at my school, I worked as a reading specialist, supporting students and teachers in various ways. Then I went into the classroom because I missed teaching. In the winter of 2022, I was working as a seventh-grade language arts teacher, teaching reading and writing, and there was a town meeting primarily organized by our local Republican committee. I was told by several sources, including some who were there, that they brought in speakers from around the state. One speaker was a woman billed as a teacher – the only teacher on the docket, by the way; she had taught for one year – *one year*, in a school in the middle of our state. She cautioned the audience, warning them to be careful because they're "teaching critical race theory in your schools. You need to know what's going on. You need to know what books they're teaching." So, some of the members of the town committee turned to a Republican member of our Board of Education and asked him if he knew what was going on. He replied, "That's really not my role." Then, another parent stood up and said something to the effect of, "Well, there's a seventh-grade language arts teacher in that school, and she's teaching…," and this parent went on to describe books I used in my classroom. While he didn't mention me by name, it was clear he was referring to me because I was the only seventh-grade language arts teacher in the school, and I had plenty of books in my room of the kind that he was objecting to. This parent claimed I was pushing books that featured LGBTQ+ protagonists and was even encouraging students to become trans, to come out as gay, et cetera. So, again, some folks at the meeting turned to the board member and said, "Do you know what books are in the classroom?" and, again, he had no idea because it wasn't his responsibility to know what books were in every classroom.

So, it was just this big, blown-out-of-proportion thing, a scare tactic to get people up in arms. After this, the word was out that these groups were brought in to stir things up and were infiltrating our town and school board meetings. From what I've heard, they were trying to get people riled up in order to take control of the schools and, ultimately, what's being taught in the schools.

The next day, I got a text with screenshots of quotes cut and pasted from a text chain about the meeting. Three different people who were at the meeting confirmed that the participants in the meeting were talking about me. I was the only seventh-grade language arts teacher in my school, so it was clearly me. In fact, I *do* have a lot of books that feature diverse kinds of folks, and conversations do come up in class about different types of gender identification, along with other identities and tough situations or circumstances *any* kid might have to navigate, regardless of identity. For example, I had books about people who live in rural contexts, books about people who live in urban contexts, books about people who live in traditional family units, books about people who live in non-traditional family units – in other words, books about people living their lives. These conversations come up because seventh graders are curious; they want to discuss these things and read these books because they're searching for information. They want to know about people around them, and they want to know about themselves. I handle these discussions respectfully. No one point of view is forced down anyone's throat, and students are certainly not pressured to read books about people who identify as LGBTQ+ – or any other identity, for that matter – if they don't want to.

This incident started, I think, with a child's conversation at home about books being offered as choices in our student book clubs. I had taught this child's sibling two years before, and the mother had raised some questions about the book *Parrotfish* by Ellen Wittlinger, which is a book about a trans boy. If memory serves, the parent wanted to know why a more traditional book couldn't be offered as a choice. I reassured her that her child didn't have to read *Parrotfish* and that there were many titles to choose from.

Of course, her child wanted to read the book because kids are curious, and they want to understand the world around them, especially people whose worlds are different from the one they inhabit. Two years later, the same parent had questions about their second child being offered *Lily and Dunkin*, by Donna Gephart, as a choice for book clubs. *Lily and Dunkin* is about a trans girl and a bipolar student who strike up this wonderful friendship. It's a powerful story about a transgender youth who doesn't initially have the support of their family. At the end of the book, though, the father really gets behind his daughter. He recognizes the threat posed by the suicide rate among transgender youth and decides he wants to support his child.

While the mother brought up her objections to the first book during a face-to-face open house night, the father was the one who spoke out about the second book and non-traditional book choices in general at the town meeting sponsored by the Republican town committee. Later in the year, both parents e-mailed me and the school administration, expressing their concerns about a Youth Summit on social-emotional learning and asking where it fit into our curriculum.

When titles like these first appeared as book club choices, they were something of a novelty. While there have always been books about diverse types of people, having titles with trans characters was a newer experience. So, with this family's first child, the book became a topic of conversation at home, prompting the mother to question it with the reading teacher who was sharing my room (and classroom library) with me that year. Apparently, it was still on the parents' minds two years later when I was their second child's reading teacher.

Every year, kids want to read these books. Every year, I've had a child who identifies as transgender or comes out as gay, and kids are aware of that. It's just life. At that age, kids are much more willing to talk about their feelings and their sense of being "other." That seems to be the trend in my school: kids will start to come out as trans or talk about different sexualities in fifth or sixth grade, and even more so in seventh grade. During the early years of the COVID pandemic, I had kids come out in a Zoom class, you know? A parent could've been walking by when our class was talking about that.

I see the kids that need to feel seen. As a mother of four, that's one reason I got into middle school teaching. That's an age when some kids don't feel safe, don't feel seen, don't feel heard, and if I'm going to be in front of them every day, they need to know that I see them and hear them and support them. I have a sign in my room that says, "All beliefs, all creeds, all races, all genders are welcome here." I have a small pride flag in my room, as does every middle-school teacher in my building. We want kids to know we're allies and that our classrooms are safe spaces.

So, that's where it started. This group of conservative parents, which was a more vocal group of any kind than we'd previously seen in our town, continued to reach out to various members of our Board of Ed about what I was allegedly doing. Shortly after that, we ended up having a youth summit sponsored by our state Department of Ed to address social-emotional needs, and these conservative parents challenged it.

They wanted to know why we were doing it and how it fit into our curriculum. I happened to be the one that was sending out the communications from my middle-school team. So, I was responding to all of these challenges, and I later found out that all of my correspondence was being fed by the parent who first objected to my book offerings to a Republican Board of Ed member.

The good part was that a board member called me at home the night before the summit to say, "You know, I've read through all your correspondence, and I can't see anything wrong with it. I think we're lucky to have you. Good luck tomorrow." So, that was a happy ending, although I still felt very uncomfortable knowing that all this misinformation was being passed around town meetings and forwarded to the Board of Ed members.

I did get support from my school administration – eventually. There was a bit of distancing at first. The parents who had the issues with *Parrotfish* were spearheading the assault on the Board of Ed, stirring people up about the Youth Summit on Social-Emotional Learning, e-mailing the vice principal, and so on. After receiving some clarification from me as the "voice" of our teaching team, they came back with more questions, and the vice principal's initial response was, "Well, I don't know anything about this." I responded to the parents, copying the vice principal, pointing out that everyone in the administration did, in fact, know about our involvement in the summit and had, in fact, supported it from the beginning, thereby clarifying that this wasn't something the teaching team had done without the administration knowing about it beforehand. Then, I went to the vice principal and said, "That's not okay. You know what's going on. You sanctioned this; you have to stand behind me."

At that point, the vice principal stepped up. He did an about-face, agreeing that the administration had supported our initiative and that it did fall within our mission as a school to support social-emotional learning. In his defense, I think he and my administration were worn down like so many administrators are. That's why I don't fault them that much for not taking my side initially.

While both members of the conservative couple who objected to *Parrotfish* and *Lily and Dunkin* were in alignment on their concerns, it's difficult to know how their children felt about these books. My job is to teach all kids and to treat each student with respect, so I wasn't going to call out a specific student about a book I was offering. Obviously, as a teacher, you know these things are going around; there are students who exchange glances when a book choice is offered. You overhear comments. I'm not going to stop a class and say to a kid, "Why are you chuckling about this book?" Knowing the families they were from and that their parents objected to these things, you just knew that there was more behind it. There were parents who would send their children to school with Let's Go Brandon T-shirts and who claimed not to understand why that was a problem. Those same kids didn't come to class on the day of our Youth Summit. So, there were many of those sentiments going around.

At the beginning of every year, I send home a letter to parents letting them know that I have a number of titles in my class library for my students to choose from. I know that kids are curious, and I'm not in the business of book censorship. Basically, I tell them, "Know what your child is reading." The parents had to sign that letter at the beginning of the year, agreeing to those terms, before I allowed their children to check out any of the books in my classroom library. Students had a lot of choices when it came to their book club books. I created a slideshow with all the book choices, links to book trailers, and so forth. So, my curriculum wasn't hidden. True, I didn't send it out to parents *specifically*, but they had access to their child's online learning platform. Everything was transparent. The parents knew their kids were free to choose the books they wanted to read.

I do a lot of writing with my students and give them opportunities to write about things they care about. It's interesting what comes out: kids will talk about the injustices they see and the things they worry about in our world today and in our government. After the murder of George Floyd, there were a lot more parents who objected to us talking about current events. There was talk about teaching a "patriot" curriculum. This didn't happen to me, but our social studies teacher got criticized for teaching current events; some of the conservative parents who thought she should be teaching a "patriot" curriculum wanted her fired.

We were hearing of this curriculum a lot at that time. Protecting white feelings and sugar-coating the past is what it sounded like to me. The parent who was the loudest advocate for the so-called patriot curriculum wasn't providing us with any specifics. Basically, this parent didn't want their children to feel bad when conversations about the murder of Black men came up. Luckily, our administration and most of the other parents supported that teacher, so the parent left the district. The teacher was reassured that she was doing the right thing and could continue to teach current events.

I link these incidents together because it felt like parents were trying to mount an attack on a number of different fronts; if one avenue doesn't work, try this avenue. What they tried to stir up at that town meeting could've been part of a larger strategy promoted by a national organization, but I don't know for sure. I'm just thinking about where it all started, at that town meeting, where there were lots of people from outside our community trying to rile parents up. Fortunately, we have enough people in our town who don't agree with that sort of extremism, so it didn't take flight here as it might have in another community.

The whole time, I was just carrying on, doing my job as a Language Arts teacher. Some primary-school teachers stopped talking to me for a time. The middle-school team, on the other hand, was strongly supportive. In the classroom, we kept discussing what was happening in the world – the Black Lives Matter rallies, Amanda Gorman's powerful recitation at Joe Biden's presidential inauguration, and the fact that voices can be used to raise awareness and unite people – and making connections to my students' lives, as usual.

There was a contingent of students whose parents may have been part of the effort to limit SEL in schools and restrict access to certain books. If I said anything about equal rights, treating people with respect, and the importance of safe spaces for people who experienced discrimination, harassment, or bullying, you'd see eyes darting between a couple of kids. There'd be little whispers. Still, I never raised the issue of the parents' allegations. I never said anything like, "I know some of your parents are upset…"

There are far more terrible stories than mine. I was able to keep doing my job. I didn't pull any books off my shelf, and I didn't steer kids away from books they wanted to read. I continued to talk about all of my students in a respectful way and to support them when they had something to share. I think it's really important that students are able to see people like them in books, and I also think it's really important that they read about people who are not like them, so they learn not to dehumanize people who are different from them.

I think about my own kids and about my someday-grandkids: I want them to live in a world where people are accepted, not discounted based on some superficial criteria, a world where everybody's story is honored. I believe that's a crucial aspect of education. This is why I'm a teacher, and I'm not going to change what I'm doing because I believe I'm doing the right thing.

MARK JOHNSON

THE SAME DOG WHISTLES ABOUT PARENTAL CHOICE, GOING ALL THE WAY BACK TO *BROWN V. BOARD OF EDUCATION.*

"My position as the first principal of color at my school was jeopardized after I was targeted for publicly supporting efforts to dismantle systemic racism in my community."

Nota Bene: I'm a non-white, racialized male. In the following testimonial, I cannot disclose identifying factors about myself, such as race, because it would put me and my professional career at risk.

So, wow, where do I begin? You know, I love education. I love working with kids. When I started my career as a younger, racialized male, that's what I thought I was going to do: just teach and coach basketball. Then, I went into administration. Never thought I would end up there, but I absolutely fell in love with the concept of creating an environment for the educators who are there to serve kids. If you get that right, you know, how much more powerful can that be?

I came to Censorville School District in the 2018-2019 school year. I'd already been a principal in another district, so I took an assistant principal job at Censor City High School. That spring, I was promoted to principal at Censor City Elementary School, which fed into Censor City High. Fast forward to March 2020: during my first year there, the pandemic shut everything down. But because of the work that the staff did and the results we were getting for our students, I had the opportunity, in May of 2020, to become the principal of Censor City High School.

A couple of weeks after I was named principal, a string of incidents of unwarranted and excessive police brutality had transpired in the surrounding area against Black individuals. Everyone was talking about it in the community and in the media. These local events mirrored other incidents of injustice at the hands of police officers across the country.

You've got all the big companies coming out, showing their support, saying, "Hey, what can we do to end systemic racism? What can we do to hold police accountable?" You have districts and their leadership teams doing the same thing in areas around me, areas that, historically, had been largely silent about systemic racism and police brutality. I had people reaching out to me I hadn't heard from in the past, parents and members of the community who just wanted to learn more about how they could help, how they could become allies. I saw people in the streets protesting. It was really encouraging.

Meanwhile, I've got this position as a high school principal. One of the things district leadership told me when I got the job was, "We want you to use this opportunity. You've got a larger platform now, and we know who you are: you're a champ for the underdogs. We want you to be that person and use your platform."

Thinking through that lens, I'm like, "Well, nobody in the district's saying anything, but I know we've got a lot of students and people in our community who are grappling with this." So, I used this moment as an opportunity to make a video that I sent to the community. In it, I said, "We're fighting this pandemic of systemic racism. We know it's real. How can we come together around this issue? We know it's gonna be hard. We're gonna have to have tough conversations, but I just want people to know I'm here for you to do the hard work of dismantling these things that are trying to hold us back."

I got nothing but positive feedback. There was not a single e-mail or phone call or anything that said, "Hey, this is not okay." It was all, "Thank you for speaking up."

The demographics of the elementary school I worked at was predominantly white. At the middle school, though, you have about a six percent African American population and another 20 percent Hispanic. When you transition to high school, it was still majority white, but growing more diverse, with almost half the student body students of color. The school looked very different than it had a decade ago, and for me, a racialized man, to be the principal of this school, well, that was very encouraging. We've got this melting pot now. There's a mix of people from all over the world, really big Middle Eastern and Southeast Asian populations in this area, because there's a city close by that's bringing in people from all over the world to work at the airport. So, this school is looking more like what we see across the world. That's part of what led to me sending out the video: I knew that we have more people of color in this community now and that they needed to hear this message, right?

That was the 2020-21 school year, my first year as principal. There had been very contentious school board elections in nearby West Censor. Their board got overrun by far-right extremists. Over the course of the year, people were sending me things from these Facebook echo chamber pages. Members of these Facebook groups were calling me, like, a lieutenant of critical race theory. They were saying that I was there to destroy the school district, that I was teaching divisive concepts. They were harping on the fact that my colleagues and I were working to disrupt inequities. They had issues with that! Friends of mine in the community would say, "Hey, have you seen this?" I just kind of shrugged it off, like, "That's crazy. Y'all know me. You know what I'm doing. I'm just here to make sure our kids have a great education, make sure teachers have the resources they need." All along, I didn't hear anything from people in the district at the administration level.

I started hearing louder murmuring during the summer of 2020. That's when I started hearing things from people in the community. But none of these far right-wing agitators were contacting me, saying, "Hey, I got a problem with you." No phone calls, no e-mails, no requests for an appointment, zero.

At the same time, though, there was an uptick in FOIA requests.* So, you start to see my name together with phrases like "critical race theory," "police brutality," "systemic racism," terms like "diversity," "equity," and "inclusion" – these were the keywords, things that they pulled from my e-mails, my social media accounts, my text messages.

They wanted access to all that to highlight their conspiracy theory that I was bringing "critical race theory" into the district. But really, they were just against anything celebrating diversity, embracing inclusivity, or trying to provide an equitable education for all kids. That's what they're about: disrupting, sowing chaos and division in the community.

You'd have people who were parents or family members of kids at my school that would go into these echo chambers to defend me, saying, "Hey, look, we know this guy. That is not what he's about." They'd quickly get kicked out of those groups.

It's hard to believe, but I had zero requests from any of these people to meet with me regarding legitimate concerns. Most rational people would think, "If you have a concern, go talk to the person," right? But this has never been about legitimate concerns. It's always been about creating this bogeyman that would create division, sow chaos in communities, sow distrust in public schools so that they can disrupt public education and divert public dollars into private school vouchers. That's what this has been about since *Brown v. Board of Education* in the 1950s.**

In the wake of *Brown v. Board*, we saw the rise of private schools along with the firing of well-qualified Black and Brown teachers. A lot of white families didn't want Black teachers teaching in their schools or, worse yet, Black principals leading them. Even today, we

---

* Freedom of Information Act allows for requests for public school records and documents related to an issue of concern including e-mails, contracts, curriculum, trainings, videos, text messages, and other records.

** *Brown v. Board of Education of Topeka*, 347 U.S. 483, the 1954 Supreme Court case, was pursued by plaintiffs who had been denied admission to public schools based on race. In a unanimous ruling, racial segregation of public schools was deemed unconstitutional. This case reversed the previous "separate but equal" doctrine and was one of the cornerstones of the civil rights movement.

talk about the representation gap in schools, by which we mean the lack of teachers and leaders who represent the student populations in our schools. We can tie this back to *Brown v. Board of Education*. You know, it's not that we can't attract Black teachers, but it became a devalued and vulnerable professional choice in the wake of *Brown v. Board of Education*. Along with white flight from these neighborhoods and the rise of private schools, white conservatives instigated the call for vouchers to pay for tuition for private education. This became the rallying call for "parent choice," framed as the right for parents to choose where their children attend school. We hear the same rhetoric now. It isn't new. This has been around, but when history is limited, you don't learn that there are these through-lines, that these are things that have been happening over time. It shouldn't surprise us that this is on your doorstep again, but in a different form, right?

So, here we are, having these same conversations, hearing these same dog whistles about parental choice. Which parents are we talking about? In the aftermath of *Brown*, white parents were talking about "having a choice." If you listen to what's being said now, it might not be as explicit, but if you listen long enough to these folks that'll get up there and speak at these board meetings, you can hear the same song being sung, just a different verse.

When you talk about *Brown v. Board of Education* today, whether it's in scholarly circles or just everyday society, people tend to think back as if it was just a great moment where we all kind of came together, and we're all good now that schools are – supposedly – integrated. But what gets lost is that we're *more* segregated now. Also, the plaintiffs in *Brown* never intended or wanted to go to white schools; they just wanted adequately funded schools and equal access to resources.

Throughout that school year, I had a gut feeling that something was gonna happen; it was just a matter of when the other shoe was gonna drop. I tried to keep my head down, even though I sensed something sinister was happening. It was a difficult, difficult year.

At the high school level, we have close to 200 teachers and support staff and 3000 students. During COVID, we had kids going back and forth because they could be remote one day and in person, the next, and teachers trying to learn Smartboards® (an interactive whiteboard with a touch-sensitive surface that enabled them to interact with digital content) and a new learning management system (that is, an instructor-facilitated learning application for documentation, content delivery, and assessment). There was so much to do that I didn't have time to be consumed with this far-right nonsense. I just kind of pushed it to the side. In retrospect, I didn't speak out as much as I should have.

In my heart of hearts, I feel like I did the right thing by just focusing on the well-being of our staff and students and trying to provide each student, regardless of where they were at, a great education. But these far-right disruptors really used the pandemic and the havoc it caused us to their advantage because, while we were focused on giving their kids the best possible education, *they* were focusing on spewing nonsense and whipping up people's fears.

In this district, the superintendent always has one campus representative as a part of his district leadership team, his executive cabinet. They meet once every two weeks to review policy. So, he had quite a few people to choose from to be that one campus representative. Well, who did he pick out of the elementary schools, middle schools, high schools, and the alternative school? Interestingly enough, me.

So, during that year, I was the campus representative that he entrusted to be the voice for the campuses. I was the only person of color in any of those meetings because the district administration wasn't representative of what the district looked like. In our meetings, I told him, "There's something coming, and unless we get really clear about who we are and what we're about, these right-wing trolls are gonna hijack the message, and they're gonna make it about all these other things." But every time I tried to sound the alarm, I was met with crickets. It's as if they knew it was coming, but no one was willing to step up and go, "Hey, we're gonna fight this."

So, fast forward to August of 2021, when a disgruntled community member aired grievances about me, and everything really hit the fan. At a school board meeting, a woman got up and was allowed to rail against me. Now, school board policy states specifically that members of the public, while they do have the opportunity to address the board during public comment during school board meetings, must adhere to the three-minute time limit, and they don't have the right to air grievances against particular employees during that time. School board meetings are not an opportunity for grievances against particular employees to be aired.

While this woman's mic was cut off at the three-minute point, she was allowed to violate the clause that says you cannot air grievances. We have a formal grievance process she could have gone through outside of a school board meeting. Even if someone has gone through the formal grievance process, they're not allowed to air those grievances at a school board meeting. Yet she was allowed to call for my termination and to broadcast the unsubstantiated claims and smears from this private Facebook group echo chamber, you know, "He's trying to bring critical race theory into our school, he's trying to destroy our schools with this social-emotional learning stuff." Within her allotted time, she managed to spew all the usual buzzwords – and no one shut her down.

The day after the meeting, I got a call from the district's executive director of communications, apologizing that the board allowed the speaker to recycle baseless far-right talking points and to attack me personally without comment from the board. I also got an apologetic call from the district's executive director of human resources, saying, "Mark, that should not have happened. We're so sorry." I got calls, voicemails, and text messages from almost all of the board members: "We got your back. We love you. We love what you're doing at that school." But no one spoke publicly.

So, I was like, "I'm gonna have to address this in some way." I put my message out there, and of course, I was contacted by a local TV and radio news station. They were like, "Man, we gotta get this message out there." At this point, I was like, well, I'm not going to allow this group of people to talk about me like this. I'm not going to sit idly by while my reputation is tarnished. I *had* to speak out because I knew my life would be a living hell for the rest of that school year if I didn't. I don't think I would have made it to Thanksgiving break. That group of people was determined to root me out, and we know what that does to educators.

Educators are already being scrutinized for every little thing. I mean, if a teacher wore a mask in school in response to the pandemic, they were called a freaking Nazi and accused of indoctrinating kids about mask-wearing. You know, that kind of crazy talk.

So, educators were already under a lot of stress and scrutiny. Then they saw my situation play out, which, even though it highlighted my decision to stand up against these people and demand a voice for educators, also made it very clear that this could happen to them.

The work of an educator is already so complex and so multifaceted. They're tasked with doing so many different things, from being a teacher to being a counselor to being a nutritionist and everything in between. And now no longer is it just those things, but now I'm having to be a politician and tiptoe around even something as basic as teaching a historical fact! This creates a chilling effect that overlays the entire system and riddles it with anxiety and stress for educators who are trying to navigate an already complex system.

Nonetheless, I thought, "I've got to speak up because if I don't, I'm giving you the keys to my career, letting you dictate what happens. It's time for me to take things into my own hands."

The teachers weren't saying much, and I understand that. They were thinking, "Well, look, this is the principal, who is beloved in the district and was able to rise through the ranks, and now this is happening to him. I'm just gonna keep my mouth shut and sit back." But the parents, the families, and the students showed up at the board meetings to defend me – in droves. Not a single one of my students or their parents had anything negative to say about me. Of course, there were Republican parents – obviously, I didn't just serve Democrat or independent families – but even those parents were saying, "No, we're okay with you speaking up for yourself."

To do that, I had to go to the media. While it could be implied that I was out in the media because I wasn't being supported by the administration due to racism or that I was being targeted because of my support for the eradication of racism in society, what's interesting is that I never specifically stated anything about racism in my comments to the media. I was intentionally trying to steer clear of that, and I was very careful in every interview I did because I didn't want to add fuel to the fire of what the people in the Republican echo chambers were trying to do.

I didn't want to make my situation about racism. Obviously, I realize the attacks on me definitely had racist undertones, but I didn't want to feed the flames. Discussing race is important, but what I wanted to turn the focus back to is what this is about, which is disrupting and destroying public education.

What I wanted to talk about in the media was that this situation where I am being attacked by outsiders without evidence and without the backing of my district is about disrupting and destroying public education and sending public dollars to private schools that accept only a certain type of student, right? So, I always flip back to that because *that* is the key point.

On top of showing up at school board meetings, the students – hundreds of them – staged a walkout. I had nothing to do with it, by the way. A group of students who were taking a full load of AP courses, very high-performing students who were trying to get into some of the most prestigious colleges in the country, took it upon themselves to organize that walkout. Even though I'd only been their principal for one year, they were able to see through this nonsense. They were walking out for me, but many of these students were students of color and their allies, and they saw what this would mean for them and for other students in marginalized populations.

Then, at the end of October 2021, I was put on leave. It was a huge shock and a devastating contradiction. I am beloved in my school community, but then the very people who entrusted me to lead that community forced me to part ways with it. All I can say is that the superintendent stated that my departure was "in the best interest of the district." He was using very broad language as a coverall, and anyone could fill in the gaps, but the district didn't have to.

The students were like, "Hell, no. That's our principal. We love him. We want answers." Of course, the district didn't *have* any answers for the students. So, students had to live with this contradiction, just like I had to. There was no valid reason for me to be forced to leave, especially because it wasn't in the best interest of the students.

So, then we went through a whole back and forth between me and the district, and finally, in December of that year, five or six months after that initial school board meeting, we came to a non-disparagement and settlement agreement. They had to pay me a substantial sum.

It's been a really challenging last year and a half. It's weighed on me, like, "What do I want to do? Do I want to do this?" I keep coming back to "Yes" because this has been my heart; this has been my passion since I was a high school kid going, "Hey, I like what my coaches do for me." I had that handful of life-changing teachers. I want to be that for the next generation of kids.

I had lunch with a mentor of mine, a wonderful lady who'd been an assistant superintendent in the area. She was like, "Mark, you know you're not going to be in a public school district around here. Wonderful as you are, nobody's going to hire you now. Have you considered relocation to another state?" I said, "You know, we've thought about that. But our family's here. I've got two older kids here."

It's discouraging to know there's a position in my home district right now, but I won't get an opportunity to even walk through the door to interview for that job despite having the experience and the credentials. I know the people, but they're not gonna bring me in for an interview.

All of these things that have happened have created an opportunity for me to advocate in ways that maybe I should have been doing more strongly in the past. I've coached a ton of educators just because I have the time to do it, and I haven't charged people a dime. So many educators are going through similar experiences. It's become so commonplace.

I fear that many people are suffering in silence. So, anytime I get a hit from an educator saying, "Hey, I just need somebody to talk to, to help me see my way through this experience," that kind of charges me up because, you know, it's an opportunity to support a lot of really good people who are trying to do good things for kids but, unfortunately, are being attacked by people with nefarious political agendas.

These far-right activists know that fear has always been a motivator when it comes to turning out a certain part of the electorate. Go back to the Southern strategy of the Republican Party, starting under Nixon, when they attracted white Southern voters by exploiting opposition to the Civil Rights Act and school desegregation. Trump has something to do with this racist fearmongering, no doubt, but if anything, he's just given them "permission" to speak what they've felt for so long.

You can't say the N-word anymore, so they use coded language. Their new bogeyman is "critical race theory," which the initiative I was promoting has nothing to do with. But they'll put anything under CRT – race, sexism, LGBTQ+-themed fiction, anything. In fact, they've *said* that. Chris Rufo explicitly said, "We're just going to hijack the term 'critical race theory' and put anything that we want to attack in the guise of CRT."* So, they know they've got this great bogeyman to scare people with, and if you're going to make people scared, what better way than to tell them somebody's doing something to your kids?

These far-right extreme folks are blaming the changes in kids today on schools alone. But kids have access to so much knowledge now. They're not going to believe stuff just because you tell them. I think that's what scares these conservative parents. There are conversations at dinner tables today that are scaring the hell out of some of these families, where it's always been their tradition that they vote a certain way, believe a certain way, and think a certain way about other people. "Those Mexican folks are trying to take our jobs, and those gay people are going straight to hell; they're this, they're that, they're Others," right?

---

* Christopher Rufo is an American conservative activist sowing distrust in public schools through rallying against critical race theory and the discussion of LGBTQ+ issues in school in order to promote school choice through privatization.

I think kids are sitting at these tables and going, "Yeah, I go to school with a kid that's from Peru and a kid that's from Colombia, and I don't think it's true that they're gonna take our jobs or rob our homes, grandpa." Or: "I really don't like that you said that about gay people, Mom, because one of my friends is queer."

These parents know that the kids are going to shift. So, even though this county is a hotbed for this nonsense, you've seen a shift in voting patterns. These parents know that, and they're afraid. Anytime, throughout our history, when you've had moments of progress, this kind of backlash is just par for the course. That's what I've tried to tell people. Anytime I have an opportunity to speak, I say, "We should be ready for this because it's happened before, and it's gonna happen again. We've got a playbook, just like they do. We shouldn't be surprised that people are lashing out in fear. This is what happens anytime we're on the precipice of progress."

what you can do to resist attacks on public education

show up

at school board meetings to advocate for teachers, students, and yourself as members of your community committed to free speech, diversity, and unbiased, fact-based curriculum.

learn to recognize

the catchphrases, political or religious agendas, and fearmongering tactics of threats to public education. For example, on a school board agenda, "book signage and content" often means there will be an attempt to censor a book. Are parents or outside operators disparaging teachers publicly for teaching "CRT," condemning educators for wearing masks, or making claims that books about sex ed, gender identity, or sexual identity are nothing other than "porn"?

know who's on your local school board

Please educate yourself about the candidates and their platforms. Are they Moms for Liberty members or funded by far-right groups? Do they hide in closed Facebook groups and ban members who offer alternate perspectives? Vote for progressive school board members or run for the school board yourself.

form collectives

If you're a parent, create a group to share information about attacks on students and teachers, write letters to administrators, and fill school board meetings with your voices. If you're a teacher, form a collective within the school to support each other and unite in solidarity.

know your First Amendment rights

to free speech in school, online, and in the community. These may vary for students, teachers, administrators, and community members.

our website Censorville.com ...

has links to legal assistance for educators under fire, First Amendment protections, and other tools for educator and community action against book bans and attacks on public education ...

- become familiar with organizations, like the AFT, NEA, ACLU, NAACP, GLAAD, the Children's Defense Fund, and encourage them to come to your district to support teachers.
- donate to *EveryLibrary*, the *Human Rights Campaign*, and teacher *GoFund-Me's*.
- learn how to talk to the media with media toolkits. See "Faculty First Responders" for sample responses to attacks by far-right extremists.

if you're a teacher ...

- know your district/institutional policies and processes. "I keep multiple copies of the [district] policy right here in my drawer to hand out to whoever needs it," says Martha Hickson, a librarian at a New Jersey high school. "Odds are, if you know the policies and processes forwards and backwards, you may be the only one in your institution who does." Knowledge is power.
- verify your employment rights by reviewing U.S. Equal Employment Opportunity policies and offices.
- consider contacting union officials and teacher organizations for legal assistance.
- alert the community not just when the house is on fire but before Moms for Liberty shows up at your BOE meeting. Good will toward your school and a clear, factual picture of the good things happening in classrooms and libraries builds support for what you do. That support will be a bulwark, if needed, against far-right activists. Share students' testimonials about books they've loved, books that have inspired, even transformed them. Let parents hear, in their childrens' words, how enriching and inspiring your students find your curriculum and classroom discussions. This is more powerful than a generic letter from the district can ever be. Share these positive takeaways in public comments at school board meetings or in parent-teacher/school newsletters to do an end-run around administrative messaging, which in the current political climate often errs on the side of bland bureaucratese.
- keep detailed daily notes about infractions: difficult conversations in the workplace, what people said, hate speech in school, threats to remove books or censor the curriculum that don't follow formal processes, appeals to help from administrators and their responses, social media trolling, etc.. Ellen Barnes, a middle-school history teacher, writes in her testimonial that her district lawyer recommends keeping a handwritten record in a personal notebook, rather than in digital form.
- if you feel unsafe at school, alert school security of any safety concerns, request regular checks on your location, and ask for a colleague to walk you to and from parking lots.
- photocopy and distribute these two spreads – *pp. 276-279* – from this book.

if you're a teacher or administrator ...

be proactive. Collaborate with like-minded colleagues and members of the community to create a school or district plan with clear guidelines and resources for responding to political attacks on employees or students, including free legal consultation, guidance from IT professionals, a support network (including other teachers who have experienced trolling or harassment), and a list of tactics, such as reaching out to well-known authors whose books are under attack.

if you're a teacher or parent ...

consider informing students about issues that affect their education, such as book bans or the freezing of library book purchasing. Teachers should be careful about not expressing your political views or directing students on how to engage but do let them know about school or district policies and administrative decisions impacting their access to resources. Their engagement will matter.

if you're a parent or student ...

get to know your librarian and teachers. Please support them. Elissa Malespina, a New Jersey high school librarian and school board member, says, "School boards pay attention to students. Use your voice. Show up at meetings. Write to school board members. Tell them how the books or teachers engage and inspire you, and make you feel seen and supported." This holds true for parents, too.

if you're a student ...

- create your own Banned Books Clubs and organize book distribution events. Create your own curriculum, invite speakers and hold a Teach-In, or explore other forms of action such as Sit-Ins or Walk-Outs.
- consider starting or joining a student rights organization or club, such as the Student Action Network for Equity.

if you're an administrator or school board member ...

be aware that your swift, decisive and, as important, public response to attacks on your school, your teachers, and your librarians – what studies call the "unconditional and public defense" of employees – is crucial. Your unequivocal support in official communications, public meetings, and the media will ensure that your teachers, librarians, and support staff have the courage of their convictions and are shielded from extremist threats to them, your school, and public education in general. Your unflinching advocacy will help foster a school environment characterized by confidence, not fear. Listen to your employees.

learn more at Censorville.com

ACKNOWLEDGEMENTS

To the teacher contributors to this book, thank you for the tremendous pleasure and honor of spending two years working with you. We are in awe of your dedication to protect the rights of all students to a real, look-the-facts-in-the-face and ask-difficult-questions kind of education and a library reflecting all identities. You each spoke up for the democratic vision of public education, even when this cost you sleepless nights and the precarity of unstable ground. We're grateful for your tenacity, moral courage, patience, generosity, and trust in guiding these stories to the public.

Thank you to the essayist and cultural critic Mark Dery, who reviewed every text in the book as a writing coach and helped us to draw out the compelling details of this, in his words, "malignant tumor on American democracy." Devon Redmond, the director for the video portion of the project, lent his ear to the spoken word and primed us to protect contributors' colloquial, regional language. Thank you to our colleagues at PEN America – Jonathan Friedman, Daniel Cruz, and Lisa Tolin – for partnering with us to amplify these stories. Thank you to the imaginative Ben Denzer for designing the book's cover. We are grateful to our project counsel, Paul Szynol, of the Film Law Group.

It was a community effort to make this book, and we're appreciative of these individuals: Eve Sarnecki – our inquisitive Research Assistant; Hilary Gustafson, co-owner of the Literati Bookstore – a hub of the Ann Arbor community – for believing in and amplifying the book; Jack Bernard, for protecting our First Amendment rights; Steven McCarthy, for his insightful design consultation; Patricia Jewell and Sanjana Ramanathan, for their careful proofreading; Ravi Pendse and Sol Bermann, for helping to make the Internet safer; Scott Creech and Olivia Cook, for setting up sponsorships; the Stamps School Finance team, especially Caitlin Walton, Dave Constant, Kristie Faust, and Michelle Hardin; Silke-Maria Weineck, for grant editing; and Melissa Levine, for pointing us in helpful directions.

This book only exists because of the funding and institutional support from the following: The Jo Ann (Jody) & Dr. Charles O. Onstead Institute for Education in the Visual Arts & Design and the encouragement and commitment of Peter B. Hyland, the Director of the Onstead Institute; and several units and people at the University of Michigan, including The Office of Research, the Penny W. Stamps School of Art and Design), the Office of Diversity, Equity & Inclusion (special thanks to Tabbye Chavous), the Ginsberg Center (thank you, Kate Livingston), and the Roman Witt Visitors Program.

From Rebekah, thank you to my family, Nick, Lucy, and Oscar Tobier, for letting me get lost in this project.

Foreword: The fight to save public education

1. Caleb Ecarma, "'I Can't Teach Like This': Florida's Education Brain Drain Is Hitting Public Schools Hard," *Vanity Fair*, May 22, 2023.; Khaleda Rahman, "Florida Combats Colossal Teacher Shortage," *Newsweek*, April 12, 2023.; Steven Greenhouse, "'The Point Is Intimidation': Florida Teachers Besieged by Draconian Laws," *Guardian*, May 13, 2023. See also Tuan D. Nguyen, Chanh B. Lam, and Paul Bruno, "Is There a National Teacher Shortage? A Systematic Examination of Reports of Teacher Shortages in the United States," *Brown University*, August 2022, edworkingpapers.com/sites/default/files/ai22-631.pdf; Hannah Natanson, "'Never Seen It This Bad': America Faces Catastrophic Teacher Shortage," *Washington Post*, August 3, 2022.

2. Leslie Postal, "Florida Teacher Vacancies Soar to Nearly 5,300 in January," *Orlando Sentinel*, January 13, 2023.

3. "The 2022 Texas Teacher Poll: Persistent Problems and a Path Forward," *Charles Butt Foundation*, accessed July 12, 2023, https://charlesbuttfdn.org/what-were-learning/2022txteacherpoll/.

4. Ashley Woo, Sabrina Lee, Andrea Prado Tuma, Julia H. Kaufman, Rebecca Ann Lawrence, and Nastassia Reed, "Walking on Eggshells—Teachers' Responses to Classroom Limitations on Race- or Gender-Related Topics," *RAND*, 2023, https://www.rand.org/pubs/research_reports/RRA134-16.html.

5. Jeremy C. Young, Jonathan Friedman, and Kasey Meehan, "America's Censored Classrooms 2023: Lawmakers Shift Strategies as Resistance Rises," *PEN America*, November 9, 2023, https://pen.org/report/americas-censored-classrooms-2023/.

An introduction

1. Elizabeth Heubeck, "What Does School Without Librarians Mean for Students?," *Governing*, November 13, 2023, https://www.governing.com/.

2. "2024 Anti-Trans Bills Tracker," *Trans Legislation Tracker*, accessed January 22, 2024, https://translegislation.com/.

3. Alice Markham-Cantor, Britina Cheng, and Paula Aceves, "28 States, 71 Bills, and an Education System Transformed," *Intelligencer*, May 8, 2023, https://nymag.com/intelligencer/2023/05/us-education-state-school-laws.html.

4. "Florida State Academic Standards—Social Studies, 2023," *Florida Department of Education*: page 6, https://www.fldoe.org/core/fileparse.php/20653/urlt/6-4.pdf.

5. Jonathan Feingold and Joshua Weishart, "How Discriminatory Censorship Laws Imperil Public Education," *Great Lakes Center for Education Research and Practice*, November 2023, https://www.greatlakescenter.org

6. "CRT Forward," *UCLA School of Law*, accessed January 22, 2024, https://crtforward.law.ucla.edu/.

7. Stephen Sawchuk, "What is Critical Race Theory, and Why is it Under Attack," *Education Week* 40, no. 34 (June 2, 2021).

8. Jason Wilson, "Colorado Springs: Far-Right Influencers Made LGTBQ People into Targets," *Southern Poverty Law Center*, November 22, 2022, https://www.splcenter.org/hate-watch/2022/11/22/colorado-springs-far-right-influencers-made-lgbtq-people-targets.

9. Tucker Carlson, "Critical Race Theory Has Infiltrated the Federal Government: Christopher Rufo," *Fox News*, September 2, 2020, The Heritage Foundation YouTube video, 6:17, https://www.youtube.com/watch?v=rBXRdWflV7M.

10. Benjamin Wallace-Wells, "How a Conservative Activist Invented the Conflict Over Critical Race Theory," *The New Yorker*, June 18, 2021, para. 6.

11. David G. Embrick, J. Scott Carter, and Cameron D. Lippard, "The Resurgence of Whitelash: White Supremacy, Resistance, and the Racialized Social System in Trumptopia," in *Protecting Whiteness: Whitelash, and the Rejection of Racial Equality*, eds. Cameron D. Lippard, J. Scott Carter and David G..Embrick (Seattle: University of Washington Press, 2020).

12. Leslie T. Fenwick, *Jim Crow's Pink Slip: The Untold Story of Black Principal and Teacher Leadership* (Cambridge: Harvard Educational Press, 2022).

13. "Labor Force Statistics from the Current Population Survey," *U.S. Bureau of Labor Statistics*, accessed January 25, 2023, https://www.bls.gov/cps/cpsaat11.htm.

14. "School-Related Protective Factors for LGBTQ Middle and High School Students," *The Trevor Project*, August 24, 2023, https://www.thetrevorproject.org/research-briefs/school-related-protective-factors-for-lgbtq-middle-and-high-school-students-aug-2023/.

15. "Acceptance of Transgender and Nonbinary Youth from Adults and Peers Associated with Significantly Lower Rates of Attempting Suicide," *The Trevor Project*, November 3, 2021, https://www.thetrevorproject.org.

16. David G. Embrick, Wendy L. Moore, and Manuel A. Ramirez, "Tearing Down to Take up Space: Dismantling White Spaces in the United States," *American Behavioral Scientist* 66, no. 11 (October 2022).

17. David Pitt, "President Jake Chapman says Press, Teachers Have 'Sinister Agenda,'" *Des Moines Register*, January 10, 2022, para. 1.

18. "Legislation of Concern Tracker, 2024," *EveryLibrary*, https://www.everylibrary.org/bill-tracking.

19. Judd Legum, "Florida School District Removes Dictionaries from Libraries, Citing Law Championed by DeSantis," *Popular Information*, January 10, 2024, https://popular.info/.

It didn't begin with Trump: The attack on public education – A timeline

1. Ta-Nehisi Coates, "The Case for Reparations," *The Atlantic*, June 2014: para. 1.

2. Nikole Hannah-Jones, "Our Democracy's Founding Ideals Were False When They Were Written. Black Americans Have Fought to Make Them True," *The New York Times*, August 14,

2019.

3. Amrita Johal, "The Change in Status of African Americans During Post-Civil War Reconstruction," *HiPo* 1, March (2018): 65-67.

4. Sarah Fling, "The Formerly Enslaved Households of President Andrew Johnson," *The White House Historical Association*, March 5, 2020, https://www.whitehousehistory.org/the-formerly-enslaved-households-of-president-andrew-johnson.

5. Greg Toppo, "Thousands of Black Teachers Lost Jobs," *USA Today*, April 28, 2004.

6. Robert Reich, "My Father and Senator Joe McCarthy," in The Roots of Trumpism, *Robert Reich* (August 26, 2022): para. 8, https://robertreich.substack.com/p/joe-mccarthy-and-my-family.

7. "Henry Wallace Criticizes Truman's Cold War Policies," in *This Day in History*, History.com, accessed February 17, 2024: para. 3, https://www.history.com/this-day-in-history/henry-wallace-criticizes-trumans-cold-war-policies.

8. Albert Wertheim, "The McCarthy Era and the American Theatre," *Theatre Journal* 34, no.2 (May 1982): 212.

9. J. Woods, *Black Struggle, Red Scare: Segregation and Anti-Communism in The South, 1948-1968* (Baton Rouge: Louisiana State University Press, 2004).

10. Leslie T. Fenwick, *Jim Crow's Pink Slip: The Untold Story of Black Principal and Teacher Leadership*, (Cambridge: Harvard Education Press, 2022).

11. Leslie T. Fenwick, "White Media Barely Noticed When 100,000 Black Educators Were Displaced," *Kappan*, November 16, 2022, https://kappanonline.org/.

12. Soheyla Taie and Laurie Lewis, "Characteristics of 2020-21 Public and Private K-12 School Teachers in the United States," *Institute of Education Sciences*, December 2022, https://nces.ed.gov/pubs2022/2022113.pdf.

13. "The Southern Manifesto," *Professor Daniel Levin's Federalism Page*, 1956, accessed February 17, 2024: para. 11, https://content.csbs.utah.edu/~dlevin/federalism/southern_manifesto.html.

14. Chris Ford, Stephanie Johnson, and Lisette Partelow, "The Racist Origins of Private School Vouchers," *Center for American Progress*, July 12, 2017, https://files.eric.ed.gov/fulltext/ED586319.pdf.

15. Karen Graves and Margaret A. Nash, "Academic Freedom Protects Both LGBTQ Topics and LGBTQ Teachers," *The Washington Post*, October 24, 2022.

16. David K. Johnson, *The Lavender Scare: The Cold War Persecution of Gays and Lesbians in the Federal Government* (Chicago: The University of Chicago Press, 2004): 3 and 116.

17. Jaweed Kaleem, "Homeschooling Without God, *The Atlantic*, March 30, 2016.

18. Jan Larson McLaughlin, "Vouchers Siphon Taxpayer Dollars from Public Education to Private Schools," *BG Independent News*, March 24, 2022, https://bgindependentmedia.org/vouchers-siphon-taxpayer-dollars-from-public-education-to-private-schools/.

19. Libby Stanford, Mark Lieberman, and Victoria A. Ifatusin, "Which States Have Private School Choice?," *Education Week*, January 31, 2024.

20. Kevin G. Welner and Preston C. Green, "Private School Vouchers: Legal Challenges and Civil

Rights Protections," *UCLA Civil Rights Project*, March 5, 2018, https://civilrightsproject. ucla.edu/.

21. Bayliss Fiddiman and Jessica Yin, "The Danger Private School Voucher Programs Pose to Civil Rights," *American Progress*, May 13, 2019, https://www.americanprogress.org/article/ danger-private-school-voucher-programs-pose-civil-rights/.

22. Keefe v. Geanakos (1969) 418 F.2d 361.

23. "Anita Bryant Confronted in 1977," SuchIsLifeVideos, *YouTube*, Accessed February 11, 2024, https://www.youtube.com/watch?v=fABwascm12s.

24. Jillian Eugenios, "How 1970s Christian Crusader Anita Bryant Helped Spawn Florida's LGBTQ Culture War," *NBC News*, April 13, 2022: para. 2, https://www.nbcnews.com/.

25. James Peron, "Ronald Reagan on Rainbow Rights," *The Radical Center*, December 4, 2018: para 24. https://medium.com/the-radical-center.

26. Board of Education, Island Trees Union Free School District No. 26 v. Pico, 457 U.S. 853 (1982).

27. Tyler Engel, "Overzealous: The Harm Caused by Parental and Administrative Censorship of Books in an Intellectually Freed Education," *Outstanding Gateway Papers* 21 (2023): 4.

28. West Virginia Board of Education v. Barnette, 319 U. S. 642.

29. David Stout, "Bush Backs Ban in Constitution on Gay Marriage," *The New York Times*, February 24, 2004: para. 3.

30. Obergefell v. Hodges, 576 U.S. 644 (2015).

31. Haas Institute Staff, "International Tolerance Day," *Other & Belonging Institute*, November 16, 2016. https://belonging.berkeley.edu/international-tolerance-day.

32. David G. Embrick, Wendy L. Moore, and Manuel A. Ramirez, "Tearing Down to Take Up Space: Dismantling White Spaces in the United States," *American Behavioral Scientist* 66, no. 11 (2022): 1582–96.

33. David G. Embrick, J. Scott Carter, and Cameron D. Lippard, "The Resurgence of Whitelash: White Supremacy, Resistance, and the Racialized Social System in Trumptopia," in *Protecting Whiteness: Whitelash and the Rejection of Racial Equality*, eds. Cameron D. Lippard, J. Scott Carter and David G..Embrick (Seattle: University of Washington Press, 2020): 3-24.

34. J.R. McNeill, "How Fascist is President Trump? There's Still a Formula for That," *The Washington Post*, August 21, 2020: para. 5.

35. Ezra Klein, "'Enemy of the People': How Trump Makes the Media into the Opposition," *Vox*, October 30, 2018, https://www.vox.com/.

36. Nikole Hannah-Jones, "The 1619 Project," *The New York Times*, August 4, 2019.

37. "2020 Impact Report," *Black Lives Matter*, https://blacklivesmatter.com/2020-impact-report/.

38. Benjamin Wallace-Wells, "How A Conservative Activist Invented the Conflict Over Critical Race Theory," *The New Yorker*, June 18, 2021: para. 16.

39. Jason Wilson, "Colorado Springs: Far-Right Influencers Made LGBTQ People into Targets," *Southern Poverty Law Center*, November 22, 2022: para. 31, https://www.splcenter.org/ hatewatch/2022/11/22/colorado-springs-far-right-influencers-made-lgbtq-people-targets.

40. Christopher F. Rufo, "Cult Programming in Seattle," *City Journal*, July 8, 2020, https://www.city-journal.org/seattle-interrupting-whiteness-training.

41. Wallace-Wells, "Conservative Activist," para. 2.

42. Russell Vought, "M-20-34, Memorandum for the Heads of Executive Departments and Agencies," *Executive Office of the President*, September 4, 2020: para. 1, https://www.whitehouse.gov/wp-content/uploads/2020/09/M-20-34.pdf.

43. V.E. Hamilton, "Reform, Retrench, Repeat: The Campaign Against Critical Race Theory, Through the Lens of Critical Race Theory," *William & Mary Journal of Race, Gender, and Social Justice* 28, no. 1 (2021): 64.

44. D.J. Trump, "Executive Order on Combating Race and Sex Stereotyping," *Trump White House*, September 22, 2020.

45. Alana Wise, "Trump Announces 'Patriotic Education' Commission, a Largely Political Move," *NPR*, September 17, 2020: para. 5.

46. Wise, "Trump Announces," para. 3.

47. D.J. Trump, "Executive Order on Combating Race and Sex Stereotyping," *Trump White House*, September 22, 2020.

48. Steven Brint, "The Political Machine Behind the War on Academic Freedom," *The Chronicle of Higher Education*, August 28, 2023: para. 22.

49. Jonathan Friedman and James Tager, "Educational Gag Orders," *PEN America*, November 2021: 4, https://pen.org/report/educational-gag-orders/.

50. Katherine Schaeffer, "America's Public School Teachers are Far Less Racially and Ethnically Diverse than Their Students," *Pew Research Center*, December 10, 2021, https://www.pewresearch.org.

51. "Moms for Liberty," *Southern Poverty Law Center*, accessed February 17, 2024, https://www.splcenter.org/fighting-hate/extremist-files/group/moms-liberty.

52. Taifha Alexander, LaToya Baldwin Clark, Kyle Reinhard and Noah Zatz, "Tracking the Attack on Critical Race Theory," *CRT Forward: UCLA School of Law*, 2023: 13, https://crtforward.law.ucla.edu/wp-content/uploads/2023/04/UCLA-Law_CRT-Report_Final.pdf.

53. Joseph R. Biden, "86, 7009, Executive Order on Advancing Racial Equity and Support for Underserved Communities Through the Federal Government," *Biden White House*, https://www.whitehouse.gov/.

54. Jennifer Liu, "Read the Full Text of Amanda Gorman's Inaugural Poem 'The Hill We Climb,'" *CNBC*, January 20, 2021, https://www.cnbc.com/2021/01/20/amanda-gormans-inaugural-poem-the-hill-we-climb-full-text.html.

55. Madeline Halpert, "Amanda Gorman's Inauguration Poem Moved by School After Parent's Complaint," *BBC*, May 24, 2023, https://www.bbc.com/news/world-us-canada-65678970.

56. Andy Sher, "Tennessee Republicans Pass Bill That Punishes Public Schools That Teach Systemic Racism Concepts," *Chattanooga Times Free Press*, May 5, 2021: para. 4.

57. "Pledge to Teach the Truth," *Zinn Education Project*, January 12, 2022, https://www.zinnedproject.org/news/pledge-to-teach-truth.

58. Eva McKend and Dan Merica, "Virginia Republicans Seize on Parental Rights and Schools

Fight in Final Weeks of Campaign," *CNN*, October 7, 2021: para. 2.

59. Laura Vozzella and Gregory S. Schneider, "Fight over Teaching 'Beloved' Book in Schools Becomes Hot Topic in Virginia Governor's Race," *The Washington Post*, October 25, 2021: para. 7 and 8.

60. Matt Krause, "School District Content Inquiry," *Texas House of Representatives: Committee on General Investigating*, October 25, 2021, https://static.texastribune.org/media/files/965725d7f01b8a25ca44b6fde2f5519b/krauseletter.pdf?_ga=2.167958177.1655224844.1635425114-1180900626.1635425114.

61. Greg Abbott, "Letter to Texas Education Agency Commissioner," *The State of Texas: Governor's Office*, November 10, 2021, https://gov.texas.gov/uploads/files/press/O-Morath-Mike202111090719.pdf.

62. Peter Greene, "New Hampshire and Moms for Liberty Put Bounty on Teachers' Heads," *Forbes*, November 12, 2021: para. 6

63. American Law Institute, "Model Penal Code: Official Draft and Explanatory Notes: Complete Text of Model Penal Code as Adopted at the 1962 Annual Meeting of the American Law Institute at Washington, D.C.," (Philadelphia: The Institute, May 24, 1962): 238.

64. David Pitt, "Iowa Senate President Jake Chapman says Press, Teachers Have 'Sinister Agenda,'" *Des Moines Register*, January 10, 2022: para. 1.

65. Katelyn Caralle, "The DeSantis Blueprint for America – from Florida Where the 'Woke go to Die'," *The Daily Mail*, January 19, 2023: para. 15.

66. Becky Sullivan, "With a Nod to '1984,' a Federal Judge Blocks Florida's Anti-'Woke' Law in Colleges," *NPR*, November 18, 2022: para. 3.

67. "New Report: Book Bans Spike by 33% Over Last School Year," *PEN America*, September 21, 2023, https://pen.org/press-release/new-report-book-bans-spike-by-33-over-last-school-year/.

68. Ileana Najarro, "Teachers Censor Themselves on Socio-Political Issues, Even Without Restrictive State Laws," *Education Week*, February 15, 2024.

69. Najarro, "Teachers Censor," para 6.

70. Ashley Woo, Melissa K. Diliberti, and Elizabeth D. Steiner, "Policies Restricting Teaching About Race and Gender Spill Over into Other States and Localities," *RAND*, February 15, 2024, https://www.rand.org/pubs/research_reports/RRA1108-10.html.

Martha Hickson

1. Board of Education Meeting, North Hunterdon-Voorhees Regional High School District, September 28, 2021, https://www.youtube.com/watch?v=Avz44fJQGrE.

2. This is the 17-page document of process improvements that the Freedom Fighters submitted to the board. "This Book Must Stay: Response to the North Hunterdon-Voorhees Reconsideration of This Book is Gay," *The Intellectual FReadom Coalition of the NH-V Intellectual Freedom Fighters*, January 31, 2022, https://drive.google.com/file/d/1dMN9LV_Y91gm-L5z-Ssb8RUDVPbjMgGWu/view.

3. Jordan Zakarin, "Exclusive: Moms for Liberty's Failure Was Even Worse Than Reported," *Progress Report*, November 13, 2023, https://progressreport.substack.com/p/exclusive-moms-for-libertys-failure.

4. Richard S. Price, "Navigating a Doctrinal Grey Area: Free Speech, the Right to Read, and Schools," *First Amendment Studies* 55, no. 2 (June 29, 2021): 79-101, https://doi.org/10.1080/21689725.2021.1979419.

"Publication Data / Materials used to develop Richard S. Price's article 'Navigating a Doctrinal Grey Area,'" *Adventures in Censorship*, accessed January 22, 2024, https://adventuresincensorship.com/publications-data.

Matthew D. Hawn

1. "Prohibited Concepts in Instruction," Tennessee Department of Education, Revised April 2023, https://www.tn.gov/content/dam/tn/education/legal/Prohibited_Concepts_in_Instruction_April%202023.pdf.

Julie Miller

1. Statute § 847.012 (Florida 2022).

2. Statute § 847.001 (Florida 2023).

3. "FLDOE Library Workgroup," *FL Freedom to Read Project*, YouTube Channel, https://www.youtube.com/playlist?list=PLGDXjdrfCeGZMOLYjHOWKzSc7HGq6I0bM.

4. Miller v. California, 413 U.S. 15 (1973).

5. Augustin Rodriguez, "Investigative Report, Case #: 2021-100272," *Flagler County Sheriff's Office*, November 2021, https://flaglerlive.com/wp-content/uploads/100272-Inves-Summary-1.pdf.

6. "District Reconsideration List," Library Media, Clay County School District, Florida, accessed January 22, 2024, https://as.myoneclay.net/academic-services-home/instructional-resources/library-media#h.27tw91ra8ul2.

7. "Tampa Free Press—Bias and Credibility," *Media Bias / Fact Check*, accessed January 22, 2024, https://mediabiasfactcheck.com/tampa-free-press-bias/.

8. Deborah Childress, "Parent Chokes Up After Reading Vile Excerpts from Florida School Library Novels. 'I Had No Idea It Was This Bad—I'm Shocked,'" *Tampa Free Press*, July 20, 2022.

9. Judd Legum and Rebecca Crosby, "How to Ban 3600 books From School Libraries," *Popular Information*, December 12, 2022, para. 34, https://popular.info/p/how-to-ban-3600-books-from-school.

10. "District Reconsideration List."

Willie Edward Taylor Carver Jr.

1. "Stamp 4S Assessment," *Avant Assessment*, accessed January 23, 2024, https://avantassessment.com/tests/stamp/4s.

2. Eric Marcus, *Making Gay History - The Podcast*, https://makinggayhistory.com/.

3. Olivia B. Waxman, "As More States Require Schools to Teach LGBTQ History, Resources for Teachers Expand," *TIME*, December 13, 2019.

4. Senate Bill 1 (Kentucky 2022), https://apps.legislature.ky.gov/record/22rs/sb1.html.

5. Rose v. Council for Better Education, 790 S.W.2d 186, 60 Ed. Law Rep. 1289 (Kentucky 1989), https://nces.ed.gov/edfin/pdf/lawsuits/Rose_v_CBE_ky.pdf.

6. For further information on the pension law and teacher protests, see: Laurel Wamsley, "Kentucky Supreme Court Strikes Down Pension Law That Sparked Teacher Protests," *NPR*, December 13, 2018, https://www.npr.org/2018/12/13/676420722/kentucky-su-preme-court-strikes-down-pension-law-that-sparked-teacher-protests.

7. "2022 National Survey on LGBTQ Youth Mental Health," *The Trevor Project*, https://www.thetrevorproject.org/survey-2022/.

8. Willie Edward Taylor Carver Jr. (@WillieETCarver), "I'm a Proud Gay Man, I Am the 2022 Kentucky Teacher of the Year, and I'm Afraid to Return to the Classroom. I Want Kids to See Me and Feel Hope, But I Am Tired." Twitter, April 22, 2022, 4:03pm, https://twitter.com/WillieETCarver/status/1517595054591860740?s=20.

9. Willie Carver, "Op-Ed: In Make or Break Moment for Education, the Cost for Kentucky's Teachers to Thrive is Change," *Northern Kentucky Tribune*, February 24, 2022, https://nkytribune.com/2022/02/willie-carver-in-make-or-break-moment-for-education-the-cost-for-kentuckys-teachers-to-thrive-is-change/.

10. Senate Bill 1 (Kentucky 2022).

11. Kentucky Governor Andy Beshear, "Veto of SB 1," April 1, 2022, https://apps.legislature.ky.gov/record/22rs/sb1/veto.pdf. (In September, 2021, the Kentucky Senate and House overrode Gov. Beshear's vetoes.)

12. The first version of Senate Bill 150, (Kentucky Feb 2023), https://apps.legislature.ky.gov/recorddocuments/bill/23RS/sb150/orig_bill.pdf.

13. "Willie Edward Taylor Carver Jr.'s Amendments to Kentucky Senate Bill 150," Amendment 1: https://apps.legislature.ky.gov/recorddocuments/bill/23RS/SB150/SFA1.pdf; Amend-ment 2: https://apps.legislature.ky.gov/recorddocuments/bill/23RS/SB150/SFA2.pdf.

14. "Medical Association Statements in Support of Health Care for Transgender People and Youth," *GLAAD*, June 21, 2023, https://glaad.org/medical-association-statements-support-ing-trans-youth-healthcare-and-against-discriminatory/.

15. For more information on Kentucky Education Commissioner Jason Glass' resignation, see: Jess Clark, "Kentucky's Top Education Official Resigns Over Anti-LGBTQ+ Law," *WYFI/NPR*, August 2, 2023, https://www.wfyi.org/news/articles/kentuckys-top-education-official-re-signs-over-anti-lgbtq-law.

16. "2022 National Survey on LGBTQ Youth Mental Health," *The Trevor Project*.

17. "U.S. LGBTQ Youth Who Experienced Conversion Therapy and Attempted Suicide," *Statista*.com, May 11, 2023, https://www.statista.com/statistics/1053024/lgbtq-youth-in-us-at-tempted-suicide-conversion-therapy-experience/.

18. Olivia Krauth, "Fairness Campaign Releases Poll Showing Most Kentuckians Oppose an

Anti-trans Legislation," *Louisville Courier Journal*, February 23, 2023, https://www.courier-journal.com/story/news/politics/2023/02/23/poll-most-kentuckians-oppose-anti-trans-legislation/69937206007/.

Gavin Downing

1. Elisabeth K. Andrie, I.I. Sakou, E.C. Tzavela, C. Richardson, and A.K. Tsitsika, "Adolescents' Online Pornography Exposure and its Relationship to Sociodemographic and Psychopathological Correlates: A Cross-sectional Study in Six European Countries," *Children* 8, no. 10 (October 16, 2021): 925, https://www.mdpi.com/2227-9067/8/10/925.
2. Hildie Leung, D.T.L. Shek, E. Leung, and E.Y.W. Shek, "Development of Contextually-relevant Sexuality Education: Lessons from a Comprehensive Review of Adolescent Sexuality Education Across Cultures," *International Journal of Environmental Research and Public Health* 16, no. 4 (February 20, 2019): 621.

   "Comprehensive Sexuality Education, 2016 report" *United Nations Population Fund*, https://www.unfpa.org/comprehensive-sexuality-education.

Ellen Barnes

1. Howard Zinn at National Council for the Social Studies," *ZinnEdProject*, August 16, 2014, YouTube video, 28:56, https://www.youtube.com/watch?v=VVjzF3meMWs&t=811s.

Carolyn Foote

1. "Matt Krause Leaves Crowded GOP Primary for Texas AG to Run for Tarrant County DA," *ReformAustin*, November 22, 2021: para. 2, https://www.reformaustin.org/elections/matt-krause-drops-out-texas-attorney-general-republican-primary-ken-paxton/.
2. Governor Greg Abbott, "Letter to Texas Association of School Boards Executive Director Dan Troxell," *Office of the Texas Governor*, November 1, 2021: para. 4, https://gov.texas.gov/uploads/files/press/TroxellDan.pdf.
3. Erin Anderson, "Activist Librarians Win Award for No-Age-Limits 'Freedom to Read' Project," *Texas Scorecard*, April 14, 2022, https://gov.texas.gov/uploads/files/press/TroxellDan.pdf.
4. Board of Education, Island Trees Union Free School District No. 26 v. Pico, 457 U.S. 853 (1982).
5. "Opposing Attempts to Criminalize Libraries and Education Through State Obscenity Laws: An EveryLibrary Institute Policy Brief," *EveryLibrary*, January 15, 2023, https://www.everylibraryinstitute.org/.